Flowering
House Plants

LIBRARY OF NATIONS

CLASSICS OF EXPLORATION

PLANET EARTH

PEOPLES OF THE WILD

THE EPIC OF FLIGHT

THE SEAFARERS

WORLD WAR II

THE GOOD COOK

THE TIME-LIFE ENCYCLOPAEDIA
OF GARDENING

THE GREAT CITIES

THE OLD WEST

THE WORLD'S WILD PLACES

THE EMERGENCE OF MAN

LIFE LIBRARY OF PHOTOGRAPHY

TIME-LIFE LIBRARY OF ART

GREAT AGES OF MAN

LIFE SCIENCE LIBRARY

LIFE NATURE LIBRARY

THE TIME-LIFE BOOK OF BOATING

TECHNIQUES OF PHOTOGRAPHY

LIFE AT WAR

LIFE GOES TO THE MOVIES

BEST OF LIFE

LIFE IN SPACE

THE TIME-LIFE ENCYCLOPAEDIA OF GARDENING

Flowering House Plants

by

JAMES UNDERWOOD CROCKETT

and

the Editors of TIME-LIFE BOOKS

Watercolour Illustrations by

Allianora Rosse

TIME-LIFE BOOKS, AMSTERDAM

THE TIME-LIFE ENCYCLOPAEDIA
OF GARDENING

SERIES EDITOR: Robert M. Jones
EDITORIAL STAFF FOR FLOWERING HOUSE PLANTS:
Assistant Editor: Carlotta Kerwin
Picture Editor: Kathleen Shortall
Designer: Leonard Wolfe
Staff Writers: Marian Gordon Goldman, Paula
Pierce, Kelly Tasker
Chief Researcher: Joan Mebane
Researchers: Diane Asselin, Muriel Clarke,
Evelyn Constable, Helen Fennell, David
Harrison, Susan Jonas, Gail Hansberry, Sandra
Streepey, Mollie Webster, Gretchen Wessels
Design Assistant: Anne B. Landry
Staff Illustrator: Vincent Lewis

EUROPEAN EDITION
EUROPEAN EDITOR: Kit van Tulleken
Design Director: Ed Skyner
Photography Director: Pamela Marke
Chief of Research: Vanessa Kramer
Chief Sub-Editor: Ilse Gray
Researchers: Jasmine Taylor, Milly Trowbridge
Designer: Joyce Mason
Copy Staff: Joanne Holland

Editorial Production
Chief: Ellen Brush
Art Department: Julia West

THE AUTHOR: The late **James Underwood Crockett** was an eminent American horticulturist, writer on gardening subjects and, on television, a teacher of plant care and cultivation. A graduate of the University of Massachusetts' Stockbridge School of Agriculture, he lived in—and cultivated a wide variety of plants in—California, New York, Texas and New England and served as a consultant to many nurseries and landscapers.

CONSULTANT, EUROPEAN EDITION: **Frances Perry** is a well-known gardening authority whose books and broadcasts have gained her an international reputation. She is a member of the Linnean Society, and was the first woman to be elected to the Council of the Royal Horticultural Society; now a Vice-President, she also holds the Society's coveted Victoria Medal of Honour. She has lectured in Australia, New Zealand and America and has collected plants in such diverse areas as Lapland, Africa and South America.

GENERAL EUROPEAN CONSULTANTS: **Roy Hay** is a horticulturist well known for his articles in English publications, including *The Times* newspaper, and for his contributions to the French magazine *L'Ami des Jardins*. He carries on a family gardening tradition—his father, Thomas Hay was Superintendent of the Central Royal Parks in London (1922-1940). Mr. Hay is an Officer of L'Ordre du Merite Agricole of Belgium and France. **André Leroy** is the emeritus chief engineer for the Paris parks and gardens. Since 1958 he has been technical consultant for the magazine *Mon Jardin et Ma Maison*. **Dieneke van Raalte** studied horticulture and landscape gardening at the college of gardening in Fredriksoord in The Netherlands. She is a regular contributor to European gardening magazines and is the author of many Dutch gardening books. **Hans-Dieter Ihlenfeldt** is Professor of Botany at the Institute of General Botany and Botanical Gardening in Hamburg. He is the co-editor of several botanical handbooks and has published in scientific journals. **Heinrich Nothdurft** is chief custodian of the Botanic Garden and lectures at the Institute of Botany in Hamburg. He is co-author of the handbook *Mittel-europäische Pflanzenwelt* (Flora of Central Europe).

GENERAL CONSULTANTS: Dr. O. W. Davidson, North Brunswick, N. J. Staff of the Brooklyn Botanic Garden: Robert S. Tomson, Assistant Director; Thomas R. Hofmann, Plant Propagator; George A. Kalmbacher, Plant Taxonomist; Edmund O. Moulin, Horticulturist. Mrs. Joy Logee Martin, Logee's Greenhouses, Danielson, Conn. Albert P. Nordheden, New York City.

THE ILLUSTRATOR: **Allianora Rosse**, who provided 120 of the 126 delicate, precise watercolours of house plants beginning on page 100, is a specialist in flower painting. Miss Rosse trained at the Art Academy of The Hague in The Netherlands and her illustrations have appeared in many gardening books.

THE COVER: Three of the thousands of varieties of African violet, one of the most popular flowering house plants. With a little care, they will bloom continuously, bearing clusters of pink, blue or purple flowers.

Portions of this book were written by Henry Moscow. Valuable assistance was provided by the following individuals and departments of Time Inc.: Editorial Production, Norman Airey; Library, Benjamin Lightman; Picture Collection, Doris O'Neil; Photographic Laboratory, George Karas; TIME-LIFE News Service, Murray J. Gart; Correspondents Jane Beatty (Philadelphia), Edward Deverill (San Diego), Michelle Dimkich (Houston), Jane Estes (Seattle), Martha Green (San Francisco), Rosemary Lewis (Los Angeles), Ann Natanson (Rome), Jeff Nesmith (Atlanta), David Snyder (New Orleans), Sue Wymelenberg (Boston).

CONTENTS

The pleasures of gardening indoors 1

"My family lives in a jungle," one of my daughters once warned a visitor. She exaggerated. But it is true that I share my office at home with a fragrant orchid, a dwarf pomegranate tree, a primrose, a fern, several pots of pink and white African violets that blossom tirelessly, a huge white poinsettia in season and a number of colourful, exotic specimens with long Latin names. It is also true that until the painters arrived, some handsome vines framed the great window in the living room.

My plants surround me with beauty and satisfy my need for having growing things close by. Almost everyone, whether country-born or city-bred, has that need. You can satisfy it no matter where you live, even if you lack as much as a narrow window sill. My own indoor garden, which includes plants from all over the world, thrives in many rooms of my home in Massachusetts. Some extraordinarily beautiful African violets that I once saw had been raised in a cellar. The florist who was selling them told me that they had been grown locally under artificial light—a technique that more and more gardeners employ each year. Even the concrete forests of cities are coming to look a little like the Hanging Gardens of Babylon. Towering tropical plants reach upwards in skyscraper foyers and reception rooms. Flowers blossom in office windows, and all kinds of potted plants contribute cheer to many desks tucked away in corners that never see sunlight.

Just as people grow potted plants almost everywhere, so do they grow almost every kind of plant in pots. Nearly every type of plant that does not need a rest period in winter can be culti vated in some form indoors with a reasonable expectation of success. True, the indoor plant must adjust to a lower level of light than it would receive outside, to the high winter temperatures that people demand indoors, to low levels of humidity and confined quarters for its roots. But to compensate, the plant does not have to stand up to wind, driving rain and wide-ranging temperature fluctuations. Disease and insects are less of a threat, and a plant-loving owner can generally be counted on

In the conservatory of Mark Twain's house in Hartford, Connecticut, a low fountain is surrounded by rosy-purple cyclamens, blue hyacinths, red gloxinias and pink begonias. In the right foreground is a pink hydrangea.

for a regular supply of food and water. Plants as diverse as ferns and vines, shrubs and miniature trees flourish indoors, but the plants that add the brightest note to a home, distilling the essence of the beauty of nature, are those that flower. Such plants are themselves a huge group, and this book will deal specifically with them, describing in detail more than 150 in the encyclopaedia section, beginning on page 101.

THE BEGINNINGS   The pleasures to be gained from growing plants indoors have attracted—and challenged—people for a long time. The Minoans, whose civilization thrived on Crete thousands of years before Christ, seem to have had flowerpots. At least, when the Minoans disappeared, about 1100 B.C., they left behind beautifully decorated potting containers with holes in the bottoms. The Greeks, the Indians and the Chinese all raised potted plants, and ancient Egyptian friezes show slaves carrying some in processions. The Romans of the Caesars' days went one better. They shaved huge chunks of mica into thin sheets and used them to make translucent roofs for heated greenhouses where they produced out-of-season lilies and roses. Seneca, the first-century Roman philosopher-statesman, who was a Stoic and therefore somewhat austere, thought his countrymen were going too far. "Do not those live contrary to nature," he asked, "who require a rose in winter and who, by the excitement of hot water and an appropriate modification of heat, force from winter the later blooms of spring?"

Whether people in what used to be called the Dark Ages grew plants inside their gloomy homes, nobody knows. A painting of a legendary martyr of those times, Saint Ursula, shows two house plants on her bedroom window sill, but the historical reliability of that picture is rather doubtful since it was made by the Venetian artist Vittore Carpaccio more than 1,000 years after Saint Ursula's death. By Renaissance times, however, there were palatial indoor gardens that rivalled those of the Romans. The great scholastic philosopher Saint Albertus Magnus built an artificially heated indoor fruit and flower garden in which he entertained a wealthy nobleman, William of Holland, in 1259.

A little later, Venetian and Genoese merchants began using their ships to import such exotic plants as hibiscus from Syria and jasmine from Persia to sell to wealthy Europeans. Semi-tropical fruits particularly caught the fancy of people who lived where it was too cold to grow such trees outdoors. The French, the Dutch, the Germans and the English all wanted oranges and lemons, and began wintering tub-grown trees in heated sheds. The sheds gave way to greenhouses that grew ever bigger and better, and eventually such plants as camellias shared the warmth and space with the citrus trees. If the favourable conditions of a specially built greenhouse were lacking, a gardener made do with whatever warm place he could find for his plants. An English glass manufacturer named Jacobs won a measure of fame in 1660 when Sir Hugh Platt, in a book entitled *Garden of Eden*, wrote about him: "I have known Mr. Jacobs of the Glassehouse to have carnations all the winter by benefit of a room that was near his glassehouse fire."

THE CONSERVATORY

From such beginnings came the conservatory, the pride and pleasure of the 19th century. (The conservatory differs from the greenhouse in that it is a place to display plants as well as to raise them, and unlike most greenhouses it is usually within a house instead of apart from it.) It achieved its maximum splendour in the Victorian decades, when parlours and bay windows were lush with palms, heliotropes, ferns, ivies, begonias, camellias, fuchsias, geraniums, carnations, cinerarias, calceolarias and aspidistras—all seeming to be carefully placed to intimidate boisterous small boys. But elaborate conservatories were the vogue even early in the century. One was described by Bory de Saint-Vincent, who entered Vienna with Napoleon's army in 1803. He wrote:

"It was a novel and enchanting circumstance, so far as I am concerned, to find the apartments of most ladies adorned with flowers. I recall among others, with a kind of intoxicated delight, the boudoir of the Countess of C., whose couch was surrounded with jasmine climbing up daturas (shrubs of the nightshade family) . . . and all this on the ground floor. You repaired from it to the sleeping chamber through clusters of African heaths, hortensias, camellias—then very little known—and other precious shrubs planted in well-kept borders, which, moreover, were ornamented with violets, crocuses of every colour, hyacinths and other flowers, growing in the green turf. On the opposite side was the bathroom, also placed in a conservatory where papyrus and iris grew around the marble basin and the water conduits. The double corridors were not less plentifully garnished with beautiful flowering plants; you might readily, in this enchanted recess, leave open the doors and windows as if an eternal spring had prevailed—the hot-water pipes which promoted and preserved the freshness of the vegetation securing in every department an equality of temperature. Yet all these marvels were kept up at no very great expense."

MODERN INDOOR GARDENING

Your own indoor garden may never rival that of the Countess of C., whoever she was, but that remark about "no very great expense" still holds true. And in most other ways, the modern indoor gardener has advantages that 19th-century Viennese who were not countesses never enjoyed. Central heating permits you to grow exotic flowering plants native to the tropics. The

Colours for all seasons

The pleasure of being surrounded by flowering plants can last all year round, since the blooming periods of different species vary enough to allow a run of colour from January to December. The array of plants on the right, arranged in four rows according to the seasons of maximum visual appeal, represent just a sampling of the palette of colours an indoor gardener might draw upon during the year.

Many of these plants remain in bloom for a generous stretch of time: for example, the ginger-coloured flowers of the chrysanthemum, (second from left in the row of autumn-flowering plants) last for two months or more. Others, like the amaryllis (third from left among the spring-bloomers) flaunt their colours for only a few days.

Some house plants are chosen as much for their leaves as for their flowers. The large, velvety ovals of the gloxinia (summer, second from right) make a major decorative contribution, as do the marbled leaves of the cyclamen (autumn, left) and the strap-like foliage of the clivia (spring, right). In other cases, the fruit of the plant may be a rich source of colour. For instance, the solanum (autumn, second from right) is at its best when bright orange and red berries replace the tiny white flowers the plant presents in summer. And when the berries fall, usually in early spring, the solanum continues to retain decorative usefulness as a small, bushy plant with tiny evergreen leaves.

SPRING

BEGONIA

CINERARIA

SUMMER

EXACUM

PELARGONIUM

AUTUMN

CYCLAMEN

CHRYSANTHEMUM

WINTER

PRIMULA

EPIPHYLLUM

AMARYLLIS

CALCEOLARIA

CLIVIA

PACHYSTACHYS

GLOXINIA

HOYA

APHELANDRA

SOLANUM

SAINTPAULIA

ANTHURIUM

POINSETTIA

AZALEA

11

large windows of today's houses admit more light than ever penetrated old-fashioned farms and city houses, and electricity supplements it with artificial light. Even the gas now used in our kitchens favours house plants. In the past it was manufactured from coal and gave off fumes that—whether anyone noticed them or not—pervaded much of the house and poisoned plants; natural gas, which has generally supplanted coal gas, is non-toxic to plants.

The materials employed for indoor gardening have also been improved. Soils and fertilizers are compounded to suit specific plants in the same way that a pediatrician's formula suits a specific infant. The plants themselves may be purchased at nurseries, florists' shops and garden centres. And the variety now available is astonishing, thanks in part to air freight, which quickly brings from remote corners of the world exotic species that could not survive an extended trip. Before you buy anything, though, you had better decide what plants will please you most and what plants among them will do well in the conditions that you can provide.

SELECTING PLANTS   Consider first what a flowering house plant is. The definition is not so simple as "a plant that flowers in the house". Besides bearing flowers, it must be suitable in size for indoor living; you do not want to be crowded out of the house even by the most beautiful of plants. It must tolerate the generally high level of heat and the low humidity in most houses. And it should grow well enough under ordinary care to delight you.

But flowers are the primary goal, and you should know what to expect of a plant before you choose one. First there are those that blossom incessantly and, when given proper treatment, live for years. Among them are the African violets (*Saintpaulia*) whose profuse blossoms of white, pink, blue or purple have made them outstanding favourites; the wax begonias, sparkling with pink, white or red flowers about as large as a man's thumbnail; and the Chinese hibiscus, which is no small plant from the forest floor, but a tropical shrub—it bears white, pink, yellow, red or orange single or double blossoms more than 10 centimetres (4 in.) across, and would grow to the ceiling if you gave it a chance. I keep mine down to 90 centimetres (3 ft) in height by pruning the roots and tops (*page 55*), and it has been bearing blossoms the year round for nearly 25 years.

A second category of house plants embraces those that bloom only part time in the house, but bear attractive foliage when not in blossom. Among such plants is the Christmas cactus (*Zygocactus*), which sends out sprawling chains of 2.5 centimetre (1 in.), dark green, elliptical, leaf-like stems linked together and suddenly, at Christmas time, produces 5 centimetre (2 in.) blossoms at the end of each chain. I have one that

A PORTABLE PLANT BOX

An inexpensive wooden container on castors displays house plants off the floor and allows the plants to be moved about according to their light and temperature needs. The inside is waterproofed with thick plastic sheeting or silver asphalt paint.
A 5 or 7.5 cm (2 or 3 in.) bed of gravel or vermiculite steadies the pots and keeps the plants above any water that reaches the bottom. Plants in large pots are set directly in the gravel; smaller ones are raised to the same level by being set on top of the inverted empty pots. Sphagnum moss stuffed around the pots provides stability and is kept moist to maintain needed humidity around the plants.

must have been 20 years old when I inherited it from my grandmother 30 years ago, and it still dresses itself up with hundreds of pink blossoms every winter. The rest of the year its unique greenery earns its keep.

In a third category are such lovely plants as the gloxinia— a relative of the African violet but bearing larger blossoms. They thrive for 20 years or more, but bloom for only a few months at a time, and need careful storage during their rest periods.

And finally, there are exceedingly beautiful house plants that are short-term but welcome guests. Grown in greenhouses by professionals and acquired by indoor gardeners at the peak of their glamour, they last but for a short while. A pot of crisp tulips blooming in midwinter can bring instant spring into the house for a week, or for several weeks, depending on the temperature; the colder the room, the longer the tulips will last, but the ideal temperature for the plant would prove far too low for you. Usually such plants fade and land in the rubbish bin because they are not truly suited to household life, although the experienced gardener will check first to see if they can be moved outdoors.

The flowering habits of the popular house plants are described in the encyclopaedia section, Chapter 6. These characteristics have nothing to do with the botanical classifications of the plants—the everblooming African violet is related to the intermittently blooming gloxinias but not to the free-flowering wax begonias. But an unusual number of house plants are drawn from just three of the 300 families in the plant kingdom: the orchids, the gesneriads and the bromeliads; they account for more than a quarter of the plants in the encyclopaedia.

Orchids, of which there are thousands of varieties that come from climates as dissimilar as Alaska's and Brazil's, share the distinction of having the most highly evolved reproductive system of all plants: the pistil and stamen are fused in a single column. A few orchids grown as house plants are terrestrial; that is, like most plants, they require soil in which to grow. Most, however, are epiphytes, or air plants; in the wild they grow mainly on trees. They are not parasites, but simply use the trees as living places, gathering their nutrients from the air, from rain water and from bits of decaying leaves caught in the angles of branches. Most orchids grown as house plants thrive in the warm temperatures we maintain in our homes, and although special attention is required to provide them with enough humidity, the species recommended in the encyclopaedia are as easy to grow as many other indoor plants.

The gesneriads, which count among their 120 genera such flowering plants as African violets, gloxinias and achimenes, are mostly plants of tropical or subtropical origin, whose family ties derive from similarities in the structure of their flowers. The bromeliads, of which there are 60 genera and perhaps 1,400 species, include such seemingly different plants as pineapple (*Ananas*) and Spanish moss (*Tillandsia usneoides*); many have stiff leaves in the form of rosettes, and bear bright flowers on spikes. Some are epiphytic; that is, like many of the orchids, they are air plants.

The biological relationships that connect so many house plants have led some indoor gardeners to specialize. Some concentrate on orchids, and there are also bromeliad and gesneriad specialists (and societies devoted to the culture of these plant families). The family connection is indicated in the encyclopaedia (which lists plants by genus) for those plants that belong to the orchid, bromeliad or gesneriad families.

MICRO-CLIMATES AT HOME

When you have decided what kinds of plants you would like to grow, take stock of the conditions you can provide for them. Since house plants come from many different parts of the world, their needs for light, temperature and humidity vary greatly. But plants are adaptable, and many inexperienced gardeners do not realize that their houses are also adaptable, that is, that each house offers a broad range of micro-climates within itself. Even with central heating, different sections of a house will be far from uniform in temperature. A window sill on the north side is usually far cooler than one on the south. A window on the south generally gets more light than one on the north. Kitchens and bathrooms are usually more humid than other rooms.

In determining the places where your plants will do best, you will find a maximum-minimum thermometer and a hygrometer (*Chapter 2*) almost indispensable. The first records the extremes of temperature that are a principal factor influencing

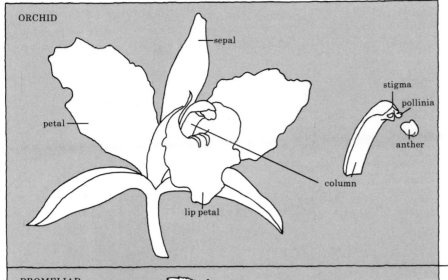

ORCHID

sepal

petal

stigma

pollinia

anther

column

lip petal

Despite their spectacular range of configurations, sizes and colours, the flowers of all orchids have the same basic structure: three sepals, or petal-like outer leaves, and three petals. One petal, called the lip, assumes a variety of shapes, often curling around a fleshy column formed of the fused male and female organs, a unique characteristic of the orchid. Insects that are attracted to the orchid's nectar easily knock the anthers off the column (inset) and deposit pollen picked up from another orchid on the exposed stigma, fertilizing the flower.

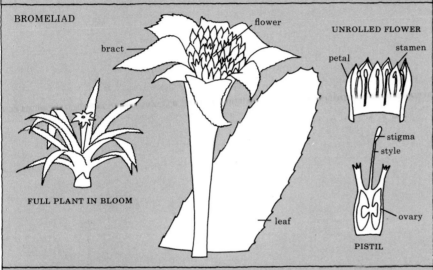

BROMELIAD

flower

bract

UNROLLED FLOWER

petal

stamen

stigma

style

ovary

PISTIL

FULL PLANT IN BLOOM

leaf

The tiny flowers of the bromeliad family of plants come in clusters, some spread out along a tall central spike, some in compact clumps like the one on the left in the drawing, which is shown enlarged in the centre view. The flowers are usually overshadowed by brilliantly coloured, scale-like leaves, or bracts, attached in various ways to the flower clump. The flowers ripen a few at a time, the petals opening to disclose male stamens (upper inset on the right) and female pistils (lower inset). Pollen deposited on the pistils finds its way down to the ovary, fertilizing the ovules to produce seeds.

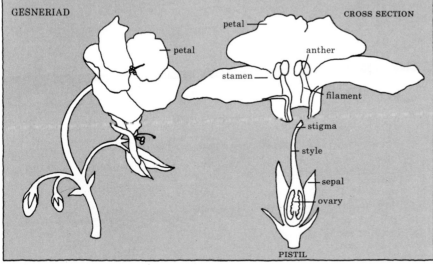

GESNERIAD

petal

CROSS SECTION

petal

anther

stamen

filament

stigma

style

sepal

ovary

PISTIL

The flowers of African violets have five petals whose bases are united to form a tubular corolla that distinguishes the gesneriad family. Each flower has but two male stamens topped by large pollen-bearing anthers (upper inset). The female pistil thrusts far above the anthers, a design that favours cross-fertilization over self-fertilization—the stigma at the pistil tip (lower inset) is more likely to trap pollen that has previously been picked up by a visiting bee than pollen the bee gathers from this flower as it pokes down past the low-set anthers.

the growth of house plants, the second measures relative humidity. With them, you can discover many micro-climates within your house and capitalize on them to grow a variety of plants.

HOW TO BUY PLANTS Since the choice is so wide, the principal problem in selecting plants to grow may be making up your mind. More objective standards apply when you come to buy individual specimens. The first rule is: acquire them from a reputable source and be prepared to pay a fair price. I am sceptical of bargains and you should be too, for horticulture, I must admit with sorrow, has its share of marginal operators who are rich in promises and poor in performance. Even when you know your nurseryman or florist is reliable, examine your plants carefully before you buy. Choose those that are of peasant build, that is, short and stocky, rather than tall and spindly, and that have abundant foliage growing right down to the top of the pot (*drawings below*); such characteristics indicate vigorous health and promise prolific blooms. Plants on which the first buds are about to open are preferable to those with full-blown blossoms because you will be able to enjoy their beauty from the beginning. And, of course, avoid plants with symptoms of pest infestation. Look at the undersides of leaves for tiny spots that are lighter than the rest of the leaf: if you find any, you know that insects have been sucking the plant's juices, to its detriment. Examine leaf surfaces near the

WHAT TO LOOK FOR IN BUYING A HOUSE PLANT

This plant is a poor buy: it has only three flower stems, two past their blossoming prime and only one to come; the plant's main stem is spindly and off centre, and the leaves are sparse.

A near-perfect plant has a thick and well-balanced array of leaves on a straight, sturdy central stem. Only one stem is in bloom, but many buds indicate a long flowering to come.

tip of new growth for the minute green, yellow, pink, black or brown insects called aphids, or plant lice. Check for evidence of spider mites, or red spiders, as they are commonly called; the mites are too small to be seen without a magnifying glass but the damage they cause is not: they manifest their presence with speckled, whitish discoloration of the leaves. Look at the leaf axils—the points where leaves and stems join—for a white, cotton-like substance that is really a community of mealy bugs.

Once you are satisfied that all is well with the plants that you have chosen, make sure they are properly wrapped if the weather is chilly. Many house plants suffer quickly from cold, and even if your car is only a few steps from the greenhouse door, your purchases will require protection in sub-freezing temperatures.

After you have a few healthy plants growing, I predict, you will want more. Fortunately, plants are easy to multiply (*Chapter 5*), and you will find that other indoor gardeners are eager to share experiences and swap cuttings. I have seen one example of such generosity in a skyscraper that revels in the beauty of several dozen pots of busy Lizzies (*Impatiens*)—a lovely plant with canes that thrust out in every direction, bright green leaves and masses of pink flowers. All the building's specimens are children or grandchildren of a single plant with a Cinderella-like history. The parent plant was given to an acquaintance of mine by two friends who had found it on a rubbish heap. It was in a sorry state. It did not even have a pot. Its stems were shrivelled, and its roots were dry and almost devoid of soil. The recipient of the plant responded to the challenge. He potted the orphan in good soil, trimmed it of dead wood, watered it cautiously while it convalesced, and set it in a cool, shaded window. It soon recovered and began to grow vigorously. But those who were pressed into accepting cuttings to grow for themselves soon became converts to house-plant gardening. In a surprisingly short time they were growing other kinds of plants as well, enthusiastically committed to the "green revolution" indoors and worthy successors to the Minoans, the Greeks, the Romans and the Countess of C.

WRAPPING A PLANT

If you have to carry a house plant outdoors in winter, wrap it in three or four layers of newspaper to prevent harm from cold. Set the pot on its side in one corner of the outspread sheets and roll it diagonally so that the paper forms a cone around the pot. Then fold the paper under the bottom of the pot, fasten the side with tape and staple across the top (inset). Such protection is essential, even for the short walk from a florist's shop to the car on a cold day; otherwise the abrupt change in temperature can shock a plant enough to cause it to lose leaves or even die.

Decorating with house plants

Whether you fill every room in your house with flowering plants or limit your indoor garden to one or two window sills, the plants you choose and how you arrange them can make all the difference in the satisfaction they provide. While foliage plants such as philodendrons and rubber plants will survive in a gloomy corner, most flowering plants need natural light in which to flourish and blossom well. This generally means putting them close to windows—the reason why window gardens continue to be the backbone of houseplant decorating schemes. A striking effect can be achieved by placing a single trailing plant like an ivy geranium in a container in front of a window. Or a wide window sill can be used to hold an entire collection of small and medium-sized plants like primulas and African violets. Flowers banked in front of glass doors or by large windows can also create a spectacular greenhouse effect, bringing the garden right in to the house (*pages 26-27*).

Small or badly lighted houses like the 16th-century cottage opposite can be transformed by house plants. Here the indoor gardener has banked pots of multi-coloured cinerarias by a glass door leading to the garden and has lined pots of cyclamens along the window ledge, transforming the low-ceilinged room into a garden spot. Sunlight streaming through the glass picks up the reds, pinks and purples of the flowers and suffuses that part of the room with colour. In the corner, large ceramic containers filled with begonias and azaleas have been set on two small tables.

Flowering plants can be used to complement colour schemes, soften architectural lines, and lend visual interest to out-of-the-way spots. Certain settings seem best served by particular plants. For instance, the long-leaved and elegant bromeliads might almost have been designed for large modern rooms with clean contours and spare decor. Small, bushy hydrangeas and marguerites, on the other hand, fit snugly into alcoves and blend with old-fashioned chintz coverings and other traditional furnishings. By taking advantage of plants with different flowering seasons, you can provide decorative enhancement to a room all year round, bringing summer lushness indoors or adding warmth to an interior on even the greyest winter day.

Rows of pink cyclamens, red and pink cinerarias, and red azaleas enliven the corner of a cottage lounge.

Positions

An indoor gardener should look at every corner of a house as a possible site for flowering plants—even when there is no direct light. Many plants can be brought to blossom at a bright window, or outdoors in mild weather and then can be transferred to an interior location; in that spot, they will retain their blooms for days or even weeks before requiring direct light again. An away-from-the-light site often seems to call for an abundance of plants, but paucity, too, has its purposes: for instance, the single vriesea (top right) looks quite at home in a large, contemporary room.

The angularities of a vriesea create an eye-catching focus for a modern living room whose colours perfectly complement the deep green-grey leaves and orange buds of the plant.

Orange and yellow chrysanthemums, red azaleas and white cyclamens supply a flaring floral surprise in the recess of an unused fireplace under a burnished copper hood (below).

The radiant red bracts of a poinsettia, banked with ivy and white and green-leaved dieffenbachias, brighten the corner of a small entrance hall (above).

Taking advantage of corners

The placement of pots of flowering plants in otherwise empty corners can pay impressive visual dividends. Below, a simple entrance hall is brightened by a small bush of marguerites that will flower from early spring to late summer; thereafter, it can be replaced by a winter plant such as a poinsettia. On the right, an indoor garden has been created around a circular staircase tucked into a sunny alcove. The spiky guzmanias, mixed with clumps of different kinds of foliage plants, thrive in this unexpected yet salubrious position.

A kentia palm (left) and a bush of delicate, white marguerites flank an entranceway. Outside is a window box of primulas.

Luminous flecks of orange and red guzmanias emerge from a clump of variegated foliage decorating an interior staircase.

Patterned and plain

Indoor gardening is at its best when the colours, sizes and shapes of plants are carefully integrated with the overall design of a room. The cottage living room below is arrayed with cyclamens, African violets and a blue hyacinth that emphasize the traditional atmosphere and pick up the blue and pink tones of the furnishings. On the right, a flash of pink on a solitary aechmea (foreground)— with its distinctive bromeliad shape—is the focal point in a spacious lounge, while tall, slender maples are silhouetted against the large, sunny windows and white walls.

In the corner of a cottage in Hertfordshire, African violets line the ledge of a tiny window, while a miniature scented cyclamen serves as an apt centrepiece for an antique inlaid table.

A bright pink aechmea enlivens the subdued colour scheme in a sunlit modern flat (right). A basket of scarlet gloxinias serves as the centrepiece on the dining room table in the background.

A sun lounge is rendered into a garden extension by a splendid array of flowering plants—among them, hyacinths, African violets,

cyclamens, begonias and an azalea. On an overcast winter day, the pink and white blossoms supply a welcome infusion of colour.

Providing light and water 2

Like people, plants need to feel at home. Otherwise they go into a decline and eventually pine away. Yet those African violets mentioned in the preceding chapter were, in their American cellar, a long way from their homeland in East Africa's mountains. Here Baron Adalbert Emil Walter Radcliffe Le Tonneux von Saint Paul-Illaire found them in 1892 so they were named *Saintpaulia*. The most popular geraniums, those with scalloped leaves and clusters of coral or pink flowers, originated in South Africa. Begonias, of which there may be as many as 1,000 species, range in their free state throughout the tropics and subtropics of the world. In the Western Hemisphere, they are found from Brazil north to the Caribbean islands and Mexico. But like hundreds of other plant immigrants, the begonias, the geraniums and the African violets can flourish away from their natural habitats as long as they are made to feel at home.

To feel at home, they demand temperatures, light, water and humidity, similar to those they were accustomed to in the old country. Plants are adaptable, but the closer you can come to creating the environment that each finds ideal, the more they will flourish and bloom. Because they come from such diverse places as deserts and jungles, their preferences differ widely, but they all share one need—light. Without light, plants starve to death, no matter how well they are fed otherwise. In fact, a fertilized plant without light will die—of indigestion—sooner than an unfertilized plant without light.

The reason plants need light is simply and mysteriously wonderful. All plants—that is, all green, chlorophyll-pigmented plants, not such fungus growths as mushrooms—depend on photosynthesis for their lives. So do many plants that do not *look* green, even those that have red or copper leaves; the green is there, but obscured by the dominant colours. Photosynthesis gets its name from the Greek words for *light* and *putting together* and it is a process that does just that. Light striking a green leaf activates the chlorophyll within the leaf. The chlorophyll sets the plant to work combining water and carbon dioxide from the

The seven flowering house plants most frequently sold as gifts make a flamboyant display in a florist shop. The plants, keyed in the drawing on the right, are poinsettias (1), chrysanthemums (2), an Easter lily (3), a geranium (4), a begonia (5), azaleas (6) and African violets (7). At the top left and in the rear are sprays of peach branches in blossom.

air to produce the sugars and starches that provide energy for the plant's life processes; as a waste product from water and carbon dioxide, plants give off oxygen vital to man. (You may have heard that plants thrive in human company. They do, although it is not your presence that they enjoy but the carbon dioxide that you exhale.) When the light fades, the synthesizing process gradually stops and the plant has to draw energy by consuming the stored-up supplies of sugars and starches. If the light does not return before the supply runs out, the plant dies. Although all flowering house plants need light to survive, each species has its idiosyncrasies about how much and what kind it needs when. Some, such as geraniums and chrysanthemums, require plenty of strong straight-from-the-source sunlight. Camellias also like bright light, but not the sun's direct rays; they do better if set a bit away from a bright window. Others prefer their light in even more moderate doses: cyclamens, primroses and African violets, for example, will tolerate the weak sun of northern winters from November to February, but need partial shade during the rest of the year. African violets and busy Lizzies, however, exemplify the adaptability of plants and will also blossom quite handsomely on a north-facing window sill where they never see the sun.

The strength of light varies of course—as any camera owner with a light meter knows—by latitude, by season, by the weather and by the time of day. These variations, and the preferences of plants in the matter of light, present together one of the challenges that make indoor gardening so fascinating—at least to me.

HOW TO PICK THE SPOT

To cope with the challenge, it is necessary to know, not to guess at, the needs of each plant, and this information is detailed in the encyclopaedia (*Chapter 6*). Where climate and weather are variables, you will not always be able to provide the optimum conditions, such as at least five hours of winter sunlight for gardenias, crossandras and lantanas, which will make them produce abundant flowers. To come closest to this ideal, put your gardenias, crossandras and lantanas in the brightest, south-facing window in your house, and if the room is painted white—which reflects light—so much the better. Make sure that the window you choose is the brightest—a tree or an over-hanging roof may make one window less desirable than another that seems less bright but is unobstructed. (The alternatives, chopping down the tree or removing the roof overhang, are not necessarily recommended.) A light meter will help you to determine which windows offer your plants the brightest light.

But suppose all your windows are bright and the plants you choose are lady's slipper orchids (*Paphiopedilum*) and African violets, which do not need much sun. Place the plants far enough back from the window to keep them out of the direct rays of the

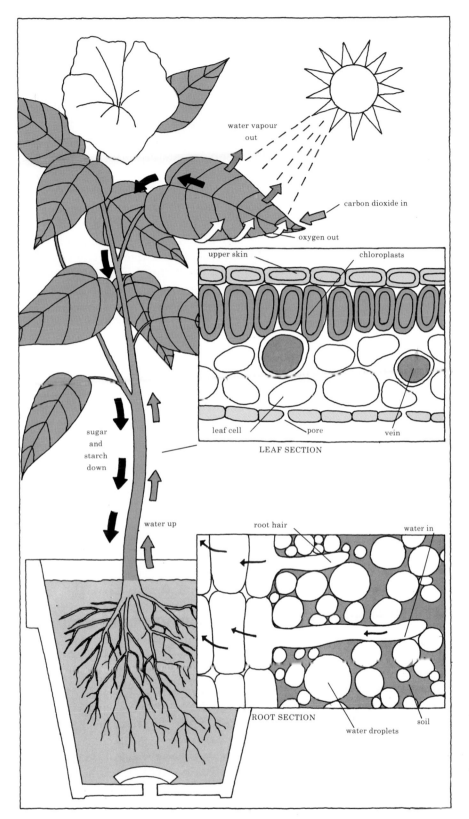

water vapour out

carbon dioxide in

oxygen out

upper skin   **chloroplasts**

leaf cell   pore   **vein**

LEAF SECTION

sugar
and
starch
down

water up

root hair   water in

water droplets   soil

ROOT SECTION

MAKING FOOD FROM AIR, WATER AND SUNLIGHT

Photosynthesis, the process by which plants convert light into food, is especially crucial to house plants, because they rarely have access to as much light energy as outdoor plants do. The process starts as tiny root hairs draw moisture from the soil and pass it on to the root cells, as indicated in the lower inset, which shows the magnified longitudinal section of a typical root. From the roots the water moves through an intricate system of tiny pipelines up the stem and into the leaves. At the same time carbon dioxide is absorbed from the air through the pores in the undersides of the leaves, as shown in the upper inset, an enlarged cross section of a leaf. Light striking the leaf activates the light-sensitive green pigment, chlorophyll, which is contained in cells called chloroplasts just beneath the leaf's translucent skin. The chlorophyll splits the water molecules into hydrogen and oxygen; the carbon dioxide and hydrogen engage in reactions to form sugar and starch. This food is conducted through the veins and eventually to the other parts of the plant. Cells in the leaves and the rest of the plant convert the food into energy and new growth. Oxygen, a waste product of the process, and excess water vapour not used by the plant are given off into the atmosphere by the leaves.

Charles Dickens, whose love for flowers and gardens is apparent in his novels, always had a small cup of fresh blooms on his desk when he wrote, and in 1869, the year before he died, he realized a long-held ambition: to have his own conservatory where he could raise living plants. Built as an addition to his country retreat in Kent, largely with the proceeds from reading his works on a lecture tour of America, this "brilliant but expensive" glass and iron structure, as Dickens described it, opened on to both the drawing room and dining room. Dickens loved to linger there after dinner, admiring his lobelias and geraniums, which he sometimes lighted at night with Chinese lanterns strung below the glass roof.

sun, or fit a net curtain across the window. Dark walls may help in a situation like this, for the darker the paint, the less light it reflects. But conditions differ so much in each house that in the end you will have to do the best you can for each plant, and then rely on pragmatism. If a plant does well, leave it where it is. If it does not do well, try another place, keeping in mind the plant's needs. You can determine whether or not the plant is doing well by looking at a distance between leaves on new stems and comparing it with the distance between leaves on older parts of the plant that grew in a greenhouse before you purchased it. If the distance has increased, the plant is—in effect, though not in truly scientific terms—stretching itself to seek more light. The same test applies to plants that you have raised yourself from infancy: if there seems to be too much stalk and not enough leaf, the light is insufficient. Move the plant closer to the window glass (but, during the winter, do not let it touch the pane, which will chill it at night), or put it in a sunnier spot. If it is getting too much light, drooping leaves will warn you. Move it to a shadier place, or draw the curtains for part of the day.

Despite all the variables and the dangers of generalization in indoor gardening, one rule holds true for almost all plants: the more light that a plant can be given without causing damage to its foliage and without depriving it of its nightly rest in the dark—which is just as vital to plants as it is to human beings—the more likely it is to produce a rewarding abundance of flowers.

USING ARTIFICIAL LIGHT

Thus far, we have been talking in terms of natural light, which in northern parts of Europe, in winter, often falls short of the optimum. Artificial light offers a solution: it improves the health of plants and increases the production of flowers so markedly that it has become one of the most useful tools of the indoor gardener. I discovered this in the Second World War. I was serving on a naval ship in the Pacific late in 1941, and I became all too aware—for the first time—how much I needed contact with the world of flowers and forests and the earth itself. I desperately desired a green, living plant to counter the grey of the ship and the ocean's mists. But I was not the captain with a sunny cabin; I was a seaman living below the water line.

I did, however, have an electric light over my desk in the store-room where I both worked and slept. And on my last shore leave at Pearl Harbor before the ship sailed on a long voyage, Dr. Harold St. John, who was then head of the Botany Department at the University of Hawaii, had given me a "ti log", a small piece of stem of *Cordyline terminalis*, which is a foliage plant. I set it in a shallow dish of water under my lone light bulb, and within weeks I had a beautiful, healthy plant with long, graceful, sweet corn-like leaves. No white-gloved officer on Saturday morning inspection ever ordered it banished as not covered by Navy Regulations, and when I went to Midshipmen's School almost 18 months later it was still thriving.

My shipboard light bulb was of the old-fashioned incandescent variety, not sufficiently bright to bring a flowering plant into bloom without daylight; but artificial lighting for plants has developed tremendously since those days. There are fluorescent lamps that emphasize certain parts of the spectrum, fostering plant growth and giving off light with much more beneficial rays than did the yellow glow in my cubby-hole. Fluorescent lamps that emit both blue and red rays promote photosynthesis, encouraging the development of foliage and promoting the production of flowers. A similar effect can be achieved by combining ordinary cool-white tubes that are strong in blue rays with warm-white tubes that are strong in red.

Artificial light can also provide supplemental illumination for plants that already get some, but not enough, sunshine. An acquaintance of mine has a deep window sill that looks east and is darkened by an overhanging roof, so the plants that crowd it receive considerably less than the natural light they need. But they flourish because, amidst them, an heirloom kerosene lamp that has been converted to electricity glows every night from dusk to 9 or 10 p.m. The lamp has a 100-watt bulb of the incandescent variety, and the sill and near-by walls are painted white. My acquaintance's plants might produce even more blossoms if

GROWING PLANTS UNDER ARTIFICIAL LIGHT

Many low-growing plants will bloom healthily even in a dark cellar if kept under fluorescent lights of a type made especially for growing plants. The standard unit shown here, two 120 cm (48 in.) *tubes set in a reflector, is adequate for two rows of pots. Cords led through ceiling-mounted pulleys and fastened to the wall by cleats allow the height of the unit to be adjusted whenever necessary.*

FRUITFUL HOUSE PLANTS

Some house plants are raised as much for their edible fruit as for their blooms: Several varieties of Capsicum *bear colourful peppers; the plums of carissas can be eaten right off the bush; and a species of kumquat,* Fortunella margarita, *can be made into a delicious preserve. Perhaps the most spectacular fruiting house plant, however, is the ponderosa lemon (*Citrus limon *'Meyeri', page 109). In addition to abundant, fragrant blooms, it bears lemons less acid than usual. One Boston housewife, who has had a lemon tree growing next to her dining room window for years, bakes lemon pies every time the large fruits ripen.*

LIGHTED PLANTERS

he turned on the light before breakfast, for it is a good rule of thumb that supplemental lighting proves most effective when, added to daylight, it provides a total of 12 to 16 hours of light a day, depending on the plant's needs.

There is a successful commercial grower of carnations who used that rule most profitably. He supplemented the natural light in his greenhouses with fluorescent lighting—to provide 15 hours a day of illumination—and tripled his output of blossoms. A supermarket operator in Alaska saves the high cost of importing tomatoes by growing his own in a greenhouse under fluorescent lights that lengthen the short sub-arctic winter days.

But it is the second use of artificial lighting—to replace sunshine completely—that many gardeners find most challenging and rewarding. Using it 14 to 16 hours a day, they grow such plants as African violets, gloxinias and *Begonia semperflorens* even in cupboards—or in cellars.

Most beginners experimenting with artificial lighting find it more practicable to buy ready-made planters, complete with lamps and almost everything else except plants. These are not always easily available, but where they can be found, they should have an automatic-timer light switch, which turns the lights on and off without you having to remember this chore.

Ready made planters come in a variety of models—and prices. Currently available are clear heavy-duty plastic covers in various shapes—round, oblong or fashioned like a miniature greenhouse. These may need only a single lamp, but converted tea trollies or tiered plant holders naturally require a lamp to each shelf; if they are enclosed with glass they will keep the interior warm and humid and the plants free from draughts.

Some gardeners-by-artificial-light prefer to build their own equipment and purchase only the fluorescent tubes and perhaps the canopy fixture. If you follow that course, be sure to make the height of the canopy adjustable; one way is to suspend it from the ceiling on chains that can be shortened or lengthened at will as the growth of the plants requires.

But whether you buy the ready-made kind or build your own, the general rules for their use are the same: use at least two tubes, allow 15 to 20 watts for each 900 square centimetres (1 sq. ft) of foliage, and keep the tubes 15 to 30 centimetres (6 to 12 in.) from the tops of your plants. And remember that almost all flowering plants need their rest, so they should be exposed to light for no more than 12 to 16 hours. Otherwise they will die of fatigue or never blossom. The importance of uninterrupted darkness, as well as of light, becomes evident when an indoor gardener keeps a poinsettia and tries to make it blossom the second year. Under natural conditions, the plant would have complete darkness from sunset until dawn. Indoors, even the ordinary house lights, turned on in the plant's vicinity after dark, will inhibit the plant from producing flowers. I once saw a single-stem poinsettia that had been grown in a greenhouse for several seasons with artificially induced very long days and very short nights. It was 3.5 metres (12 ft) tall, but it had yet to produce a single flower bud.

Artificial lighting is not yet the perfect substitute for sunlight, for its rays lack the intensity and some of the life-giving qualities of the sun's. Nevertheless, most plants will at least survive under electric light, and some will do much better than others. The types of plants that thrive best, producing rich foliage and an abundance of flowers, are those that in nature prefer subdued light—a category that includes African violets, gloxinias and *Begonia semperflorens*.

While the proper amount of light is indispensable to a healthy plant, equally critical is the amount of water it receives. Years ago when I was a retail florist, I found that every customer waiting for me to finish wrapping his purchase asked the same question, "How often should I water it?" It was easy to specify the needs of any given plant, but when the question is applied to house plants in general, the reply has to be, "It all depends."

WHEN TO WATER

Before I explain, I want to warn you that, in my opinion, over-watering is the No. 1 killer of house plants, and inexperienced gardeners are its well-meaning but dangerous accomplices. One of my daughters, for example, refuses to allow a certain big-hearted member of our household to enter her room. "She'll kill my plants with kindness," she explains. Some people are so afraid that their plants will die of thirst that they keep their soil saturated. Plants cannot grow in waterlogged soil because the over-abundant water drives out air, which is vital to root growth and to the activity of beneficial soil organisms. Roots rot. The soil becomes foul smelling. When this happens to a house plant, it is usually beyond salvation. Throw the victim away, start with a healthy young plant—and do not repeat the crime.

Watering correctly is so important that there is a saying among professional greenhouse horticulturists that "the profit depends on the man with the hose", who can tell at a glance whether or not to shower a given plant.

So—how often to water? The generally accepted advice that a plant should be allowed to become moderately dry between thorough waterings is sound, to a point, but not entirely accurate. There are some exceptions, which I have noted in the encyclopaedia (*Chapter 6*). And there is another important exception to the rule, which is to spare the water in the case of a dormant, or "resting", plant. Just as they rest at night, many plants also rest between their flowering periods. An otherwise healthy plant that is getting enough light and warmth and still shows no new growth is probably dormant; gloxinias, for example, actually shrivel up like old people during this period. A dormant plant needs less water than one that is blossoming. Those that become completely dormant and lose all their top growth should not be watered until they start to grow again, generally in spring at the time of repotting.

The best time of day for watering all plants is in the morning, so they can utilize the nourishment during the hours of daylight. Any excess water should be removed from their saucers or trays within half an hour or so to prevent waterlogging of the soil.

HOW TO WATER

How to water is nearly as important as *when*. The first rule is: do not use cold water, which will set back many plants severely —especially in winter. African violets are so sensitive to cold water, in fact, that if water below room temperature is spilled on their leaves, the leaves will develop ugly yellow blotches. This characteristic has given rise to the widespread belief that African violets cannot stand water on their foliage. Not so. It is just water of the wrong temperature that they detest: in commercial greenhouses, African violets get water as warm as the greenhouses themselves. For my house plants I use water at a temperature of about 32°C (90°F). You do not need a thermometer to test it. If it feels pleasantly tepid, it will do.

THREE WAYS TO WATER HOUSE PLANTS

Watering from the bottom, by filling the saucer under the pot, allows the soil to draw up as much moisture as it can absorb. To avoid root rot, empty the saucer half an hour after watering.

Top watering is best done with a long-spouted can, which allows you to reach in without wetting the leaves or dripping water on the floor. Occasional top watering flushes away accumulated salts.

To give a very dry plant a thorough soaking, immerse the pot in a bucket or sink filled with water to a level that barely covers the top of the pot. Remove the plant when bubbles stop rising, and drain.

Of less importance than the water's temperature, but of concern to some gardeners, is the chemical content of the water. Plants are highly adaptable in this respect, and despite the wide variations in water across Europe, excellent house plants grow in all parts. If water is highly chlorinated—as your tongue and nose will warn you—it is a good idea to let it stand in a shallow pan for a day so that the chlorine will evaporate before you pour it on your plants. The very qualities that make chlorine a disinfectant make it somewhat injurious to vegetation. Highly saline water also has a deleterious effect—and if by chance you have any doubt about your water's salinity, check with your local water authority. Where salinity is a problem, and the air is relatively clean, you would do well to use rain water, collected in a water butt set beneath a drain pipe. Some of the finest plants I have ever seen drank only rain water—just like the flowers that bloom in meadows and forests. But rain water in many big cities and small but heavily industrialized towns is far from pure; in fact it can be so heavy with the floating filth in the air that it may be harmful to plants. If you live in such a place, let it rain for a few minutes to wash the air clean before you collect the rain water for your plants.

The perfect water for plants is the kind that is low in soluble salts. Water that has passed through certain—but not most—kinds of water-softening devices is also excellent. Most

(continued on page 41)

CARE OF HOUSE PLANTS

For a few weeks during the summer, most house plants can take care of themselves if placed outside in light shade in a bed of gravel to keep them cool and moist. In dry climates, use moss peat.

To tide plants over holidays at any time, set them out of direct sun in a tray of moist gravel or vermiculite, water them and cover with clear plastic. Support the plastic on stakes; tuck the ends under the tray.

Notables who shared their names with plants

JEAN NICOT

The genus *Nicotiana*, which includes the fragrant flowering tobacco plant as well as leaf tobacco, is named after the scholar and diplomat Jean Nicot, French ambassador to Portugal from 1559 to 1561. While at the court in Lisbon, he was introduced to tobacco, which had been brought back from the New World in 1558. Intrigued with the new plant, he sent seeds to the Queen Mother, Catherine de Medici of France, to whom he owed his position. After his return home, Nicot also raised tobacco himself on his country estate and promoted the fashionable new custom of smoking among the members of the elegant French court, as Sir Walter Raleigh later did in London.

NICOTIANA

BEGONIA

Begonias are named after an amateur botanist who was a patron of the sciences, the French magistrate and administrator Michel Bégon. Posted to the French Antilles in 1681 to introduce legal reforms after a series of civil disorders there, Bégon brought begonias back with him and introduced them to the botanists of Europe. His large collection of botanical books, illustrated with original paintings, was open to any interested student or amateur.

MICHEL BÉGON

JOEL ROBERTS POINSETT

Joel Poinsett, whose name the familiar Christmas plants bear, served as the first U.S. Minister to Mexico from 1825 to 1829. His indiscreet support of local revolutionaries had previously led to his recall from posts in South America, and his brash enthusiasm for Mexican politics finally resulted in his being asked to leave that country as well. On his return to his South Carolina home, he brought back cuttings of poinsettias and of the similar Mexican fireplant, which grow wild in the Mexican countryside. At first thought to be two species of a new genus, which was named in Poinsett's honour, these plants were later found to be members of the genus *Euphorbia*, so he is remembered only in the poinsettia's common name.

POINSETTIA

VRIESEA

The genus of bright tropical plants known as *Vriesea* is named in honour of a brilliant 19th-century Dutch botanist Willem Hendrik de Vriese. By painstaking experiments he proved that plants, like animals, absorb oxygen and use it in converting food into heat energy. He spent some time in Batavia in the Dutch East Indies and sent a collection of native plants to the Royal Gardens at Kew, London.

W. H. DE VRIESE

CARL PETER THUNBERG

Thunbergia, the black-eyed-Susan, is named after the 18th-century Swedish botanist and explorer Carl Peter Thunberg. A pupil of the famed classifier of plants and animals, Carl Linnaeus, at Uppsala University, and like his teacher a doctor of medicine as well as botany, he joined the Dutch East India Company as a physician so he could study the plant life of Japan, a land closed to all Europeans except the Dutch. He landed in 1775, the first botanist to visit the country in nearly a hundred years and the last one for almost half a century after he left in 1776. During his trip he stopped off in Java, Ceylon and South Africa, exploring and collecting plants. His career was crowned by his appointment as Linnaeus' successor at Uppsala in 1781.

THUNBERGIA

COLUMNEA

The bright-flowered tropical columnea commemorates in Latin the name of Fabio Colonna, the botanical star of a talented and noble Roman family that included statesmen, generals, cardinals, popes (Nicholas IV, Martin V) and a poetess to whom Michelangelo wrote love sonnets. Fabio is noted mainly for compiling in 1592 all the botanical data then known; he was also a member of the exclusive Society of Lynxes, a club of about 30 eminent early scientists, including the astronomer Galileo.

FABIO COLONNA

L. A. DE BOUGAINVILLE

The name of the brilliant-blooming bougainvillea commemorates the French navigator and commander Louis Antoine de Bougainville, who explored much of the world for King Louis XV during a globe circling voyage in 1766-1769. The man who named the genus was the naturalist on board, Philibert Commerson, who undoubtedly saw the plants when the ship put in along the coast of South America, where they are native. On the Pacific leg of the voyage, Bougainville, Commerson and their crew touched at Samoa and Tahiti, the New Hebrides, the Solomon Islands, the Moluccas and the Tuamotus, charting the unfamiliar waters, studying native populations and making further botanical observations. The largest of the Solomons and two straits also bear Bougainville's name.

BOUGAINVILLEA

RRUNFELSIA

The chameleon plant, whose showy flowers turn colour from deep purple to white as they mature, was named brunfelsia by an unknown botanist after Otto Brunfels, a 16th-century botanist—a wry tribute, for Brunfels had himself turned colour: a Catholic monk, he became a Protestant early in the Reformation. In 1530 Brunfels published the first German herbal, an illustrated study of Rhineland plants. In it he included some of the earliest botanical renderings of life-like quality done directly from nature, in hopes of starting his own small reformation in the world of plants.

OTTO BRUNFELS

MARCELLO MALPIGHI

The delicate-flowered, bright-fruited plants of the genus *Malpighia* honour the 17th-century Italian physician Marcello Malpighi, who in the days of ruthless and drastic medical practices was known as the "gentle doctor". Best known for his pioneering use of the microscope to study anatomy and physiology, Malpighi also explored the world of plants. In 1662, two years after he discovered the principle of capillary circulation in the lungs, his probing microscope and analytical mind made a valuable contribution to botany: he was the first to prove that a tree's age can be determined by counting the number of rings in a cross section of its trunk.

MALPIGHIA

FUCHSIA

The dainty-blossomed plants of the *Fuchsia* genus were named in honour of the German physician Leonhard Fuchs, author of a handsome 1542 herbal that contained woodcuts of over 500 specimens gathered near Tübingen, where Fuchs taught medicine. The herbal is still used as a reference work by botanists and horticultural historians.

LEONHARD FUCHS

QUEEN CHARLOTTE SOPHIA

Strelitzias, the flamboyant South African plants known as "bird-of-paradise flowers", commemorate the maiden name of a Queen of England whose happiest hours were spent among the flowers of the Royal Gardens at Kew. Charlotte Sophia of Mecklenburg-Strelitz was only 17 when she left her family's tiny duchy to marry George III and dutifully bear him 15 children. In 1771, when she was 27, Sir Joseph Banks, the British naturalist travelling with Captain Cook on his voyage around the world, came across specimens of the bright-flowered bird-of-paradise plants near the Cape of Good Hope and named them after his Queen. On Banks' recommendation Charlotte later sent an official plant collector to seek out other exotic plants for Kew Gardens, soon turning it into one of the most famous collections of horticultural specimens in the world.

STRELITZIA

GAZANIA

The colourful South African genus *Gazania* is named in honour of a Greek-born scholar of the 15th century, Teodoro Gaza, who translated into Latin the ancient Greek of *Theoretical Botany* and *History of Plants*, two third century B.C. works by Aristotle's pupil Theophrastus. These versions of Theophrastus, prepared while Gaza was a refugee in Italy from the Turkish invasion of his homeland, remained the only books on botanical theory for nearly two centuries.

TEODORO GAZA

softening units work by substituting sodium for the calcium or magnesium that makes the water hard. If the sodium is not removed, it draws water out of plants and thus proves more harmful to them than the calcium or magnesium of the hard water would be. Some of the more expensive softening devices are equipped with de-ionizing units that do eliminate the sodium and other harmful salts, and the water that they produce is almost the equivalent of distilled water and is fine for plants. But if you have a water softener without the de-ionizer, your plants should get rain water or untreated hard water, perhaps from an outside tap that serves the garden hose.

Now, to the actual watering of your plants: there are three common methods—watering from the top of the pot, placing water in the saucer or tray in which the pot stands, and immersing the whole pot. It is generally poor advice to suggest that any plant should always be watered the same way. A combination of methods is preferable, for reasons that calceolarias and cyclamens, for example, demonstrate. If you water them from the top when there is not enough sunshine to dry them, the crowns of the plants—which have dense foliage close to the top of the pot—become wet and it is not uncommon for decay to set in close to the surface of the soil. But if they—or other plants —obtain all their moisture by soaking up water from saucers, fertilizer salts in the soil will rise to the top, accumulating on the soil's surface and on the top edges of the pots, where they will burn the near-by growth. This occurs commonly in African violets, with injury to leaf stems. Although I usually water my African violets by the saucer method, I occasionally give them copious top-of-the-pot watering to leach away the secretions of fertilizer salts on the surface. But I do so only when the air is dry and the weather bright, so that the plants' crowns will not stay wet for too long. This same approach of alternating watering methods works well with almost all of my house plants.

The third method, immersion of the pot in a bucket of tepid water, is time-consuming and laborious, but worth using once in a while because most plants benefit from a thorough soaking occasionally. When you use this method, make sure the water in the bucket rises above the soil level in the pot. Immediately the soil will begin to emit bubbles that gurgle noisily. When the bubbling stops, take the plant out of the bucket and let it drain for 20 minutes before putting it back in its saucer on the window sill. Some gardeners use this dip method exclusively. But I still prefer to water my plants from the top with a long-spouted nondrip watering can. Such a watering can does not have to be followed around with a mop. (A can like that makes a fine house gift for a friend who wants to become an indoor gardener.)

Whatever method you are using at the moment, do the job thoroughly. Do not apply only a little water at a time, because much of the soil deep in the pot is apt to remain dry—and so will some of the roots. But remember that a plant's need for water varies not only with its life cycle—as in the waning gloxinia I mentioned—but with external conditions: on sunny days plants need more water than they do on cloudy days, and even on the sill of a curtained window they respond to the weather. Plants that have just been moved to larger pots need less moisture than they will when they have settled down in their new homes and their roots have filled the balls of soil.

Because the demand for water varies so much, some gardeners use self-watering devices that reduce the frequency of watering and keep the soil uniformly moist for long periods. One simple method, called wick-watering, involves installation of a wick, preferably of glass fibre, when potting or repotting. The usual drainage material (pebbles or crocks from a broken flower pot) is omitted from the bottom of the pot. The wick is spread out on the pot's bottom (*drawings below*) and one end is drawn through the drainage hole and allowed to rest in a tray, saucer or other container of water below the pot. (The pot does not sit in the water, but is raised on legs or a little platform.) The wick, by capillary action, draws water from the container up into the pot. Some plants that need to be kept constantly moist—azaleas, for example—benefit from wick-watering. But the water requirements of most plants vary so much that the

WATERING WITH A WICK

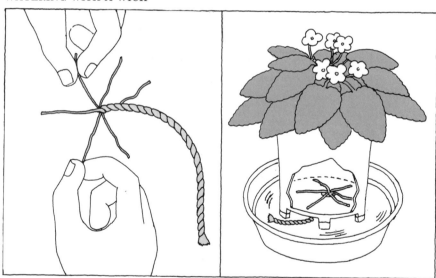

Plants which thrive with constant moisture can be watered by a glass-fibre wick that draws water up into the soil. Prepare the wick by unravelling one end so it will cover the bottom of the pot.

Before potting the plant, insert the wick through the drainage hole of a raised wick-watering pot and spread the unravelled ends flat on the inside. The water should cover the wick but not touch the pot.

wick may provide an excess of water on dull, cloudy days, and too little on bright, sunny ones, and even experts have had difficulty determining just what size wick will serve what plant best. If you are in an experimental mood, however, you may want to try. There are also several commercial devices, such as hydro-culture, that provide a steady supply of moisture, including at least one that senses how dry the soil is and waters accordingly.

HOW TO INCREASE HUMIDITY

Moisture in the air is quite as important to plants as moisture in their soil. Except for kitchens and bathrooms, most houses in winter are frequently as dry as deserts, and in such arid air house plants never attain the full beauty for which they have the potential. Indeed, many of them go brown around the edges of the leaves; if dry air draws off enough moisture the leaves will simply shrivel up. So to increase the humidity—which human beings need as much as plants do—I keep many of my potted plants sitting in large trays. These should be about 5 centimetres (2 in.) deep and can be made of plastic or any painted or non-rusting metal; a welder might make them for you if you cannot find them in the right size or shape. Cover the bottoms with at least 2.5 centimetres (1 in.) of sand, pebbles or pea-sized granules of charcoal, and add water, keeping the water level below the surface of the material selected. The material on which the pots rest serves as a reservoir of moisture and will raise the humidity in the immediate vicinity, depending on the hour and the room temperature, by 100 to 500 per cent. If you doubt my word, measure the humidity around your plants with a hygrometer and find out for yourself.

Plants themselves contribute generously to raising the humidity level. Every plant exhales moisture constantly through its leaves. When a number of plants grow together in one part of a room, they constitute an informal mutual-aid society: the moisture that each gives off serves to raise the humidity and benefits them all. (Come to think of it, I have never seen a lonely plant—the only one in the room or house—that was doing more than barely surviving.) Consider how much water you provide your plants in a week. After they have used it, the moisture they give off hangs suspended in the air. You can add to it by misting your plants with a bottle-type atomizer that emits a fine vapour. Use water of at least room temperature and spray the plants' leaves lightly—not so much that moisture will form beads on the foliage. The aim is not to wet the plants, but to increase the humidity of the air around them. Try it and see how much better your plants will grow.

THE PROPER AIR TEMPERATURES

Air temperature, especially at night, is as important to house plants as the temperature of the water you pour in their pots or spray on their leaves. Most people, I suspect, keep their thermostats set in winter at from 20° to 22°C (68° to 72°F), day and night. That is much too warm for potted tulips, for example, but fine for African violets. But no matter how much people may cherish their plants, they quite rightly cherish their own comfort more. And even if they were willing to forgo it for the sake of their plants, they could hardly reconcile the preferences of the African violets with those of the tulips. But thermostat or no thermostat, the thermometer in the living room does not really reflect the temperatures of different parts of the house. The exposure, the presence or absence of double-glazed windows, and the position of heating ducts and radiators cause surprising variations. In an enclosed but unheated sun porch or in a spare bedroom where the radiator is turned off, you will be able to grow many plants that cannot stand the heat of the kitchen. In my house, the temperature on a wide window ledge in a guest bedroom upstairs drops to 8°C (46°F) on winter nights with the heat turned low—in the absence of a guest, I had better add. The ledge is bright with cyclamens, azaleas and winter-flowering bulbs.

All plants, indoors or out, grow better if you have cooler temperatures at night than by day, and before central heating, indoor temperatures fell at night as they do outside. Many plants will adapt to average house temperatures, but others will not: fuchsias, calceolarias and many other plants will not set flower buds, and camellias will drop theirs if night temperatures are above 18°C (65°F); they prefer rooms much cooler than that. On the other hand, African violets and gloxinias and their relatives will come close to perishing if night temperatures fall to 7° or 10°C (45° or 50°F). So to some extent it depends on which plants you prefer.

A tale to the point was recounted to me recently by a friend. He owns a large garden centre and maintains a "hot line" for gardeners with questions. He received a phone call from a man who said that his philodendron did not look quite right—in fact, he insisted, it was turning blue. The plant was in a big tub, and repotting it would have been difficult, so my friend advised the inquirer to dig out some of the old soil and replace it with rich, fresh potting soil. About five minutes later the man called back. He could not dig out the old soil because it was frozen. He had neglected to mention in his first call that the plant was placed in his bedroom—and that he slept with the window wide open. It was midwinter and the thermometer had hovered well below freezing point for a week.

THE USEFUL THERMOMETER

In the encyclopaedia, I specify the ideal night temperatures, as well as the recommended day temperatures, for each plant. When you start looking for these ideal temperatures—and there are many micro-climates in our houses—you will find the maximum-minimum thermometer helpful. As a matter of fact, I consider it one of the greatest boons to indoor gardening. This device is not always easy to come by; you may have to ask your local ironmonger to order one for you, but it will prove well worth the trouble and the price. A maximum-minimum thermometer differs from ordinary thermometers in that its column of mercury is U-shaped rather than vertical and records the day's highest temperature on one side of the U and the lowest on the other. (Tiny slivers of metal remain in place at the high and low temperature marks until the thermometer is reset with a magnet that comes with the device.) It was with a thermometer of this sort that I discovered the chilly window ledge in the guest bedroom.

One temperature problem often encountered by flat dwellers —and lots of other people—who would like to grow house plants but complain that they cannot, is presented by radiators. The heat and the dryness around radiators make their immediate vicinity inhospitable to most vegetation. But if the radiator is beneath a window, or anywhere that has sufficient light for plants, its presence need not defeat you. The solution is to deflect the heat. Install a shelf, using a board at least 15 centimetres (6 in.) wider than the radiator and about 15 centimetres (6 in.) above it. Cover the top of the shelf with a layer of asbestos insulating board (available at hardware shops) or any other non-conductor of heat. Put a tray on top of this, with the usual layer of pebbles or sand on the bottom. Use your maximum-minimum thermometer to determine the range of temperatures on the shelf, day and night, and then find suitable plants in the encyclopaedia. But be sure to keep water in the pan always and, except when watering your plants, never let the water level rise to the bottom of the pots.

One final word about environment. Plants need some circulation of air; even in wintertime, greenhouse operators keep their ventilators ajar. Plants do not, however, like draughts—that is, cold air blowing on them suddenly from an open window or door near by. When you want to freshen a room, open a window at the top, and choose one that is farthest from your plants, even the hardiest ones. But do not worry that plants such as cyclamens and primroses on a sill of a closed window will suffer from cold at night, for they can tolerate 4°C (40°F) temperatures without damage as long as their foliage does not touch the cold glass. Tropical plants such as African violets and gloxinias, however, should not be chilled. Move them away from the cold at night.

Now you know (I hope) how to create the proper environment for growing green flowering things. This is not as complicated as it may sound. All it takes, really, is a degree of dedication, a reasonable amount of intelligence, a watering can—and a careful eye on temperature and light.

PLANTS AND COLD DRAUGHTS

45

Soils, pots and potting 3

Of all the near miracles of gardening that we take for granted, one of the most impressive is the ability of plants to thrive in containers—a variety of pots, boxes, trays, wooden tubs, tins, virtually anything that will hold soil. It seems so unnatural. Out of doors, plants in the wild can pick and choose their preferred growing conditions—coniferous trees the sandy, acid earth of a hillside, flowering annuals a sunny meadow rich with nourishment, saw grass a swamp. But indoors we toss a few cupfuls of soil into a container, embed a plant's roots in it, and say "Now grow". The marvel is that the plant usually does grow. And if it does not flourish, it will at least survive, for plants possess a determination to live that enables them to make the best of even the poorest soil—and in the case of so-called air plants, no soil at all.

But you want your plants to do more than survive. You want them to thrive, and whether or not they thrive depends on the kinds of soil and containers they live in. Although some plants have unique requirements, most will do well in any container in which water does not collect and remain unused to drown the plants or rot their roots. But they will need better than average soil if they are to bear rich foliage and masses of bright flowers. Your garden soil, no matter how rich it looks, is not well suited to potted plants. For one thing, it may contain insect eggs, weed seeds or disease spores; more important, it lacks sufficient organic matter to make it porous enough for proper drainage in the confines of a pot under frequent watering. The lack of porosity also blocks air, which the roots of plants need just as much as they do moisture. The soil is soon compacted into a hard, impenetrable mass.

So when growing house plants, your first concern should be to make sure that you have the right kind of growing medium for each kind of plant. Generally speaking, orchids raised as house plants are air loving and require a special medium, a porous fibrous mixture; and many bromeliads and gesneriads flourish in a mixture including twice as much moss peat or leaf-

The ancient Greeks used potted plants as tokens of yearly rebirth. In this detail from a fifth century B.C. vase, Eros, god of love, hands seedlings to a girl celebrating rites for Adonis, symbol of plant fertility.

mould as you would give most house plants, approximating the natural environment in which they grew wild. But the majority of house plants will do well in a more or less standard mixture. You can make such a mixture by sterilizing ordinary garden soil in the kitchen oven to get rid of weeds, insects and diseases, and then mixing it with various supplements. But most indoor gardeners buy pre-packaged potting soil, available at garden centres, florists' shops and many hardware shops. Packaged potting soil has been sterilized and packed with enough moisture to make handling and potting easy. It comes in airtight plastic bags that retain moisture; any left-over soil will not dry out if the bag is resealed. Many potting soils also contain soil-loosening agents such as moss peat, and enough nutrients to start plants off well.

IMPROVING POTTING SOIL If I have any complaint about packaged potting soils, it is only that they have been screened too finely; perhaps the packers do that to forestall complaints from misguided gardeners about twigs, pebbles or lumps of moss peat in the product. The truth is that plants, except for very tiny seedlings, benefit from a little roughage in their soil. So although most packaged soils can be used as sold, I prefer to add coarse organic matter, which opens up the soil structure, and also some gritty material, which facilitates drainage. The most widely available organic

HOW MUCH SOIL TO PUT IN A POT

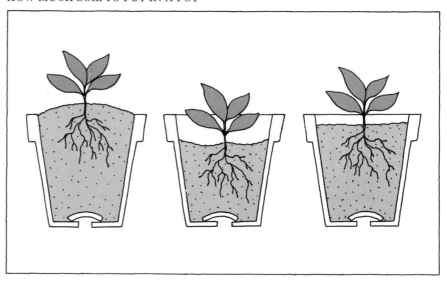

If the soil level in a pot is too high (left), water will spill over the side of the pot and the plant will not get enough moisture when you water it. A low level (centre) presents an almost irresistible temptation to

fill up the empty space, and too much water may cause the plant's roots to rot. The correct level (right), is about 12 mm ($\frac{1}{2}$ in.) from the top; 2.5 cm (1 in.) in pots 15 cm (6 in.) or larger.

material is moss peat, the partially decayed fibres of bog mosses. (The best kind of moss peat for potting mixtures is sphagnum moss peat; this material should not be confused with sphagnum moss, the dried but undecayed form of the moss used for packing plants, holding moisture in hanging baskets and rooting cuttings.) Another good organic material is leaf-mould, which consists of decayed, compacted leaves. Whichever you use, make sure it is coarse. The best kind of moss peat is the poultry grade, so called because it used to be spread on the floors of chicken coops to absorb droppings. Unlike the finer garden variety of moss peat, it comes in chunks 6 to 12 millimetres ($\frac{1}{4}$ to $\frac{1}{2}$ in.) in diameter, and this rough texture makes an ideal addition to the packaged potting soil.

For gritty material, some professional growers use the mineral called perlite, a synthetic product that is light in weight and spongy; it not only loosens the soil so that air can enter but absorbs and stores moisture. Vermiculite can be used equally satisfactorily where perlite is not obtainable. Cheaper than perlite or vermiculite is coarse, or "sharp", sand; it can be bought at most garden centres and horticultural sundriesmen.

To prepare a potting mixture that contains the essentials for most house plants, start with a bag of packaged soil, a similar quantity (by volume) of coarse moss peat or leaf-mould, an equal amount of a coarse sand, a trowel or small shovel and a tightly woven basket or a large bucket.

Using the trowel or shovel, place some of the soil in the basket or bucket, then add equal quantities of the moss peat or leaf-mould and the sand, and mix them together thoroughly. Repeat the procedure several times until you have enough for the job at hand. Then add ground limestone, at the rate of 75 to 140 grams (3 to 5 oz) per 36 litres (1 bushel) and mix thoroughly again. The limestone will counter the mixture's acidity, giving it a suitable pH of about 5.5 to 7.0, which approaches the neutral middle of the scale between extreme acidity (pH 0) and extreme alkalinity (pH 14). If the mixture is intended for acid-loving plants such as azaleas or gardenias, use 2 parts moss peat to 1 part potting soil and 1 part sand to provide the acidity these plants need, and do not add limestone.

With properly mixed soil, almost any type of container can be adapted to any kind of plant. The most common containers, of course, are pots—but pots come not only in many sizes but in different materials and in several different shapes that are designed for different uses.

Whatever its use, a pot's size is described by its top diameter. The smallest pot in common use is 5 centimetres (2 in.) across and the largest 30 centimetres (12 in.), although some can be found in larger sizes. In shape, regular flowerpots

LILIES FOR EASTER
The great trumpet blossoms of the pure white, sweet-scented Easter lily seem as much a part of Easter as bunnies and coloured eggs. Yet Lilium longiflorum is a comparative newcomer to the Christian world. The Madonna lily of Europe, Lilium candidum, was long the Easter flower, but it has one disadvantage: it is difficult to be sure of bringing it to blossom in time for the festival. About a hundred years ago, a missionary returning from the Orient stopped in Bermuda and presented a friend there with some early flowering wild lily bulbs he had gathered. They thrived in the island's mild climate. Soon their similarity to the Madonna lily— and their more convenient blossoming season—attracted florists. They promptly adopted the "Bermuda" lily, and the importation of longiflorum bulbs, from both Bermuda and the Orient, became big business.

SELECTING THE POTS

49

DISPLAYING PLANTS IN DECORATIVE CONTAINERS

1. *Plants in clay or plastic pots can be set inside many kinds of ornamental containers to display them to advantage. A formal urn suits well-pruned, symmetrical plants such as hydrangeas. To reduce weight, use a plastic pot on a bed of vermiculite to keep it above drainage water.*

2. *A heavy brass tub on the floor makes a suitable base for a tall, substantial plant such as a hibiscus. The plant is potted in a heavy clay pot that has been surrounded by vermiculite.*

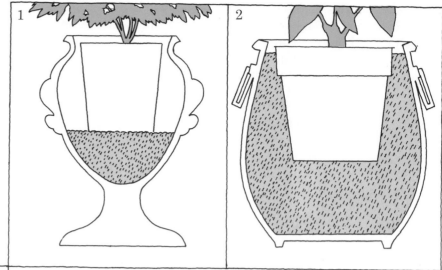

3. *A shallow round interwoven basket can be filled with several small pots of profusely blooming plants such as cinerarias, giving a room a focal point and a massive splash of colour. To provide an attractive, unifying background for the plants as you look down at them, place the pots in a metal liner made to fit and filled with gravel or vermiculite up to the pot rims; if the basket is too high for the plants, prop the liner up on blocks. Sprinkling the gravel occasionally will raise the humidity around the plants.*

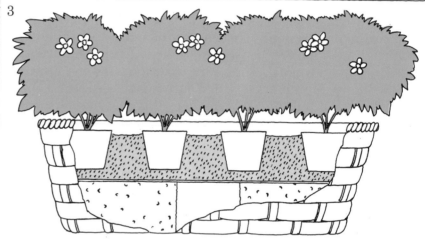

4. *A tall wicker basket can be used for displaying large, bushy plants such as gardenias. Push a deep metal liner into the top of the basket; a cake or biscuit tin may fit, or you can have one made. Set the potted plant in the tin, or use the tin itself as a pot, but put a 5 cm (2 in.) layer of crocks or coarse gravel on the bottom for drainage.*

5. *A pewter or silver pitcher holding a delicate plant such as a lantana makes a charming table centre-piece. If necessary, elevate the plant on vermiculite.*

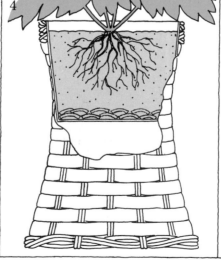

are as tall as they are broad across the top, and are used for most plants from African violets and begonias to geraniums and primroses. Three-quarter pots, often called azalea pots, are three-quarters as tall as their diameter and are used for azaleas and other large plants, to provide stability and to suit their bushy proportions. Pans, which are half as high as they are wide, are used for bulbs because bulbs are planted close to the soil's surface and have a short growing season; they do not need the depth of soil required by other plants.

Most pots are made of clay or plastic, and both have advantages and disadvantages. Clay pots are heavy and thus do not tip over easily. More important, they are porous, so that moisture moves through their walls; this transpiration lessens the danger that waterlogging may rot plant roots, and it adds humidity to the air, which helps most plants. On the other hand, the moisture a clay pot loses through its sides—about as much as its plant uses—is so great that plants in clay pots must be watered more frequently than those in plastic and other non-porous containers. Moreover, with the transpired moisture go dissolved nutrients from the soil; these accumulate on the pots' outside walls, sometimes leading to an unsightly encrustration of fertilizer salts, but more often simply providing a comfortable moist place for unsightly green algae to develop. (The saying that successful gardeners are those with green fingers may have originated with the handling of algae-covered clay pots.) Some manufacturers prevent transpiration—and algae—by coating the outsides of their pots with the moisture-resisting substance silicone, and some house-plant enthusiasts achieve the same result by painting their pots a decorative colour. Most just scrub them clean. Though relatively durable, clay pots do occasionally break, but even the crocks can be useful in achieving proper drainage at the bottoms of other pots.

Plastic pots come in most of the sizes that clay pots do, and in most of the shapes; they also come in square and rectangular versions and in various colours. They are light, and thus both easier to carry and more likely to tip over. Because their walls do not permit passage of moisture, they do not collect algae or fertilizer salts on the outside. But the danger of drowning the plant with waterlogging increases; for this reason many plastic pots have four drainage holes in the bottom instead of one. Nevertheless, it is important that plants in plastic pots have well-aerated soil and be watered with great restraint. The same applies to plants in containers of such materials as glazed earthenware, glass and various metals, some of which are more attractive than clay or plastic but are otherwise not particularly advantageous.

In choosing pots of any material, select the smallest size that will accommodate your plant without immediately over-

THE ORCHID MONKEYS
Part of the almost mystical attraction of the tropical epiphytic, or air-growing, orchids—aside from the rarity of many species—is due to the fact that they make their homes in the tops of giant jungle trees, where they are all but impossible to reach. Orchid hunters solved the problem in Malaysia, where trained berok monkeys have long been employed to collect coconuts, by retraining the monkeys to climb the tall trees and bring the orchids down. The champion, a monkey named Merah, set a record in 1936, when he collected specimens from more than 300 trees.

A DIPSTICK WATER GAUGE

A simple dipstick device, like those used to check the oil level in car engines, can help you prevent over-watering a plant set in a decorative container that lacks drainage holes. The dipstick—a thin wooden plant stake or a length of 6 mm ($\frac{1}{4}$ in.) wooden dowelling—is contained in a length of thin plastic or aluminium tubing set upright at the side of the pot before the plant is potted; it should reach to the bottom of a layer of coarse gravel 2.5 to 5 cm (1 to 2 in.) deep in smaller pots, 5 to 7.5 cm (2 to 3 in.) deep in larger ones. From time to time insert the dipstick in the tube; do not water the plant unless the stick comes out bone dry.

crowding the roots, which should extend to within about 12 millimetres ($\frac{1}{2}$ in.) of the pot walls, all around (in the case of large plants in large pots, no closer than 2.5 centimetres—approximately 1 in.). Non-porous pots are ready to use as they come from the shop. But before using clay pots I recommend that you try a trick that many professional gardeners use—soaking them overnight. If you leave the pots unsoaked, the dry walls will absorb moisture from the potting soil, making it dry out too quickly. It is also a good idea to soak old clay pots every time you re-use them, not only to get them moist but to loosen dirt and old bits of roots so that they can be scrubbed clean easily with a stiff brush or a kitchen scouring pad. After soaking a pot, whether it is an old or a new one, allow it to dry just enough so that soil will not cling to the inside of the pot; then it is ready for use.

GETTING GOOD DRAINAGE

Any pot needs to be filled with more than dirt. First comes material to promote drainage. If the pot is larger than 10 centimetres (4 in.), place a piece of crock from a broken clay pot over the drainage hole or holes, convex side up, to allow water to drain out while keeping the pot's contents in. In pots that are 15 centimetres (6 in.) or larger in diameter, a 2.5 centimetre (1 in.) layer of crocks or pebbles at the bottom is helpful in improving the drainage.

If you are using an ornamental container with no drainage holes in the bottom, special arrangement for drainage should be made. You can set the plant in a slightly smaller pot inside the container, raising the pot on a 2.5 centimetre (1 in.) layer of stones if necessary to avoid having the pot stand in water. Or you can plant directly in the container, using a bottom layer of broken crock pieces, 12 millimetre ($\frac{1}{2}$ in.) pebbles or pea-sized charcoal to act as a drainage layer. Such a container, if it is 25 centimetres (10 in.) high or higher, should have 5 to 7.5 centimetres (2 to 3 in.) of drainage material, which should be lightly covered with a layer of long-strand sphagnum moss, a few autumn leaves, coarse peat or other material to keep the potting soil from sifting down into the drainage area. Care must be taken to avoid overwatering such a closed container, for the only way moisture can leave the container is by evaporation from the soil's surface and from transpiration through the plant's leaves. For the beginner who may be prone to overwater, I suggest the addition of a length of thin pipe reaching from the drainage material to the rim of the pot. Bury this as you fill in with soil. Then by using a dipstick—be sure that water is not accumulating beneath the plant (*drawing, page 52*).

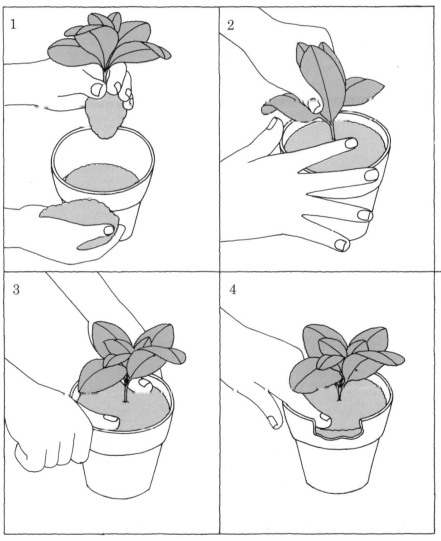

POTTING A PLANT

1. *To pot a plant correctly, hold the plant gently while you put it into the pot, adding enough soil mixture to bring the top of the soil ball to just below the pot's rim. Rest the plant in the pot with one hand and, using the other to add mixture, fill in around the soil ball. The mixture for each type of plant is specified in Chapter 6.*

2. *When the mixture is at the same level as the base of the stem, press down with your forefinger all around the stem to bring the roots into contact with the soil.*

3. *Press down with both thumbs around the edge of the pot to firm the mixture; this will eliminate air pockets and will prevent water from draining too rapidly down the sides.*

4. *With your forefinger, measure the distance between the top of the pot and this mixture; it should be about a finger's breadth, or 12 mm ($\frac{1}{2}$ in.), in pots up to 12.5 cm (5 in.) wide, up to two fingers or 2.5 cm (1 in.), in larger ones. If necessary, add or remove mixture. Water thoroughly.*

Once you have arranged the drainage layer at the bottom of the pot, pick up a handful of your potting soil mixture and make a fist. If the mixture barely holds its shape when you open your hand, crumbles apart at a touch and does not stick to your skin, it is just damp enough for the pot. If it clumps and sticks, it is too damp and needs to dry out a bit. On the other hand, if it is so dry that it will not hold together when squeezed, it should be moistened slightly.

POTTING THE PLANT Now scoop potting mixture into the pot, and rap the pot on a workbench or table to settle the soil and eliminate air pockets. Hold the plant in the pot to see if the top of the soil ball comes to about 12 millimetres ($\frac{1}{2}$ in.) from the top of the pot (2.5 centimetres—1 in.—in larger pots). If the plant is a newly rooted cutting that lacks a ball of soil around its roots, spread the roots gently and sprinkle the mixture in and around them until they are covered. If the plant does have a ball of soil, disturb the ball and the roots as little as possible, although it may be necessary to trim back some of the long straggly roots. Use your hands to fill in around the ball with the potting mixture, and firm down as shown in the drawings on page 53.

Having completed the potting, water the plant thoroughly (*Chapter 2*) and then do not water again until the soil begins to look dry and crumbly.

HOW TO REMOVE A PLANT FROM A POT

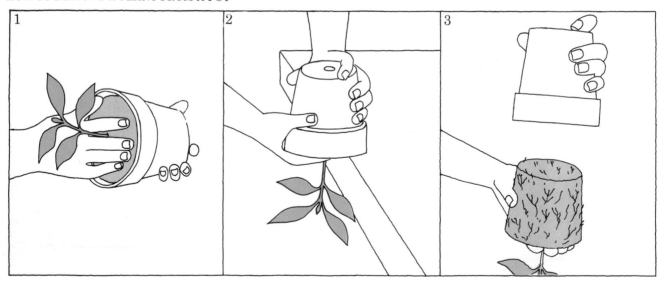

To "knock out" a plant—that is, to remove it from its pot for inspection or repotting—hold the main stem between the fingers of one hand, the pot in the other. Watering beforehand will make the job easier.

Without changing your grip on plant or pot, turn them upside down and knock the rim sharply on the edge of a workbench. The impact will jar the plant loose, with roots and soil intact.

Pull the pot up and away, allowing the plant to slide out while you hold it in your lower hand. You can now check to see whether the roots have grown enough to need repotting.

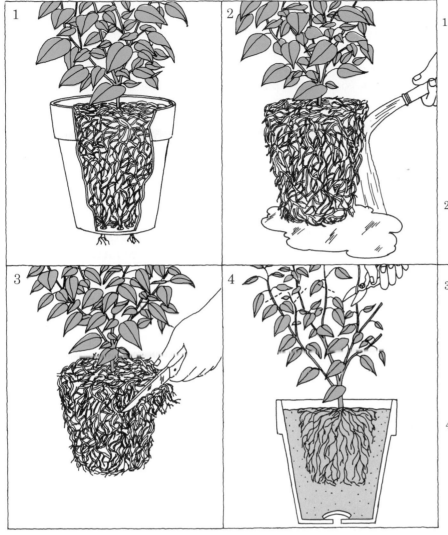

ROOT AND TOP PRUNING

1. *Woody-stemmed flowering plants such as camellias and hibiscuses may become unmanageably large if you use larger pots whenever their growing roots require repotting. When the roots become tightly crowded—even cropping out on the surface of the soil and growing down through the drainage holes—prune both roots and top growth.*

2. *After knocking the plant out of its pot (opposite page), hose it down to remove as much soil as you can from around the roots.*

3. *With a sharp knife, trim the outer roots, shaving down all around the root ball; then turn the plant on its side and slice an equal amount off the bottom. The roots must be 12 mm ($\frac{1}{2}$ in.) from the edge of a pot 25 cm (10 in.) or less in diameter, 2.5 cm (1 in.) away in larger pots.*

4. *Repot the plant (page 53), using the old pot scrubbed clean and filled with fresh soil. To keep the plant in balance, prune the stems (dotted lines)—if you cut a third off the roots, cut a third off the stems.*

A properly potted plant should thrive in its new home for a year, or several years, depending on the spread of its growth. But eventually its roots will outgrow the pot, and it will have to be repotted in a larger container. Only then, when it has more root space, can a healthy plant continue to grow.

Repotting does wonders for plants that seem lethargic, but it cannot restore health to a plant that is already in its last days. Yet many people put all their faith in repotting, as I was reminded not long ago, when I was parking my car close to a florist's shop. I noticed a well-dressed woman carrying into the shop one of the most woebegone plants I have ever seen. My heart went out to the florist for I knew he was going to be asked to repot it, with repot being a euphemism for rejuvenate. The woman obviously did not want the same old straggly plant back in a new pot; she wanted the florist to restore its health and youth

—an impossibility at this late stage. But the small disaster might easily have been averted had the plant been repotted when there was still time.

WHEN AND HOW TO REPOT Repotting is in order when a plant has become pot-bound—that is, when its roots have completely filled the ball of soil and the pot. (A few plants, such as agapanthus, aeschynanthus and crindonnas, blossom more profusely when they are slightly pot-bound and for this reason are repotted less frequently; such plants are so noted in the encyclopaedia.) Sometimes a plant will signal its need for repotting by wilting between waterings and producing only small new leaves and little growth. Sometimes it will give no signal, and continue to grow actively, but if its roots have filled the pot it is soon going to need soil and more room in which to flourish. There is only one way to determine with certainty whether or not a plant needs repotting, and that is to slip it out of its pot and examine its roots, a procedure that is not difficult and will not injure the plant if done properly.

A few hours before removing the plant for examination, water it just enough to ensure that the soil is moist throughout; this extra moisture will help hold the soil ball together and will also prevent the tender tips of the roots from clinging to dry spots on the pot walls—they may be damaged when they are pulled away. Then, with the fingers of one hand outstretched over the top of the pot and around the plant's stem or stems, turn the pot upside down and rap it on a wooden bench or table edge (*drawings, page 54*). Plant, earth and roots will drop intact into your hand. If the roots are tightly matted, and resemble the contents of a tin of spaghetti, the plant has reached the stage at which it needs repotting. With plants that have a dormant period, repotting should coincide with the start of new growth,

(continued on page 61)

Orchids you can grow as house plants

The orchid is something special. Mere mention of the name inspires visions of wondrous beauty in dark jungles, a beauty unattainable by any but the wealthiest or the most adventurous. Yet the orchid, far from being rare, is numerous, varied and ubiquitous. There are at least 25,000 known species, growing on every continent except Antarctica and in nearly every climate from the Congo to Alaska. Despite their seeming fragility, orchids are relatively disease resistant and long lived; despite their aura of exoticism, many are no more expensive than other house plants and take just as comfortably to life in an ordinary living room. Pictured here are some of the many different orchids, from the long-lasting, fragrant Brassavola nodosa to the tawny miniature Cymbidium 'Minuet' (opposite), that have thrived in the author's home without any extraordinary care. Instructions for the culture of these and other orchids will be found in Chapters 3 and 4 and in Chapter 6.

TOP TO BOTTOM:

Brassavola nodosa LADY-OF-THE-NIGHT
ORCHID

Cattleya labiata

Paphiopedilum callosum 'Balinese Dancer'

Angraecum distichum

BELOW:
Cymbidium 'Minuet'

BELOW:
Oncidium varicosum var. *rogersii* DANCING LADY ORCHID

BOTTOM LEFT: *Laelia flava*   BOTTOM RIGHT: *Sophrolaeliocattleya* x 'Miami'

58

BELOW:
Phalaenopsis amabilis MOTH ORCHID

TOP TO BOTTOM:
Epidendrum cochleatum COCKLESHELL ORCHID
Maxillaria tenuifolia
Trichocentrum tigrinum
Rodriguezia venusta 'Ann'

BELOW:
Odontoglossum pulchellum LILY-OF-THE-VALLEY ORCHID

which generally occurs in midwinter or early spring; in the case of plants that grow all year round, repotting can be done any time you think it is necessary.

For repotting a plant that needs more room choose a pot one size larger; soak the pot if it is new, soak and scrub if it is not, and let the surface dry. As in original potting, place a piece of crock at the bottom, and in larger pots, add a layer of drainage material. Remove the plant and its ball of soil intact from its old pot, as you did to inspect the roots. Set it in its new pot to try it for size. The ball of soil should be about 12 millimetres ($\frac{1}{2}$ in.) away from the new pot's walls, all around (2.5 centimetres—1 in.—away in the case of 25 centimetres— 10 in.—or larger pots). Estimate at the same time how much soil the new pot will need at its bottom to raise the ball of soil to the proper level—when you finish, the surface should be 12 to 25 millimetres ($\frac{1}{2}$ to 1 in.) below the pot's upper rim, depending on the size of the plant (*drawings, page 48*). Raise the plant out of the new pot for a moment, and spread the requisite amount of potting mixture at the bottom. Rap the pot to settle the mixture. Replace the plant and its ball of soil in the pot, and fill with potting mixture, firming it down with your thumbs. Water thoroughly and do not water again until the soil begins to dry out.

Sometimes plants need repotting in the same pot, or in a new pot of the same size. This procedure should be followed when a plant needs fresh soil, but must be kept from growing too large for the house—my hibiscus would reach to the roof if I did not restrain it by keeping it in an undersized pot. The need for fresh soil may be indicated by a diminution in the size of new leaves and by a slackening in the production of blossoms. To carry out this same-size repotting, lift the plant out of the old pot, shake off some of the old soil on the outside of the soil ball or wash it off with a garden hose, then prune the roots and top growth as shown in the drawings on page 55. Replace the plant in the pot in fresh soil mixture with a drainage layer at the bottom. Water thoroughly, and do not water again until the soil is nearly dry. If the soil is kept too wet immediately after repotting, the roots will not penetrate the new soil mixture since there will be no need for them to go in search of moisture.

REPOTTING ORCHIDS

The techniques of potting and repotting orchids differ somewhat from those used for most house plants. Repotting should be undertaken when plants are just starting new roots, which will be visible above the potting medium. Ordinary clay or plastic pots can be used as long as good drainage is provided. The orchids generally grown in the home, being epiphytes, or air plants, require fresh air and excellent drainage.

The most popular potting medium for orchids is the bark of fir trees; it comes in three sizes, finely ground for tiny seedlings, intermediate for larger plants and coarse for mature plants. An equally suitable medium is the shredded fibre of the roots of the royal fern, *Osmunda regalis*, which is sold as osmunda fibre. This makes an ideal growing medium for orchids as it breaks down very slowly, providing an adequate supply of the necessary nutrients to maintain the plant in a healthy condition.

Whether you use fir bark or osmunda fibre it should be mixed with coarse moss peat (at a ratio of 2 parts bark or fibre to 1 part moss peat) to retain moisture. Tree-fern fibre is occasionally sold in the form of chunks, suitable as a growing medium for larger orchids, and in slabs or "logs", on which some of the air-loving orchids, particularly the smaller varieties, will grow especially well.

Before potting, consider where your orchids will sit in the pot; some types of orchids should be centrally placed and others planted at one side. Those that require a central position are of the so-called monopodial type: they have stems that grow upright like the majority of plants and send out clusters of flowers from the base of each leaf, or opposite each leaf, part way down the stem. A second type of orchid, called sympodial, grows horizontally; the older growth should be set close to the pot wall to permit expansion of the new inwards growth. All the orchids listed in the encyclopaedia section except *Angraecum* and *Phalaenopsis* are of this type.

POTTING AND CARING FOR A MONOPODIAL ORCHID

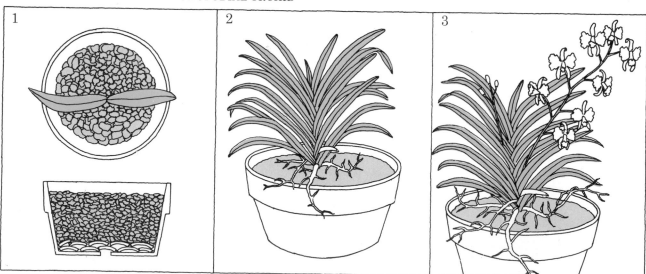

A single-stemmed, or monopodial, orchid should be set in the centre of a shallow clay pot 20 to 22.5 cm (8 to 9 in.) in diameter, in fir bark mixed with moss peat. Two layers of crocks ensure good drainage.

Properly watered, humidified and fed (see entries in the encyclopaedia for Angraecum *and* Phalaenopsis*), the orchid grows steadily, adding new leaves alternately on either side and sending out aerial roots.*

When the plant is about five years old, flower stems appear and the flowers themselves finally unfurl. Do not cut flowers until they have reached full firmness and colouring, usually 48 hours after opening.

Sympodial orchids have non-rigid multiple stems that generally require support to keep from sprawling. Bend one end of a piece of stiff aluminium or galvanized wire, available at hardware shops, into a semi-circle that will fit tightly at the bottom of the pot, and let the rest of the wire rise like a flagpole just to one side of the pot's centre (*drawings below*). The upright segment of the wire should extend far enough above the pot's top rim so that it will serve to support the vertical stems of a plant that is tied to it—25 to 30 centimetres (10 to 12 in.) should be more than adequate. As stems develop along the rhizome, loop them to the stake with raffia.

From this point on, the potting of monopodial and sympodial orchids is the same. Line the bottom of the pot with one or two layers of crocks, then fill the pot half full with the mixture of bark or fibre and moss peat. Hold the plant over the pot so that the top of its root crown is level with the pot's rim and its roots are dangling lower. Fill the pot almost full with the mixture, covering the roots and packing the mixture tightly. Water newly potted plants lightly, then mist them twice a day until the new roots become established in the potting medium; at this point follow the watering instructions for the particular species of orchid given in the encyclopaedia.

Your orchid is now ready to take its place among your display of favourite house plants.

POTTING AND CARING FOR A SYMPODIAL ORCHID

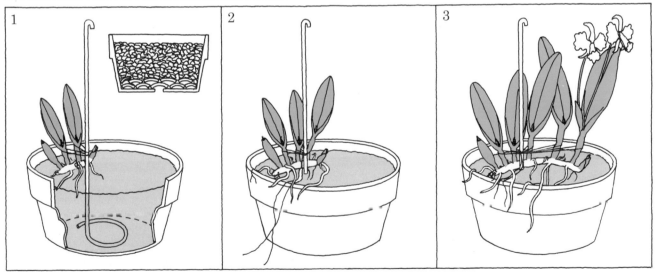

Multiple-stemmed, or sympodial, orchids (including most of the orchids in the encyclopaedia) should be planted to one side and supported by a bent wire set in a pot filled with crocks, fir bark and moss peat.

As the orchid's ground stem, or rhizome, creeps across the pot, bind each new vertical stem to the wire stake (bent over to prevent accidental injury); use lengths of raffia fibre looped like slings.

A mature sympodial orchid produces flowers when it is about five years old, but only on the leading, or forward, stem. As with other orchids, do not cut off the flowers until they have become firm and fully coloured.

What your house plant is trying to tell you

Some people talk to their house plants. In fact, some contend their plants will cringe if they are scolded. There is no evidence that a house plant ever talked back, but if one is feeling poorly it has its own ways of letting you know what is wrong. The leaves may droop, spots may appear, growth may stop. One symptom may mean a plant is getting too little light, another too much water, a third that mealy bugs are attacking. A quick, accurate diagnosis is half the battle in controlling the problem before it gets out of hand.

SYMPTOMS	CAUSE	WHAT TO DO
1 Stems grow abnormally long, leaves become long and pale, and new leaves are undersized.	Not enough light. Too much nitrogen.	Give plant more sunlight (see encyclopaedia, Chapter 6, for specific plants' needs) or move closer to plant-growing lights. Reduce strength of fertilizer or frequency of application.
2 Leaves curl under; new leaves are undersized.	Too much light.	Give plant more shade or move it farther away from plant-growing lights.
3 Stems become mushy, dark in colour and rotten; lower leaves curl and wilt; soil at top of pot is constantly wet.	Too much water.	Do not water so much or so frequently; water only when top soil is dry to the touch and reduce watering while plant is dormant. Make sure the pot's drainage hole is not clogged and do not let plant stand in water in its saucer for more than half an hour.
4 Tips of leaves become brown and leaves wilt. Lower leaves turn yellow and fall off.	Not enough water.	Water until the water runs out the bottom of the pot, then do not water again until the soil is dry to the touch. Spray an affected plant with a foliar feed to aid recovery.
5 Leaf edges are crinkly and brown.	Lack of humidity.	Increase humidity by placing pots on a bed of moist pebbles in a tray (*page 43*) or by grouping plants in a planter with moist moss peat around them (*page 13*). Mist the leaves (*page 43*). Install a humidifier in the hot-air heating system, if the house has one, or use a cool-vapour room humidifier.
6 Plant bears few or no flowers and an excessive amount of foliage. Stems may be elongated. Green scum may be present on the sides of clay pots.	Too much fertilizer, especially nitrogen.	Fertilize less often, or at half the suggested rate, particularly during winter months when the plant is receiving less light. Do not use high-nitrogen fertilizers during the blooming season. Do not fertilize dormant plants.

Illustrated here and on the following pages are 22 signs that indicate house-plant trouble. A diagnosis and cure for each are also given, but keep in mind that your house is not a plant hospital; discard plants that are obviously in bad shape and replace them with fresh, healthy ones. To forestall problems, wash the leaves regularly (*page 76*) and remove any faded flowers and withered leaves. When you bring new plants into the house, isolate them from other plants for two weeks to make sure they are not carriers of insects or disease.

	SYMPTOMS	CAUSE	WHAT TO DO
7	Lower leaves turn pale green and drop off. New leaves are undersized; stems are stunted.	Lack of fertilizer.	Fertilize more often during the plant's growing season (see encyclopaedia for specific recommendations).
8	Leaves turn yellow or curl and wilt.	Too much heat.	Move the plant to a cooler spot in the house (see encyclopaedia for optimum night and day temperatures for specific plants). Be sure plants are not close to a radiator or hot-air outlet.
9	Yellow or brown spots appear on leaves, often appearing as bands across the leaf surface.	Sun scorch.	Give the plant more shade, especially during summer, by filtering sunlight through blinds or curtains or moving the plant to a window that does not receive full midday or afternoon sun. (See the encyclopaedia for sunlight requirements of specific plants.)
10	White or yellow spots appear on leaves, particularly on African violets and other plants with hairy foliage.	Cold water on leaves.	When watering plants, use water at room temperature or slightly higher.
11	White crust appears on soil surface or on sides and rims of clay pots; leaves touching the rim wilt, rot and fall off.	Build-up of salts from fertilizer.	Water the plant thoroughly to dissolve the salts; after half an hour, water again generously to carry the dissolved salts off through the pot's drainage hole. Wash salts off the pot rim and sides; coat the rim with melted wax to prevent future salt build-up from harming leaves and stems.
12	Roots fill the pot completely and may reach down through the bottom hole. Plants may wilt in between waterings and bear only a few small new leaves.	Plant is too big for its pot.	Repot plant in a container one size larger (*drawings, page 53*), and spray with a foliar feed to hasten root growth into the new compost.

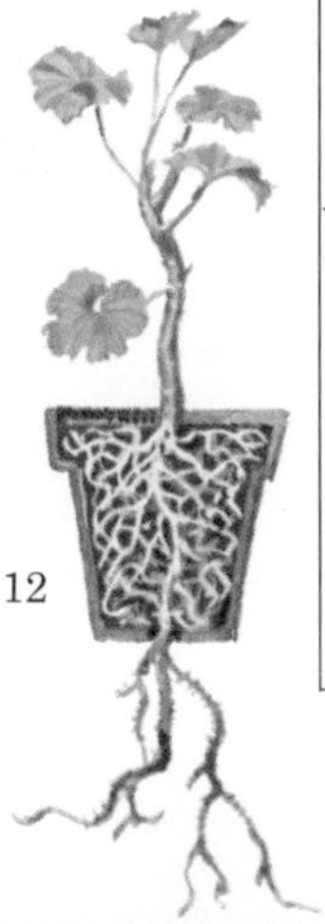

		SYMPTOMS
1	2	**1** Plant is stunted; flowers are malformed or streaked with darker colour; leaves curl and stems are twisted and darkened. Heavily infested plants may not bloom, or if they do, buds may fail to open.
		2 White, woolly spots appear on stems, at junctions of stems and leaves, and at base of buds, generally in areas hidden from bright light. Leaves develop sticky patches and entire plant looks stunted.
3	4	**3** Leaves show pale speckles, then slowly turn yellow. Tiny spider webs appear, first on undersides of leaves or at junctions of leaves and stems, then on stems or bridging from leaf to leaf. In severe attacks leaves turn brown and drop.
		4 Leaves and stems become shiny and sticky to the touch. Leaves curl and buds may be malformed. On close examination tiny insects are visible on undersides of leaves, along stems, at the base of buds and particularly on new shoots.
5	6	**5** Leaves become pale, turn yellow and drop off. Leaf surfaces are covered with a sticky substance. When plants are moved, tiny insects resembling fine white dust take flight.
		6 Plants become stunted and stems and leaves are often sticky to the touch. White, yellow or brown scales appear on stems and undersides of leaves.
7	8	**7** Leaves look as if their surfaces have been scraped, or may have large, ragged holes. Trails of silvery slime appear on leaves. Slimy, legless creatures can be seen during the day under pots or pot rims and among fallen leaves in the pot; at night they can be seen feeding on plants.
		8 Spots of varying colour and size appear on leaves and may merge to form large blotches. Leaves wither and die.
9	10	**9** Stems, leaves, flowers and buds become rotten and covered with grey mould. Leaves turn brownish-black.
		10 Stems and roots turn mushy, dark coloured and rotten; lower leaves become dark and waterlogged and collapse; top of plant may die.

CAUSE	METHODS OF CONTROL
Cyclamen mites, microscopic spider-like pests, suck plant juices from leaves and stems.	Spray with dicofol. Destroy badly infested plants. Space plants so they do not touch. Wash hands well after handling infested plants to avoid transferring mites to healthy plants.
Mealy bugs, oval-bodied insects that are up to 6 mm ($\frac{1}{4}$ in.) long and are covered with a white powdery wax, suck plant juices and excrete honeydew on which a sooty black fungus may form.	If insects are few, pick them off by hand or dab them with a cotton swab dipped in alcohol. Wash foliage with a lukewarm spray in the sink. For heavier infestations, wash the plant in tepid soapy water and rinse in clear tepid water. Severely infested plants may be sprayed with malathion.
Spider mites, red or green eight-legged creatures, barely visible, suck plant juices.	Direct a spray of lukewarm water on foliage to dislodge mites. In the case of severe infestations, spray with malathion or dicofol.
Aphids, pear-shaped, usually wingless insects less than 3 mm ($\frac{1}{8}$ in.) long, suck plant juices and excrete honeydew. The insects may be green, black, yellow, brown or pink in colour.	Remove individual aphids with fingers or kill them with an alcohol-dipped cotton swab. Wash by dipping the plants upside down in warm soapy water and rinse in tepid clear water; larger plants can be washed with a sponge. Spray heavily infested plants with pyrethrum, derris, malathion, or nicotine.
White flies, white-winged insects about 1.5 mm ($\frac{1}{16}$ in.) long, lie on the undersides of leaves, where they suck plant juices and excrete a mould-forming honeydew.	Spray with malathion, pyrethrum or BHC.
Scales, 3 mm ($\frac{1}{8}$ in.) flat, oval or rounded insects with hard shells, can be seen on plants as they suck plant juices and excrete honeydew.	Wash off scales with a sponge dipped in lukewarm soapy water and rinse in lukewarm clear water. Spray with malathion, nicotine or diazinon.
Slugs and snails, ranging in size from 1 to 10 cm ($\frac{1}{2}$ to 4 in.) and in colour from yellowish to black, chew holes in leaves and flowers.	Pick snails and slugs off plants at night and destroy them, or set out a saucer of beer or grape juice near the plant to attract and drown them. Get rid of hiding places by removing plant debris. Apply slug pellets to the soil.
Fungus leaf spot.	Cut off and destroy infected leaves. Keep water off foliage and space plants wider apart for air circulation and lower humidity. If further spots appear spray with captan, maneb or zineb and check with the encyclopaedia that cultural conditions are suitable.
Botrytis blight, grey-mould.	Avoid overwatering, overfertilizing and overcrowding of plants. Keep water off leaves. Destroy infected plants or plant parts. Plants may be sprayed with benomyl, captan, thiophanate-methyl, thiram or zineb.
Crown, stem and root rot.	Destroy infected plants. To avoid future infections, avoid overwatering, overfertilizing and overcrowding of plants, and keep water off foliage. Slightly affected plants can sometimes be saved by dusting the crowns with dry Bordeaux powder.

The basics of day-to-day care

4

When my aechmea or vriesea refuses to bloom, I give it an apple for company. I slice an apple, place the pieces in the pot with the plant, then put the whole thing inside a clear plastic bag and tuck the bag end underneath the pot. The apple remedy works, too. The aechmea or vriesea (or any other house plant of the bromeliad family), even if it has never flowered or given a hint it might, is stimulated to bloom several weeks or months later, depending on the variety.

This trick sounds like an old wives' tale, but it depends on a well-established chemical reaction. A cut-up apple gives off ethylene, a gas used in manufacturing plastics; the gas acts as a ripening hormone to induce blossoming. Unless you raise nothing but bromeliads—and there are people who do just that, out of affection and admiration for them—most of your house plants will not need an apple and you will not need to know more about the bloom-promoting properties of ethylene. But scientific knowledge of your house plants' needs, applied daily throughout the year, will pay generous dividends in enhanced beauty for your indoor garden, whatever you grow. While most house plants respond to the same sort of general care, each genus has a particular regimen that suits it best, and this is described under the genus entry in the encyclopaedia (*Chapter 6*).

The care of house plants is no dull chore; as I make my rounds each morning before beginning work, I find inspiration and surprise. My tour of inspection has a practical as well as a pleasurable purpose. It is the starting point for effective care of my plants. I look for plants that need repotting—if one requires watering daily, this unusual thirst is a sign that its roots have filled its ball of soil. I turn each pot 90°, because plants always grow towards the light from the window and will become lopsided if left unturned. I pick off faded flowers and leaves. I consider whether lanky stems should be pruned, or pinched back, to induce more compact growth, and whether I should root the cut-off tips (*Chapter 5*) to produce new plants for friends. I examine tips of stems, the undersides of leaves and leaf axils—

The predecessor of today's popular Easter lily, Lilium longiflorum, *is the beautiful and ancient Madonna lily,* L. candidum, *shown here in a pen-and-ink-and-chalk detail from the notes of Leonardo da Vinci.*

the points where leaves rise from the stems—for signs of insect infestation (*pages 66-67*)—and take immediate action at the slightest suspicion. And, I look for dust on the leaves.

Occasionally I add fertilizer, which ranks next to light and water in importance to the health of plants. House plants depend on regular feeding more than do outdoor plants, because water dissolves and carries off some of the nutrients in their limited soil, and their roots, confined by the walls of pots, cannot reach for more, as garden plants can. But fertilizer supplied in excess or at the wrong times can prove as harmful as incorrect watering. So understanding when and how to apply fertilizer is an important step to maintaining healthy, handsomely blooming plants.

FEEDING POTTED PLANTS First, just any kind of fertilizer will not do for your house plants. You may not be able to use indoors the fertilizers you prefer in your garden. Organic fertilizers, which are so valuable outdoors, can be used on house plants. But most of them break down and release their nutrients slowly—too slowly for ideal feeding of indoor plants, which do better when given small amounts of fertilizer regularly. Moreover, many organic fertilizers are too messy and smelly to be used indoors. So most house-plant gardeners depend on the cleaner and faster-working chemical fertilizers for the compounds of nitrogen, phosphate and potassium that all plants require.

Almost any fertilizer specifically designed for house plants is satisfactory because it will contain all three of the elements plants need; these may be in various ratios of nitrogen, phosphate and potassium compounds, but must always be diluted and used according to the maker's instructions. Some mixtures have a particularly high percentage of nitrogen to make up for the fact that nitrogen is dissolved more rapidly out of a pot under constant watering than in an outdoor garden. Plants such as azaleas and gardenias need fertilizers that leave an acid residue after they have broken down; these fertilizers contain such compounds as diammonium phosphate or ammonium sulphate and are often labelled "for acid-loving plants".

In addition to varying in chemical composition, house-plant fertilizers also vary in physical characteristics. They are sold in four forms: powders, crystals or tablets that are mixed with water to make liquid fertilizer; concentrated liquid fertilizers that are diluted with water; sticks, pills or tablets that are inserted dry into the soil to dissolve slowly when plants are watered; and dry powders that are forked into the soil.

I have used all four kinds, and they all work well. Some indoor gardeners use the dry powders, but many amateurs find this method of application a time-consuming chore. The fertilizers that are dissolved in water make their nutrients available quickly and are convenient to use; most people prefer them.

Since the concentration of active ingredients varies from brand to brand, follow the instructions on the label when preparing the solution. Never feed a plant until you have determined that its soil is moist; when the soil is dry, even fertilizer that is dissolved in water may burn tender roots. Water dry soil lightly, then pour on enough of the solution to soak through the soil—when it drips out the bottom of the pot, the plant has had enough. It is also a waste to apply fertilizer to plants that need repotting.

The fertilizing schedule must be modified, of course, when you use the "slow release" sticks, pills or tablets, since they are specially compounded for spreading out the application over a long period of time. They are meant to be buried about 2.5 centimetres (1 in.) deep in the soil, and as close to the pot walls as possible to avoid burning the plant roots. When used up, they must be replaced, and this requirement is their chief disadvantage, since it is not always easy to tell when the last bit has dissolved. They are easy to dispense, however, and especially handy if you are going away and leaving the care of your plants to someone you do not trust with the fertilizing.

Do not get the idea from what I have said that your flowering house plants should be fed fertilizer constantly. They can utilize it only when they are growing well, and they grow best only under ideal light conditions. So in northern regions, where winter suns are wan, most house plants should be fed sparingly, if at all, from November to February. A dormant plant—as for example gloxinias in their resting period—should not be fed at all; neither should a plant that is obviously sick, with wilting, withering or drooping foliage. Neither dormant nor ailing plants can convert the fertilizers' nutrients into new growth. A newly transplanted one should not be fed for two or three weeks, to give it time to re-establish its roots and cope with the extra nourishment.

With these cautions in mind, begin regular feeding of your flowering house plants as the days lengthen and new growth starts, and continue applications on the schedule prescribed for each plant. But do not overdo the feeding. I know the temptation common to so many indoor gardeners. They pick up a bottle of liquid fertilizer and read the label that says, perhaps, "One teaspoon to 1 litre (2 pt) of water". They think: "How could such a little be enough?" And they decide to use a tablespoon instead. If ever you are so tempted, apply a taste of fertilizer to your tongue. It will not hurt you, but it will sting, and you will reach for a glass of water. Imagine how it will burn the tender roots of your plants. In case honest error leads to an overdose, give the plants the drink of water you would demand for yourself. Set them where their pots can drain quickly and safely, and water them over and over again for an hour or two. That may save them from an overdose of fertilizer.

A LEAF IN THE MAIL

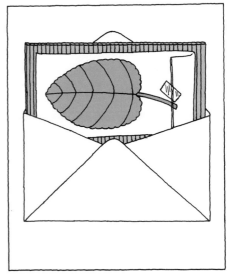

African violet enthusiasts often mail a leaf from a prized variety to a faraway friend so that he can raise a new plant from it (page 89). The packaging technique is simple: cut the leaf stem as long as possible so that the withered end can be trimmed back on arrival, before rooting; insert the leaf in a plastic bag, seal the bag with tape and slip it into an envelope with a sheet of corrugated cardboard as a backing to prevent its being crushed by the post office stamping machine.

SHOWER AND SPONGE BATHS

In the routine of house-plant care, cleanliness ranks next in importance after food, drink and light. A bath will get rid of most insects, insect eggs and mites, which may or may not be visible, but which will damage the plants if left undisturbed.

Plants light enough to carry should be taken to the sink at least once every two weeks and given a tepid shower. Use the rinsing spray attachment with which some modern kitchen sinks are fitted, and apply a firm but not overly forceful spray to both sides of the leaves and to the stems, taking care not to bruise soft new growth with too much pressure. Alternatively, spray the leaves with tepid water in a watering can fitted with a fine rose or use a plastic houseplant misting sprayer. Plants can also be taken to the bathroom and given a light, tepid spray with a hand shower. In the case of fuzzy-leaved plants, I do not use a direct spray, which can injure the leaves; instead I turn the plant upside down, holding it lightly in its pot, and swish the leaves around in a sink of tepid water. If the plant is too large to be moved wash it with a damp cloth or sponge. Whatever you use to wash down the plants, do the job early in the day, with water warmer than room temperature. Then set the plants to dry where there is good circulation of air and no direct sunlight. I never use anything but plain, tepid water on my plants in their fortnightly baths. It makes old leaves look young again. Specially formulated baths seem unnecessary to me, for I am not convinced that normal soft green leaves become more attractive when they are made shiny with oil or chemical preparations. Part of the joy of plants lies in the variety of their leaf textures.

CONTROLLING THE PESTS

Regular baths wash away most insects before they can do any harm, but some pests are tenacious. The worst are frequently those that arrive on newly purchased plants or that move indoors

(continued on page 76)

A Dutch auction

One of the most spectacular sights in Europe for a gardening enthusiast is the profusion of flowering house plants that arrive five mornings a week in the small market town of Aalsmeer in The Netherlands. Here, in the pre-dawn hours, more than 3,000 Dutch growers bring their freshly cut flowers and potted plants to be sold at the world's largest flower auction, where some five million potted plants alone go under the hammer each month. The 2,000 buyers—exporters, wholesalers, shopkeepers and street vendors—compete for lots that range from a few pots to whole trolleys filled with plants in every imaginable colour and size. Registration, bidding and distribution are computerized, and in a matter of two or three hours the halls are empty and the flowers are on their way to small shops and houses all over Europe.

Buyers prepare for bidding as a trolley of brightly coloured begonias, kalanchoës and calceolarias move by rail into the Aalsmeer auction room.

72

Bidding against the clock

Success in the Aalsmeer auction rooms requires a quick-silver mind and steely nerves rather than a green thumb. Prices, indicated on a device resembling a clock, start high and work progressively downwards—until a buyer presses a concealed button beneath his desk, stopping the clock and securing the offered trays of blooms. The bidders are allowed no chance to catch their breath: on average, a sale is completed every five seconds in each of the five halls of the vast Aalsmeer auction complex.

Outside the sale rooms, a buyer checks a list that records his identifying number and the pick-up point for any flowers procured during the auction.

A trolley of flowering house plants undergoes inspection by a potential buyer before the auction. The lot number is posted on the side.

In front of the large price-clock, an attendant displays pots of African violets.

Trays of purple and pink African violets start their rail journey from the 4 hectare (10 acre) warehouse to the auction rooms.

in autumn on plants that have spent the summer in the open. So it is good practice to isolate such plants for a few weeks until their freedom from pests has been established.

The most common invaders are aphids and white flies. Aphids are tiny, pear-shaped insects, and white flies look like tiny white moths. Aphids and white flies both suck the juices from the tender tips of plants and can also be found on the undersides of leaves. Less common than white flies and aphids are red spider mites and cyclamen mites, both tiny members of the spider family. Red spider mites spin fine webs on the undersides of leaves of such plants as impatiens and miniature roses, and suck their juices until the foliage becomes speckled white. Cyclamen mites assault African violets and begonias as well as cyclamens. Too small to be visible, they suck the juices from the plant cells, deforming the plants, causing their leaves to curl and wither, and preventing buds from opening.

Fortunately most of these pests can be controlled, one way or another. If aphids or white flies defy the fortnightly bath of tepid water, douse the plant's leaves and stem in a tub filled with tepid soapy water—but be sure to use old-fashioned mild soap, not a detergent. Swish the plant around, then rinse it in plain tepid water. If any pests survive, spray with pyrethrum, which is harmless to human beings and other mammals (it is toxic to fish, though, and should not be used near an aquarium).

GIVING A HOUSE PLANT A BATH

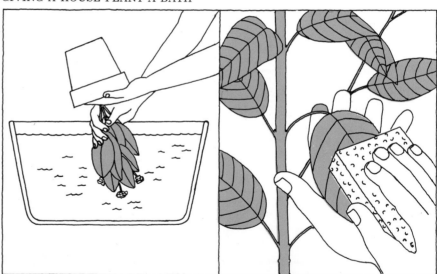

To wash dust off a small plant or one with tender, hairy leaves, swirl it around upside down in tepid water. If the dirt sticks, use mild soap (not a detergent), then rinse the plant in clear tepid water.

To bathe larger plants that are too cumbersome to carry to the sink, wipe off their leaves with a sponge dipped in tepid water; if you use soapy water to remove sticky dirt, sponge off with clear water.

If mealy bugs persist, wipe them off with a cotton swab dipped in alcohol. Only if that remedy fails should you turn to an insecticide spray. The most suitable kind for mealy bugs is malathion, which is available at garden supply centres. Since it is slightly toxic and has an obnoxious odour, use it with the windows open or move the plants outdoors before spraying.

Malathion is also effective against red spider mites. For cyclamen mites, use dicofol. This treatment will salvage plants that have not been too seriously infested, but badly damaged plants should be destroyed.

Before using any insecticide, read the label on the package carefully. Make sure that the treatment is suitable for your plants, for some species are dangerously sensitive to certain preparations. If the chemical must be mixed with water before use, adhere strictly to the instructions for dilution. If the insecticide comes in an aerosol spray can, as many insecticides do, spray only at the distance specified on the label—usually 45 centimetres (18 in.). The spray is squirted out of the can by a pressurized gas that emerges very cold; it may severely chill a plant that is too close to the jet.

Disease is less of a problem than insect attack because most plant diseases are caused by fungi, which need moisture to spread, and house-plant foliage is ordinarily dry, so long as you are careful with your watering. When diseases appear, the usual cause is excess moisture from overwatering or from watering so late in the day that daylight warmth cannot dry out the plants. Powdery mildew, particularly on begonias, is most troublesome on plants that have been kept dry at the roots. Dinocap usually controls it. When the improper practices cease, so do the diseases —generally. The chart on pages 64-65 describes the symptoms of important house-plant diseases, as well as common pests, and prescribes specific treatments.

Treat your sick plants but never maintain a plant hospital on your window sill. Diseased plants or plants infested with insects should be kept away from other healthy plants. And when the disease seems incurable or the pest infestation defies control, the plants should be consigned to the dustbin, pots and all. Otherwise they may set off an epidemic in your indoor garden.

Apply the same Draconian measures to plants that simply look worn out, particularly when you notice spindly growth during your rounds of inspection in late spring. However, you should save plants like glory lilies and gloxinias, which may simply be in a period of dormancy before putting out new growth. Bulbs such as hyacinth, tulip and narcissus, that blossomed during the winter, should also be saved for setting out in the garden in the autumn. And woody plants—hoya, hibiscus, calliandra, jasmine—which may look as if they are on their last legs, will gain a new lease on life in a summer outdoors.

Spring is also the time to prepare your potted plants for a season in the fresh air outside the house. Many of them benefit from a summer outdoors, either in the garden itself or on a terrace or patio. But some should not go outdoors at all. I never put my African violets outside, although some gardeners find that they do well enough in a shady, protected place on a covered terrace. Among the plants that gain the most from a few months in the fresh air are calliandras, which like full sun, camellias, which prefer shady spots, and potted citrus trees—orange, lemon and lime—which perk up splendidly on sunny patios. No plants should be transferred abruptly to direct sunlight outdoors from the limited light that they have been used to indoors. Make the move a gradual one, first putting the plants in a relatively shady spot, then closer to the sunlight, and finally in full sun. Positions that get morning sun are preferable; the heat of the afternoon sun in summer is often too intense and can burn the leaves of some plants.

When moving plants outdoors, try to put them in a spot that is sheltered from strong winds, which can dry out the plants and even knock the pots over. It is best to set the plants on a hard surface such as a paved terrace or wall; if they are set on the ground or on grass, they may send roots down through the pot's drainage hole into the soil. I find that the best way to take care of house plants outdoors in summer is to sink them below ground

PINCHING BACK STEMS FOR FULLER GROWTH

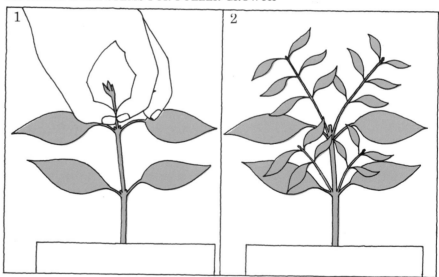

To get compact, bushy house plants with many flowers, pinch off the ends of new stems, using your thumbnail to sever the stem. Pinch as close as you can to the top leaves without injuring the buds.

The energy that the tip would have put into flowering now goes to the buds, producing new branches, all of which can bear flowers. Repeat the process on the new stems to maintain the plant's shape.

level; this shields the pots and roots from the sun and wind and helps them stay cool and moist. To do this, choose a well-drained spot within easy reach of a hose. Dig a bed 15 to 20 centimetres (6 to 8 in.) deep, and as long and as wide as necessary to accommodate your plants without crowding; each should have its full share of light and air. Fill the bed with gravel or with 7.5 to 10 centimetres (3 to 4 in.) of gravel topped by a similar layer of moist moss peat to hold moisture; roots are not likely to grow down into a bed of gravel. Set the pots in the bed, burying them up to their rims. Do not actually set the plants in the bed until both night time and day time temperatures are mild enough so that they will not be damaged by chill.

Every week or so give each pot a twist in its bed to make doubly sure that, despite the gravel, no roots are spreading out through the drainage hole. This method makes it easy to retrieve your plants at summer's end and return them to the house. Some house plants, such as begonias and impatiens, can be knocked out of their pots and set, ball of soil and all, in a hole in the garden; many gardeners do this to fill in empty spaces in their flower beds. But don't do this unless you are willing to leave the plant in the garden. By the time summer is over the roots will have spread so much that you may find it impossible to repot the plant without drastic—possibly harmful—pruning.

The first few weeks in the garden are a time for house plants to renew their strength. But they will require help from you. To protect them against diseases and harmful insects, spray the plants thoroughly. Outdoors you can use an all-purpose pesticide that might be unsuitable inside the house. You can also begin foliar feeding, a very effective method of fertilizing that is generally too messy for indoor use. In this process, plant nutrients dissolved in water are sprayed on the leaves, which absorb them to supplement food the plants take in with their roots. Foliar nutrients should be administered at the same frequency as other fertilizers. Never use a solution stronger than that recommended on the label, for it may burn the leaves. The practice of foliar feeding has its critics among some horticulturists who doubt that certain plants absorb much nutrient through their leaves, but it is my experience that potted plants respond well to it when they have been moved outdoors; some older plants that have occupied the same large pots for a long period seem to benefit especially from foliar feeding.

When the temperature drops below the ideal night temperature indicated in the encyclopaedia for your plants, it is time for them to come indoors. Hose them down to knock off any bugs that may be on them and thoroughly clean off the outside of the pots before bringing them in to settle down for the winter.

Whether or not they have spent the summer outdoors, all plants except annuals and some tropical plants need a period of rest. Without it they weaken and die, and one of the most important aspects of house-plant culture is recognizing when a plant is entering this period and understanding how to take care of the plant while it rests. Many an inexperienced gardener, misreading the symptoms, has tossed out a plant that would have flourished the following year. I know one indoor gardener, by no means inexperienced, who received an orchid cactus as a gift and kept it in his greenhouse. When it had failed to flower by the following May, he asked the donor's advice. "Throw it away," she suggested. He tossed it, pot and all, behind the garage and forgot about it. A month later he happened to look behind the garage and discovered that the plant had produced six blossoms.

Different plants rest in different ways and at different seasons—times that were apparently fixed ages ago by the climatic changes in the regions where their ancestors originated. Some merely cease to flower, but retain their green leaves. Some stop growing, but give no other sign that they are resting. Some drop their leaves, but retain moisture in their stems and branches, and stand like green skeletons. Some go into the extreme form of rest that horticulturists call dormancy: all vegetation above ground dies down and the plant appears dead.

The requirements of resting or dormant plants vary widely and are described, species by species, in the encyclopaedia section. It is important to follow them closely—the future

CATCHING DRAINAGE FROM HANGING PLANTS

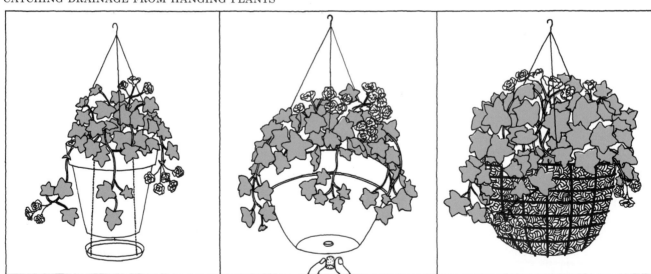

A small sandwich tin will catch water that drips from a hanging plant pot. To hang the tin, punch three holes in its rim, tie a string to each hole and to short stakes driven into the soil inside the pot rim.

To eliminate messy dripping without suspending a saucer beneath a hanging pot, plug the drainage hole with a cork. Water the plant at the sink, then let it drain before you hang it up again.

Plants hung outdoors can be placed, unpotted, in baskets lined with sphagnum moss. To water them, take the basket down and immerse it in a sink or tub, then set it aside for a while to drain.

production of blooms and even a plant's very survival often depend upon the care given during its resting period. Success with Christmas cactus, for example, depends largely on the treatment given the plant during its resting season. It will show no sign of needing any kind of special care, but if it is not kept quite dry, unfertilized and at a temperature of about 13°C (55°F) during November and December, it may not flower when flowering time arrives.

The general guidance given above applies to virtually all house plants—even orchids. While they are often held in awe as delicate, exotic plants, they are so easy to grow that they are found in homes all over the world.

Orchids are normally kept under cover all the year round. Here some protection from direct sunlight is necessary from March onwards and some form of shading is generally applied. In the case of cymbidiums, greenhouse blinds are usually sufficient, but other, more delicate, orchids may require a semi-permanent type of shading to the glass. By the end of August this can be reduced until by the end of September it will no longer be necessary and can be washed off.

But as too much shading inhibits flowering, particularly in the case of cymbidiums, the question of shading has constantly to be reviewed. The aim is to prevent scorching of the leaves, and in the home it is usually easier to pull a plant away from a sunny window or give it an airy light position in a good sunless situation. Additional artificial light at night helps in some instances, for it has been observed that greenhouses with side lighting produce twice as many flowering plants as those grown with semi-darkness round the bulbs.

While you can grow lovely orchids without any expertise, you will find it easier if you understand some of the peculiarities of these plants. First of all, do not start out by trying to raise them from seeds. A single pinch of seeds, often as fine as talcum powder, will produce thousands of plants, but even if you had room for them, tending them might tax your patience; some orchids require five to seven years to progress from germination to flowering. In any case, raising orchids from seeds is a job for experts, requiring special growing materials, tools and skills.

If you are willing to wait several seasons for flowers, and you have had some experience in cultivating orchids, you can raise plants from seedlings. They cost little, and if you buy those that are 5 to 7.5 centimetres (2 to 3 in.) tall, they will thrive under the care prescribed for mature plants—but they will not bloom for two to five years. Most people want flowers right away, and they buy established plants as they would rose bushes or azaleas. Although some rare specimens have sold for small fortunes, the popular orchids cost no more than other good house plants.

Orchids are often thought to be delicate plants, but their innate toughness is demonstrated by the discovery of cattleya orchids—the familiar corsage plants with the large lavender, pink or white flowers. The first cattleya to come to the attention of Western botanists arrived in England in 1818—as packing material for rare mosses and lichens shipped by boat from Brazil. A curious horticulturist, William Cattley, decided to pot some of the odd-looking roots and stems. Six years later, the first magnificent cattleyas to be grown in cultivation blossomed under his care.

When buying, however, inspect the plants carefully. For growing in the house, it is best not to buy bare-root divisions or plants that were collected in the jungle, for they will take too long to accommodate themselves to indoor conditions. For your first few orchids, it is best to buy plants that are already in bud; with an orchid-grower's help, select types that blossom at different times of the year.

The special care that orchids require consists mainly of attention to their specific needs for ventilation, humidity and light. Light, in particular, has a powerful influence on blooming; give the plants too much or too little and you will get few flowers or none at all. Whether or not the quantity of light is right is indicated by the colour of the foliage. Generally, a light green colour signals that all is well, a deep rich green means that the light is inadequate for optimum production of flowers, and a yellowish green means that there is too much light. Natural light is generally regulated by curtains. In the north of Europe, most orchids can stand full winter sunshine from November to March; during the rest of the year a thin curtain should be drawn between them and the sun from mid morning to mid afternoon. In very warm areas, the curtain should be drawn during the hottest part of the day throughout the year.

Many orchids will also grow satisfactorily under artificial light. But for mature plants, limit the hours of artificial lighting

THE DISPLAY AND CARE OF ORCHIDS

To show off orchids attractively and give them the light and moisture they need, set the pots in a window in a large ceramic dish or other decorative container that will act as a humidifying tray

(page 43). Water in the bottom of the pebble-filled tray will supply the surrounding air with moisture as it evaporates (orchids do best in humidity of 60 per cent or more). Mist the foliage at least twice a day.

to the season's normal period of daylight, and keep the plants in rooms that remain dark at night. The length of the daily period of darkness controls the plants' internal regulating mechanisms, and if it is too short, the plants may not flower, or may flower erratically. Young plants, however, reach maturity faster if they get 16 hours of artificial light daily.

Orchids' tastes in humidity are rather finicky. The ideal level for plants indoors in winter is 60 per cent or higher, far greater than that usually maintained in a heated house. You can install a room humidifier, but it is simpler to increase humidity in a limited region around the plants. An atomizer or misting device that sprays a fine mist over the plants will accomplish the purpose, but only if used several times a day. You will have less routine work if you keep the plants in humidifying trays. Set the pots in plastic or metal trays that have been filled to a depth of 2.5 centimetres (1 in.) or more with pebbles, charcoal, marble chips or other material and up to 2.5 centimetres (1 in.) of water. The pots should rest on this material without sinking; if it proves too soft to support the plants' weight, put half a brick beneath each pot before filling in the tray with the pebbles.

Although orchids prefer fairly high humidity, they are paradoxically averse to excess water. Overwatering is particularly harmful to the group of orchids that does not grow in the earth, the epiphytes, which cling to the bark of trees or perch in their crevices. They are accustomed to alternating periods of moisture and dryness about their roots, and the *Cattleya* genus of epiphytes—the plants most orchid fanciers begin with—can survive for long periods without water. Orchids that grow on the ground in soil—the terrestrial orchids—demand that the medium they live in be kept slightly moist but not wet. The signs of excess moisture are little brown spots on flowers, brown watery spots on the foliage, and blackened stems. Treat these conditions by withholding water and humidity and moving the plant to a spot where air circulates more freely and dries the plants between waterings. But you are unlikely to encounter such problems if you simply water your orchids sparingly early in the day, and keep them potted properly (*page 62*) and well ventilated.

When orchids are growing rather than resting, every third or fourth watering should be accompanied by a feeding. Orchids grown in fir bark should be given a high-nitrogen fertilizer because bacteria breaking down the bark absorb part of any nitrogen given to the plants.

If orchids, for all their delicate beauty, turn out to be easy to grow once you know how, the same cannot be said for all house plants. Some are indeed delicate and require continual skilled attention. If your time is limited, choose among the undemanding plants. There are many of them, in all shapes and sizes, that are equal in beauty to their more difficult companions.

HOW THE PASSION FLOWER
GOT ITS NAME
During the 16th century, the Catholic missionaries who discovered the passion flower vine (page 136) blooming in the jungle of South America used it to teach the story of the Passion of Jesus Christ. Its 10 outer petals, they taught local Indians, represented the 10 apostles present at the Crucifixion; the rays of the inner corona were the Crown of Thorns; the pollen-bearing anthers were Christ's wounds; and the three pollen-receiving stigmas were the nails used to fix His body to the Cross. The missionaries even likened the vine's coiling tendrils to the cords and whips that bound and scourged the Lord, and the lobed leaves to the hands of His tormentors.

Growing new plants from old ones 5

In one way, indoor gardeners often resemble those old-fashioned Latin Americans whose code of hospitality requires them to offer you any of their possessions that you admire. ("You really like my cravat, señor? Please, you must take it. I insist.") If you praise an indoor gardener's plant, the chances are that he will press on you a leaf, a segment of stem or even a bit of root so that you may grow a plant like his. I would not be surprised if that pleasant custom went back to the oldest Latins of them all, the Romans. For Pliny the Elder (A D 23-79) wrote in his *Natural History* about the ways in which plants can reproduce themselves without going through the process of producing seed, and he refers familiarly to "slips" and "cuttings" and "layering"—which are among the subjects of this chapter, and all of which have the same purpose: to make roots grow where no roots grew before.

When plants reproduce themselves by seed, as most of them do, they are behaving sexually, uniting male and female. But almost all of them can reproduce asexually as well. Bulb plants such as tulips produce not only seeds but little bulbils, each a potential plant of its own, surrounding the mother bulb the way chicks surround a hen. Many types of plants send out long shoots called runners that spread along the ground and take root to start independent life as they go. A single leaf cut from an African violet can soon become the parent of one or more identical plants. The methods that plants have developed for asexual increase—or vegetative reproduction, as botanists call it—are manifold, and gardeners have not only been able to adapt them, but to devise a few of their own. (Pliny attributes the first ventures in this field to "mere accident", which, he says, "taught us to break off branches from trees and plant them because stakes driven into the earth had taken root".) Even bits of a leaf can grow into plants. All these methods work because many parts of every plant contain cells capable of reproducing the whole plant. In practice, a method of vegetative reproduction that succeeds with one kind of plant may not succeed with another. The rex

A window greenhouse is ideal for starting plants (in trays on floor) and displaying mature ones. The roof opens to adjust warmth and humidity; a timer and an electric eye control artificial light.

begonia, for example, will grow from bits of leaf, but not from root cuttings; gardenias and impatiens, among others, reproduce themselves from sections of stem, but not from leaf cuttings; and regal pelargoniums can be multiplied from sliced-off chunks of root and from stem cuttings.

But with seeds so plentiful and so cheap, the amateur gardener may well wonder, why bother? The compelling answer is that only by asexual or vegetative reproduction can you be sure that you will obtain a young plant just like its parent in leaf and blossom characteristics, if not in exact shape and size. In fact, I should not even use the word parent, for the young plant is really a continuation of the plant from which it came, a duplicate rather than an offspring. They are such exact copies because they contain only the inherited characteristics of one progenitor. Seeds, contrarily, may not breed true, as horticulturists say. This means that a young plant grown from seed may or may not closely resemble its parents. The fertilized seed contains inheritance factors from both parents, and the result is likely to be a mixture of the parents' characteristics.

Many house plants are the result of cross-breeding because cross-breeding, by deliberately mixing inheritance, can enhance the beauty and vigour of plants and produce new varieties as well. But most indoor gardeners prefer the certain results of vegetative reproduction. It has several other important advantages as well. Not the least of these is the fact that the new plants will reach maturity and begin to produce flowers much more rapidly than those started from seed. When young, they are much less vulnerable to disease and injury than young seedlings. And seeds, no matter how sparingly you spread them, yield far more seedlings than the indoor gardener is likely to be able to or want to accommodate.

TAKING STEM CUTTINGS Of the methods of vegetative reproduction illustrated on these pages, stem cutting is probably the simplest and most frequently successful. It works well with geraniums, gardenias, *Begonia semperflorens* and the many other plants that develop firm stems. The best time to take a stem cutting is during a plant's period of active growth, usually spring and summer, unless the encyclopaedia (*Chapter 6*) specifies otherwise. In looking for a likely piece to cut, choose the upper part of a stem of the current year's growth, but a section that is fairly mature; if it is light green and succulent, it is too young and may rot before new roots develop, and if it is brownish and tough, it is too old and will lack the vigour to develop roots easily. If possible, avoid making the cutting on a stem that has flowers or flower buds; such a cutting will root but usually will not produce as good a plant as a non-blossoming shoot. If you do use a flowering stem, remove the buds or flowers before rooting. The length of the cutting will vary

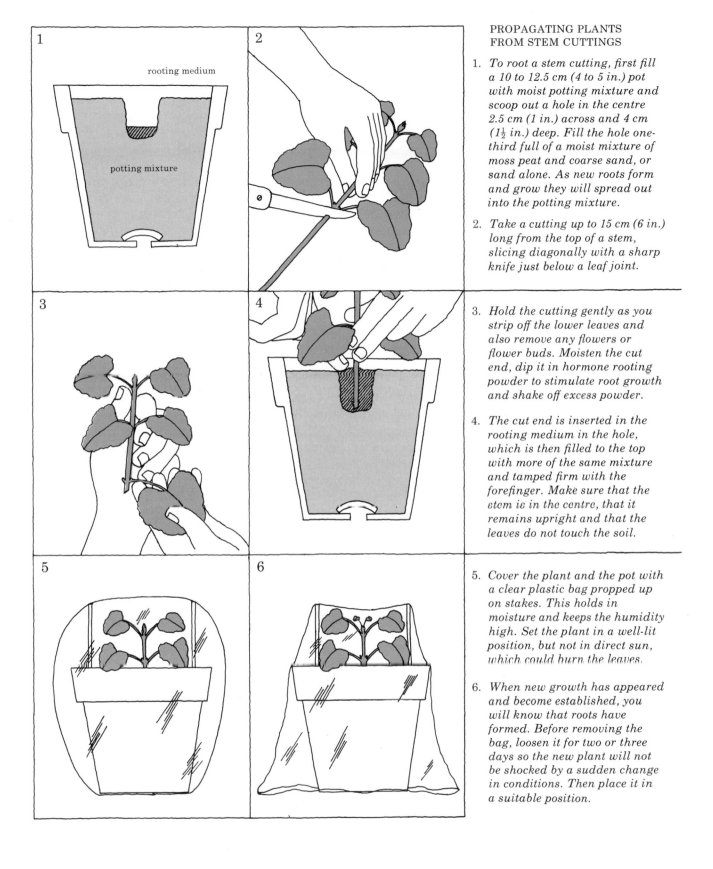

PROPAGATING PLANTS FROM STEM CUTTINGS

1. *To root a stem cutting, first fill a 10 to 12.5 cm (4 to 5 in.) pot with moist potting mixture and scoop out a hole in the centre 2.5 cm (1 in.) across and 4 cm (1½ in.) deep. Fill the hole one-third full of a moist mixture of moss peat and coarse sand, or sand alone. As new roots form and grow they will spread out into the potting mixture.*

2. *Take a cutting up to 15 cm (6 in.) long from the top of a stem, slicing diagonally with a sharp knife just below a leaf joint.*

3. *Hold the cutting gently as you strip off the lower leaves and also remove any flowers or flower buds. Moisten the cut end, dip it in hormone rooting powder to stimulate root growth and shake off excess powder.*

4. *The cut end is inserted in the rooting medium in the hole, which is then filled to the top with more of the same mixture and tamped firm with the forefinger. Make sure that the stem is in the centre, that it remains upright and that the leaves do not touch the soil.*

5. *Cover the plant and the pot with a clear plastic bag propped up on stakes. This holds in moisture and keeps the humidity high. Set the plant in a well-lit position, but not in direct sun, which could burn the leaves.*

6. *When new growth has appeared and become established, you will know that roots have formed. Before removing the bag, loosen it for two or three days so the new plant will not be shocked by a sudden change in conditions. Then place it in a suitable position.*

THE WALKING IRIS

Neomarica (page 132), a relative of the common iris, spreads across the ground by "walking"; its long stalks repeatedly droop over, take root and grow up again. Given the chance indoors, it will do the same from one pot to another. As its flowers fade, baby plants develop in their place on top of each stalk. When the little plants grow large enough, they weigh down the stalk, which bends in a graceful arc until its tip touches down. If the baby plants make contact with moist soil, they will take root, and a new walking iris will rise to begin the odd ambulatory process all over again.

from plant to plant but it will usually be 7.5 to 15 centimetres (3 to 6 in.). The exact length of the cutting is determined by the fact that it should contain at least two but not more than six nodes, or joints, where leaves have been attached; if the leaves have fallen off, nodes manifest themselves by a slight thickening of the stem, like the knuckles on fingers. The best place to cut is about 3 millimetres ($\frac{1}{8}$ in.) beneath the lower node. Use a sharp knife or a razor blade, not scissors, which squeeze and often injure the plant cells. It is usually easiest to cut diagonally. Strip off the lowest leaves, but retain the upper ones: the cutting will need a few leaves to manufacture food while roots are being established, but it must not have so many that the root-less cutting cannot supply them with enough water. (If you retain too many, you will soon know, for the leaves will wilt; you may be able to save the cutting by stripping off more leaves.)

The simplest way to make the cutting develop roots is to drop it into a translucent jar of tepid water and put it in a shaded spot, but this system may have drawbacks. Many hardy foliage plants such as English ivy (*Hedera*) and philodendron will root that way, but flowering plants tend to form weak, brittle roots in water, and I recommend that you use something more solid to initiate a strong root system in the new plants. There are a number of rooting techniques, and normally even-tempered gardeners argue with the vehemence of medieval theologians about which is the best. For most of the methods—whether you are rooting a geranium stem or a begonia leaf—you will need much the same supplies:

○ Rooting hormone powder, a chemical that stimulates and accelerates root formation. It is obtainable at florists' shops and garden centres, generally in easy-to-use powder form.

○ A potting mixture, prepared to suit the needs of the plant you are rooting (*encyclopaedia, Chapter 6*).

○ Enough 10 or 12.5 centimetre (4 or 5 in.) clay or plastic pots to accommodate each of the cuttings individually.

○ Enough clear plastic bags to create a miniature greenhouse over each pot.

○ Rooting mediums, such as coarse sand, half-and-half coarse sand and moss peat, shredded sphagnum moss or vermiculite (the agricultural type of expanded mica).

Coarse sand from a horticultural shop or garden centre is often the cheapest and most effective medium; it drains well and permits air to get down where the roots are to form. The half-and-half mixture of coarse sand and moss peat retains moisture better than pure sand does, and may be used where extra moisture will spread root formation, as in the case of gardenias and azaleas. Vermiculite and shredded sphagnum moss also hold water well while permitting air to enter; you might want to try all three to see which works best for you. If you use sphagnum

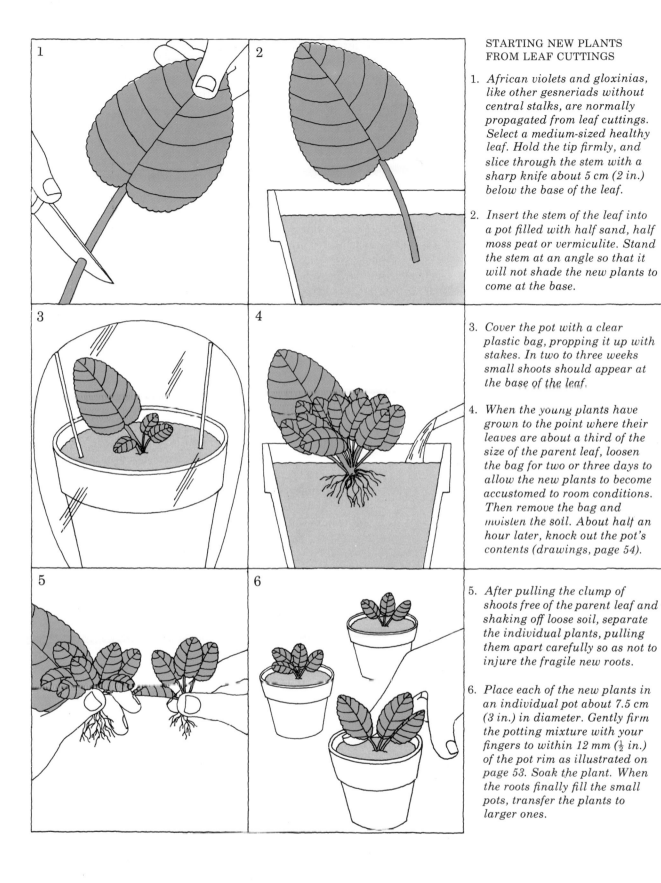

STARTING NEW PLANTS FROM LEAF CUTTINGS

1. *African violets and gloxinias, like other gesneriads without central stalks, are normally propagated from leaf cuttings. Select a medium-sized healthy leaf. Hold the tip firmly, and slice through the stem with a sharp knife about 5 cm (2 in.) below the base of the leaf.*

2. *Insert the stem of the leaf into a pot filled with half sand, half moss peat or vermiculite. Stand the stem at an angle so that it will not shade the new plants to come at the base.*

3. *Cover the pot with a clear plastic bag, propping it up with stakes. In two to three weeks small shoots should appear at the base of the leaf.*

4. *When the young plants have grown to the point where their leaves are about a third of the size of the parent leaf, loosen the bag for two or three days to allow the new plants to become accustomed to room conditions. Then remove the bag and moisten the soil. About half an hour later, knock out the pot's contents (drawings, page 54).*

5. *After pulling the clump of shoots free of the parent leaf and shaking off loose soil, separate the individual plants, pulling them apart carefully so as not to injure the fragile new roots.*

6. *Place each of the new plants in an individual pot about 7.5 cm (3 in.) in diameter. Gently firm the potting mixture with your fingers to within 12 mm (½ in.) of the pot rim as illustrated on page 53. Soak the plant. When the roots finally fill the small pots, transfer the plants to larger ones.*

moss, be sure to soak it first in very hot water to make it absorbent; in cold water, it is likely to float and remain impermeable.

Like most lifelong gardeners, I have a favourite way to root a stem cutting. Step-by-step instructions are shown in the sequence of drawings on page 87. The reason I like this method is that it is not necessary to transplant the cutting after it has taken root and become an independent plant. The cutting goes into a little bit of rooting medium that is poured into a cup-shaped hole poked in a pot of potting mixture. After the roots appear and grow through the rooting medium, they can keep right on growing into the potting mixture that fills the rest of the pot; unlike the rooting medium, this contains nutrients that the new plant now must have. The plant develops completely from a cutting into a flowering specimen just where it is, without any need for repotting.

For successful rooting, take pains with watering and with the use of the hormone powder. Shake a small quantity of rooting powder on to a piece of paper. Dip the cutting's lower end in water, let it drip until it is barely moist, then dip the end into the powder, some of which will stick to it. Then shake the cutting to remove any surplus powder and insert the cut end in the rooting medium. Fill in the rest of the cup-shaped hole with more of the rooting medium and tamp it down quite firmly so that the cutting stands upright.

PROPAGATING BEGONIAS BY LEAF VEIN CUTTINGS

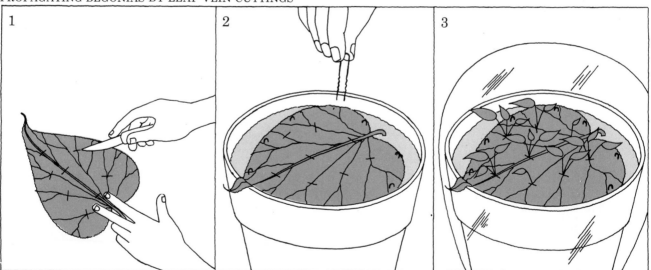

To start a number of rex begonias from a single leaf, cut the leaf from the plant, turn it upside down so that you can see the veins easily and then make six or seven cuts through the larger veins.

Lay the leaf right side up on moist sand in a pot. Poke the stem into the sand so that moisture can continue to enter the leaf. Keep the cuts in contact with the sand by securing the leaf with hairpins.

Cover the pot with a plastic bag. In two to three weeks new plants should appear at the slits. When they are 5 cm (2 in.) high, loosen the bag; remove it after two or three days and pot up each plant.

After you have watered the pot lightly and placed it in its clear plastic bag, set it in a well-lit spot out of direct sunshine—a window sill behind a sheer curtain will be just right. Do not water it again unless the inside of the bag looks dry; fine droplets on the bag indicate there is about the right amount of moisture, but if the droplets form large drops that run down the sides, open the bag and drain the excess water out; leave the bottom of the bag slightly loose for a while to make sure excess moisture does not build up again. Then be patient. Rooting takes at least two weeks for most plants, and it may take several months depending on the species, the health of the plant and the time of year you make the cutting. I know of a stubborn 11-year-old girl who waited almost ten months for an azalea cutting to root. She won—it finally did.

Once the cutting has rooted—you can tell because it will send out new growth—loosen the bag to give the new plant a chance to become acclimatized to the conditions of the room. Two or three days later, remove it. The new plant can then be treated like any others of its kind, and allowed to keep on growing where it was born, so to speak, until it gets too big for the pot. This system has one disadvantage—which never bothers me much because I usually start only a few cuttings at a time: you can put only one cutting in a pot. In the conventional method, which uses rooting medium only, you can put several cuttings in

INCREASING BEGONIAS BY LEAF SECTIONS

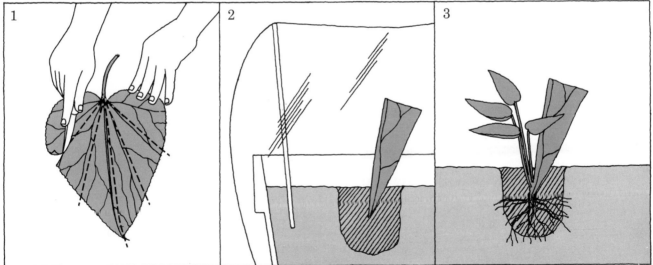

To propagate rex begonias without having to transplant new shoots, turn a leaf upside down and cut it into elongated triangles, each with a main vein and a segment of stem at the leaf base.

Stand each leaf section, point down, in a pot prepared as for stem cuttings (page 87). Cover the pot tightly with a clear plastic bag propped up by stakes; loosen the bag if droplets run down the sides.

In two to three weeks, shoots should appear from the base of the leaf. When they become 5 or 7 cm (2 or 3 in.) tall, loosen the bag for two or three days before removing it entirely.

one pot. But then you have to transfer them to separate pots when they have rooted.

Growers in the horticultural trade often pot three to five cuttings of certain plants—particularly ivies—in one pot. The famous English firm, Rochford, pot or keep about three African violets in the same pot. Any leaves in the middle of the clump are removed so that the final result resembles a Victorian posy, with many small flowers surrounded by a ring of foliage.

STARTING LEAF CUTTINGS

Many house plants, such as African violets and gloxinias, lack stems suitable for cuttings, but they can be rooted from leaf cuttings, for which there are two techniques. The method best suited to African violets and gloxinias involves snipping off a leaf and its petiole, or stem, close to its base with a sharp knife or razor blade. The rooting procedure (*drawings, page 89*) differs from that prescribed for stem cuttings only in three aspects. The leaf stem should be set in the rooting medium at an angle rather than straight up in the manner used for stem cuttings. Then the leaf will not shade the new plants. When the roots have formed, new petioles and leaves will shoot up at the base of the parent stem, and you have to leave room for them. Also, several new plants usually appear, and these are divided by being pulled apart and then planted each in its own pot. Finally, in leaf cuttings, you do not need to use rooting powder.

Rex begonias do not even need a leaf stem from which to send out new roots. They will root from the leaf alone, if you cut the leaf's major veins—the thicker of the lines branching from the stem—and pin the leaf, with hairpins, vein side down on the rooting medium (*drawings, page 90*). Roots and new plants will start wherever you cut the veins. This works because rex begonias apparently have very vigorous regenerative cells in their veins. They are so vigorous, in fact, that you can even cut a single leaf into wedges and root each wedge separately (*drawings page 91*). But in order to ensure the growth of a new plant each wedge must have at least one major vein in it as well as a piece of the leaf stem—otherwise roots are not likely to form.

NEW PLANTS BY DIVISION

Many plants, notably African violets, develop what horticulturists call multiple crowns; that is, they send up a number of stems from the surface of the soil in clumps or clusters. Although they are joined at the base, like Siamese twins, they are in effect separate plants and dividing them is an easy method of multiplication. When the plant has formed such clumps, knock the whole plant out of its pot; the best time to do this is while plants are dormant, or if they have no dormant period, either before or after flowering period. Separate the crowns or stems by hand where there are natural divisions that come apart easily; if no natural divisions are obvious, cut them apart with a knife and forestall infection by dusting the cuts with a fungicide powder. Make sure each division has its own set of leaves and roots. Plant each division in a separate pot filled with potting mixture —no rooting medium or hormone powder is necessary. Just make sure that the stem is planted at the same height in relation to the soil surface as it was before. Water lightly once, then water sparingly until the new plants have become well established.

Saxifraga stolonifera, episcias and some other plants propagate themselves by sending out runners—trailing stems that creep along the ground and put out roots beneath each cluster of leaves as they go. The easiest way to capitalize on this characteristic in the case of indoor plants is to guide a runner to an adjacent flowerpot filled with potting mixture. Wherever the runner begins to develop leaves, just pin it to the soil with a hairpin: it will root without help from hormone or rooting medium. But do not sever the runner from its parent until the new plant is growing vigorously.

RUNNERS AND OFFSETS

Instead of runners, many bromeliads develop offsets, or shoots, around their bases. You can create a new plant from such a shoot after it has formed roots of its own—poke in the soil mixture to find out. Then simply sever an offset with a sharp knife and plant it in its own pot. No hormone treatment is necessary.

For plants that have long, flexible branches—jasmines and

PROPAGATING PLANTS FROM RUNNERS

Plants that develop runners, such as Saxifraga stolonifera, *normally multiply by creeping out along the ground, rooting as they go—as the longest runner from the potted plant shown above is attempting to do.*

Leaving the runner attached to the parent plant, place it in a separate pot containing potting mixture. Fasten the young plant down with a hairpin behind the leaves growing from the node where roots will form.

When new leaves have appeared in abundance and have begun to fill the pot, the plant has established its own root system; it is no longer dependent on the parent plant and the runner can now be severed.

daphnes, for example—an easy method of vegetative reproduction is soil layering. In this method a branch is notched about half-way through on its underside 10 to 20 centimetres (4 to 8 in.) from its tip. The notch is dusted with rooting powder and buried about 12 millimetres ($\frac{1}{2}$ in.) deep in potting mixture—rooting medium is unnecessary—in a pot adjacent to the parent plant. The buried portion is held down with a hairpin or layering pin and the end of the branch is left exposed. When new growth at the tip or around the notch indicates that roots have formed at the notch, the new plant can be severed from its parent. Some plants—calliandras, for example—have inflexible branches and for them soil layering is impractable, but air layering (*drawings, below*) achieves the same result.

Vegetative reproduction is the quickest and easiest way of getting new flowering plants, but do not overlook seed propa-

PROPAGATING PLANTS
BY AIR LAYERING

1. *A woody plant can be propagated by a method that is called air layering. First make four or five slits about 2.5 cm (1 in.) around a stem 10 cm (4 in.) from the tip, cutting only through the bark, not into the wood (inset). Dust each of the slits with rooting powder.*

2. *Wrap a clear plastic bag around the stem below the slits and stuff it with moistened sphagnum moss. The bag should be tied with raffia fibre or with cotton string.*

3. *Tie the bag firmly at the top, then wind more raffia or string around the rest of the moss ball to give it support. In a few weeks you will see small roots spreading into the moss.*

4. *After about eight weeks, when the moss is filled with roots, the plastic can be removed and the new plant cut free. Sever the stem from the parent just below the moss and pot the new plant, moss and all, in the potting mixture recommended for the parent (see the encyclopaedia, Chapter 6).*

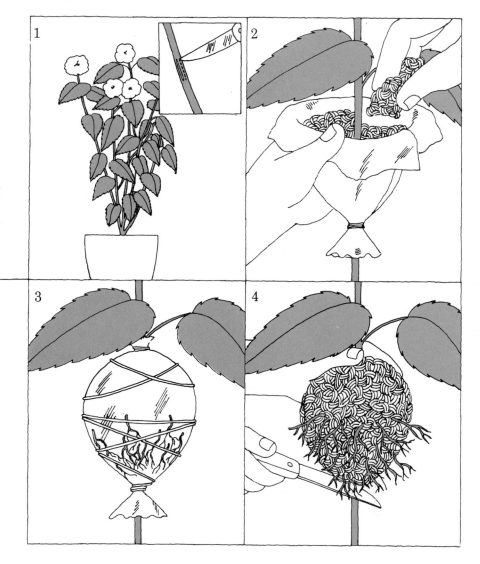

gation if you want lots of plants, and are willing to wait. The essentials for seed germination are moisture, fresh air and the proper temperature, which for most plants is between 18° and 21°C (65° and 70°F). You will need, besides seeds, finely shredded sphagnum moss, potting mixture, 10 centimetre (4 in.) pots, and clear plastic bags. Fill each pot with potting mixture and firm the mixture with the heel of your hand so that its surface is 12 to 18 millimetres ($\frac{1}{2}$ to $\frac{3}{4}$ in.) below the pot's rim. Then sow the seeds on the surface of the soil. Scatter the seeds sparingly to avoid crowding the future seedlings; each tiny plant must have light, air and soil of its own to thrive and to avoid the common fungus disease known as "damping-off", which can kill young seedlings overnight. Unless the seeds are extremely fine, like those of gloxinias and begonias, cover them with a thin layer of moist sphagnum moss, then sprinkle water on the surface with a fine spray, or let the pot stand in a tray of water until the surface appears moist. (Remember to soak sphagnum moss with water before you cover seeds with it). If you are planting very fine seeds, first cover the soil with a 6 millimetre ($\frac{1}{4}$ in.) layer of moistened sphagnum moss. Then spread a pinch of the seeds sparingly on top of the layer of moss—they will slip into the proper depth. Do not water from the top you would wash the seeds too deeply into the moss. Instead, let the pot stand in a tray of water until the surface is moist.

The next step is to slip the pot into a clear plastic bag and place it in a well-lit place out of direct sun. As soon as the seedlings have germinated, take off the plastic bag. Plants that like sun (*encyclopaedia*) can be moved into direct sunlight in a few days; others should stay behind a net curtain. Do not be tempted to transplant the seedlings as soon as you see what looks like a pair of leaves. Those first deceptive bits of green are not true foliage, but what are called seed leaves. When the first real leaves have appeared—they will be unmistakably typical of the parent plant—you can transplant each seedling to its own pot.

It is all quite simple, really. But if you want to try something a little different, do as I sometimes do and substitute a jar for the plastic bag and the pot. I use a square wide-mouthed jar because it will not roll over. After cleaning it, I lay it on its side and put in a layer of about 2 centimetres ($\frac{3}{4}$ in.) of moist potting mixture. I spread the mixture and tamp it lightly with a spatula, then scatter the seeds sparingly with a long-handled spoon. Then I mist the interior with an atomizer, put the jar's cover on loosely, and set my miniature greenhouse on a window sill behind a net curtain until the seedlings are large enough to transplant. The long-handled spoon will get them out. If you keep several jars of seedlings in various stages of growth, you can always delight a visitor with a gift of a young plant.

A GLASS-JAR GREENHOUSE

An encyclopaedia of flowering house plants

What colours do African violets come in? Does your living room window provide enough sun for a pot of azaleas? How do you propagate fuchsias? Which species of orchids are most easily grown? These questions, and many others, are answered in the following encyclopaedic chapter, which lists the characteristics and needs of 146 genera of outstanding flowering house plants.

The entries specify the natural-light requirements of each plant and note those plants especially suited to growing by artificial light. Each entry also includes the preferred ranges of temperature, with emphasis on night temperatures, which are critical if the plant is to get rest for flowering and general health. The need for coolness at night often determines where plants can be located; camellias, daphnes and hyacinths, for example, should have night temperatures of 4° to 10°C (40° to 50°F) and thus should be placed in a room that gets little or no heat. But plants are adaptable; if their environment falls short of the ideal, they probably will thrive, though they may grow less vigorously or blossom less spectacularly.

Most flowering house plants respond to standardized growing procedures. Unless a special potting mixture is indicated, use one consisting of 1 part packaged potting soil, 1 part coarse moss peat and 1 part sharp sand; add 100 grams (4 oz.) of ground limestone per 28 litres (1 cu ft) except where indicated otherwise. Unless a special fertilizer is recommended, use any standard complete fertilizer that is specifically designed and labelled for house plants.

All the plants are listed alphabetically by their Latin botanical names, which are recognized throughout the world. In the case of the white Italian bellflower, *Campanula isophylla* 'Alba', for example, the genus name, *Campanula*, is followed by the species name, *isophylla*; the third name, 'Alba', indicates the white-flowered variety. Common names are cross-referenced to their Latin equivalents in the index. For quick reference a chart with the characteristics and requirements of the illustrated plants appears on pages 152-154.

A sampling of the year-round colour that can be enjoyed indoors is provided by artist Allianora Rosse in a grouping of 24 of the flowering house plants described and illustrated in the following encyclopaedia.

FLOWERING MAPLE
Abutilon megapotamicum 'Variegatum'

CHENILLE PLANT
Acalypha hispida

HOT WATER PLANT
Achimenes hybrid

A

ABUTILON

A. x *hybridum*; *A. megapotamicum* 'Variegatum'; *A. striatum* 'Thompsonii' (all called flowering maple)

Flowering maples, which have maple-like leaves 5 to 7.5 cm (2 to 3 in.) long, bear drooping bell-like flowers, about 5 cm (2 in.) across, that bloom from spring to autumn. *A. megapotamicum* 'Variegatum' has red-and-yellow blossoms with large, dark brown pollen-bearing anthers; old plants trail as long as 1.5 metres (5 ft) and are suited to hanging baskets. Bushy varieties, which are generally pruned to stay about 60 cm (2 ft) tall, include *A. striatum* 'Thompsonii' with orange-salmon flowers, and *A.* x *hybridum*, with white, yellow, salmon or purple blooms.

HOW TO GROW. Give flowering maples at least four hours of direct sunlight a day. Night temperatures of 10° to 13°C (50° to 55°F) and day temperatures of 20° to 22°C (68° to 72°F) are ideal. Keep the soil moist and fertilize once a month. Propagate in spring from stem cuttings of new growth or from seeds.

ACALYPHA

A. hispida (chenille plant, red-hot cat's-tail); *A. wilkesiana* (copperleaf, beefsteak plant)

The chenille plant is notable for its 20 to 50 cm (8 to 20 in.) plumes of fuzzy red flowers, which seem ready-made for drapery fringes; a cultivar, *A. hispida* 'Alba', bears pinkish-white flowers. Both bloom profusely in autumn and winter, and will blossom the year round under optimum conditions. They have coarse, 7.5 to 12.5 cm (3 to 5 in.) dark green leaves. The other species is noted more for its striking foliage than for its flowers, which are small and inconspicuous. The 7.5 to 10 cm (3 to 4 in.) long leaves of the species *A. wilkesiana* have tones of red, copper and pink, while *A. wilkesiana* 'Godseffiana' has 5 to 7.5 cm (2 to 3 in.) long dark green leaves edged with white. All acalyphas are upright, bushy plants that are usually pruned to 60 or 90 cm (2 or 3 ft).

HOW TO GROW. Acalyphas need considerable heat and humidity, and flourish in direct sunlight, but also do well in a bright room without direct sun. Ideal temperatures are 16° to 18°C (60° to 65°F) at night and 21°C (70°F) or higher during the day. The soil should be peaty and kept moist; fertilize monthly for continuous bloom. To rejuvenate old plants, prune severely in early spring, leaving only 20 to 30 cm (8 to 12 in.) of growth. Propagate from stem cuttings of new growth in summer and root at a high temperature of 21° to 27°C (70° to 80°F).

ACHIMENES

A. hybrids (hot water plant)

Aglow with masses of satiny flowers, 2.5 to 6 cm (1 to 2½ in.) across, achimenes offer a brilliant floral display from spring to autumn. Relatives of the African violet, these bushy gesneriads ultimately grow 20 to 30 cm (8 to 12 in.) tall; their spreading branches are lined with glistening, often hairy leaves 4 to 7.5 cm (1½ to 3 in.) long. Available flower colours include pastel blue, deep pink, yellow (with silvery foliage), deep red with yellow throats, deep purple and bright rose pink. All are attractive when used in hanging containers, but also do well when the pots are plunged in containers filled with moist peat or sphagnum moss.

HOW TO GROW. Achimenes do best in bright indirect or curtain-filtered sunlight and can be grown in 14 to 16 hours of artificial light a day. Night temperatures of 18° to 21°C (65° to 70°F) and day temperatures of 24°C (75°F) or higher are ideal. Plant in a mixture of 2 parts moss peat to 1 part packaged potting soil and 1 part sharp sand. Water with tepid soft water and keep the mixture moist; fertilize monthly during the blooming season. After flowering, let plants die to the ground. Store dormant rhizomes at 16°C (60°F) over the winter in plastic bags with dry moss peat or vermiculite. Propagate during dormancy by dividing the tiny rhizomes that appear on roots or leaf stems, or sow seeds or take stem cuttings in spring.

AECHMEA
A. caudata; *A. chantinii*, also called *Billbergia chantinii*; *A. fasciata*, also called *Billbergia fasciata* and *Billbergia rhodocyanea* (urn plant, exotic brush)

Aechmeas are spectacular bromeliads with central floral spikes up to 60 cm (2 ft) tall and 20 to 25 cm (8 to 10 in.) long spiny-edged leaves that form water-holding cups at their bases. They may flower at any time of year. *A. caudata* is topped by branched clusters of bead-like yellow flowers; the leaves of the cultivar *A. caudata* 'Variegata' are striped lengthways in white. *A. chantinii* has 4 cm (1½ in.) red petal-like bracts tipped with yellow, and brownish-green leaves with silver stripes. *A. fasciata* bears pink 4 cm (1½ in.) bracts dotted with tiny blue flowers; its light green leaves have silver bands. The inflorescence stays colourful for about four months.

HOW TO GROW. Aechmeas do best in bright indirect or curtain-filtered sunlight, night temperatures of 16° to 18°C (60° to 65°F) and day temperatures of 21°C (70°F) or higher. Pot in equal parts of pine-needles, leaf-mould and peat. Keep the mixture moist. Keep the cup at the base of the leaves filled with water at room temperature and add a very little liquid manure to this once a month, in summer only. Propagate from shoots that appear at the base of the plant after it flowers; and pot up separately when these have rooted.

AESCHYNANTHUS, also called TRICHOSPORUM
A. lobbianus, also called *A. parvifolius* (lipstick plant); *A. pulcher* (royal red bugler); *A. speciosus* (all called basket vine)

Basket vines, so named because they are best displayed in hanging containers, are gesneriads with gracefully trailing stems 60 to 90 cm (2 to 3 ft) long, tipped with 5 to 10 cm (2 to 4 in.) tubular flowers. *A. lobbianus* has waxy, yellow-throated scarlet flowers with deep purple leaf-like outer petals (calyces); the flowers of *A. pulcher* have green sepals. Both bloom in spring, producing buds that resemble lipsticks. *A. speciosus* bears waxy, scarlet-tipped orange flowers in winter and spring.

HOW TO GROW. Basket vines do best in at least four hours direct sunlight a day in winter and bright indirect or curtain-filtered sunlight for the rest of the year. Night temperatures of 18° to 21°C (65° to 70°F) and day temperatures of 24°C (75°F) or higher are ideal. Pot in a mixture of 2 parts moss peat to 1 part packaged potting soil and 1 part sharp sand. Keep the mixture moist and fertilize monthly. After the plants have flowered, cut the stems back to a height of about 15 cm (6 in.) to produce new growth. Propagate from stem cuttings, preferably in spring.

AGAPANTHUS
A. africanus, also called *A. umbellatus*; *A.* hybrids; *A. praecox* ssp. *orientalis*, also called *A. orientalis* (all called agapanthus, blue African lily, lily of the Nile)

Agapanthus is prized for its 30 to 60 cm (1 to 2 ft) long

URN PLANT
Aechmea fasciata

LIPSTICK PLANT
Aeschynanthus lobbianus

AGAPANTHUS
Agapanthus africanus

strap-like leaves and great clusters of 2.5 to 12.5 cm (1 to 5 in.) lily-like flowers, which bloom in summer. *A. africanus* bears blue flowers (as many as 30 to a cluster) and grows 45 to 60 cm (1½ to 2 ft) tall. Among the hybrids, are countless varieties, ranging in colour from white and pale blue to light navy blue and in height between 45 and 75 cm (1½ to 2½ ft). *A. praecox* ssp. *orientalis* is much larger, growing 1.2 to 1.5 metres (4 to 5 ft) tall and has 100 or more blue or white flowers in a cluster.

HOW TO GROW. Grow agapanthus in large tubs, where it can be allowed to become very congested before being repotted. Use a loam-based compost and give the plants plenty of sun and light. They do better on a south-facing terrace outdoors than inside; and in winter they should be stored in a cold but frost-free place and kept almost dry. During the growing season, they do best in temperatures of 10° to 13°C (50° to 55°F) at night and 20° to 22°C (68° to 72°F) during the day. Keep the soil moist and fertilize every two weeks during the growing season. Propagate in February or March by dividing the fleshy roots, or sow seeds in spring.

AGATHAEA See *Felicia*

ALLAMANDA
A. cathartica (golden trumpet); *A. neriifolia*

Allamandas are vigorous tropical climbers, best suited to light, warm, airy positions as in sunrooms, conservatories or office-block entrance halls with plenty of glass. The evergreen leaves are obovate and arranged in whorls of three; the flowers, golden-yellow and funnel-shaped, fragrant in some species, can be 7.5 to 10 cm (3 to 4 in.) across. Hybrids of *A. cathartica* include 'Grandiflora' with 10 to 12.5 cm (4 to 5 in.) flowers and 'Schottii', yellow with brown lines on the inner petals; 'Williamsii' can be trained as a bush. *A. neriifolia* is an erect shrub, growing to 90 cm (3 ft) with golden flowers streaked with orange.

HOW TO GROW. Allamandas do best in at least four hours of direct sunlight a day, night temperatures of 16° to 18°C (60° to 65°F) and day temperatures of 21°C (70°F) or higher. Keep the soil moist and fertilize every two weeks from April until September; apply less water and no fertilizer for the rest of the year. Good drainage is essential. Prune the plants back in spring and use the tip cuttings for propagation purposes.

x AMARCRINUM See x *Crindonna*
AMARYLLIS See *Sprekelia*

ANANAS
A. comosus 'Variegatus'; *A. sagenaria*, also called *A. bracteatus* (both called pineapple)

A. sagenaria, the most common pineapple plant grown indoors, has arching, 30 to 37.5 cm (12 to 15 in.) greyish-green leaves surrounding a 37.5 cm (15 in.) spike of red buds resembling a pincushion; the buds open into purple flowers, which are followed by a 5 cm (2 in.) high, fragrant, edible pineapple. A larger variety of these bromeliads, *A. comosus* 'Variegatus' has green, cream and pink striped leaves forming rosettes 60 cm (2 ft) or more across. Violet flowers on top of a 60 to 120 cm (2 to 4 ft) spike are followed by an edible fruit.

HOW TO GROW. Pineapples do best in at least four hours of direct sunlight a day, night temperatures of 16° to 18°C (60° to 65°F) and day temperatures of 21°C (70°F) or higher.

ALLAMANDA
Allamanda cathartica 'Williamsii'

PINEAPPLE
Ananas comosus 'Variegatus'

Pot in a mixture of 2 parts moss peat to 1 part packaged potting soil and 1 part sharp sand; do not add lime. Keep moist and fertilize monthly. Propagate from shoots that appear at the base of the plant after it fruits and dies, or plant the rosette of leaves from the top of the fruit.

ANGRAECUM
A. distichum. Also called *Mystacidium distichum*—see also *Neofinetia*

This charming miniature orchid, which grows only 7.5 to 12.5 cm (3 to 5 in.) tall, may bear 100 or more sweetly fragrant, milky-white 6 mm ($\frac{1}{4}$ in.) blossoms, set closely together on loosely spreading 15 cm (6 in.) stems (*photograph, page 57*). The flowers bloom profusely in late summer and autumn and intermittently through the rest of the year. Thick 6 mm ($\frac{1}{4}$ in.) wide leaves are folded tightly and evenly on the stems like plaits.

HOW TO GROW. *A. distichum* does best in bright indirect sunlight, night temperatures of 13° to 18°C (55° to 65°F) and day temperatures of 20°C (68°F) or higher. It grows especially well on a slab of tree fern, but will also thrive in a mixture of 2 parts fir bark or shredded tree-fern fibre and 1 part coarse moss peat. Place the pot on a humidifying tray (*page 82*) and keep the potting medium slightly damp at all times. Fertilize monthly with a high-nitrogen formula, diluting $\frac{1}{4}$ teaspoon in 1 litre (2 pt) of water.

ANTHURIUM
A. andreanum (tailflower, painter's palette); *A. scherzerianum* (flamingo flower, pigtail plant)

Visitors to the tropics are captivated by the strange petal-like leaves, or spathes, of anthuriums. The spathes, orange, red, pink or white, and glossy as patent leather, bear yellow tail-like structures called spadices, on which are crowded the plant's minuscule true flowers. *A. andreanum* has spathes 10 to 15 cm (4 to 6 in.) wide on top of upright stems 60 to 90 cm (2 to 3 ft) tall. *A. scherzerianum*, seldom over 30 cm (12 in.) tall, has nearly oval 5 to 7.5 cm (2 to 3 in.) long spathes that bear curly spadices. Both species will bloom continuously; single spathes usually last up to a month.

HOW TO GROW. Anthuriums do best in bright indirect or curtain-filtered sunlight, night temperatures of 16° to 18°C (60° to 65°F) and day temperatures of 20°C (68°F) or higher. Pot in equal parts of fir bark and coarse sphagnum moss. Set the pot in a humidifying tray or spray regularly in dry atmospheres. Keep moist and fertilize every two weeks. As high crowns and aerial roots develop, cover the crowns with moist sphagnum moss. Propagate from the offsets at any time of the year.

APHELANDRA
A. aurantiaca; *A. squarrosa* (zebra plant)

Favourites in Victorian conservatories, aphelandras, with gaudy flower clusters 10 to 20 cm (4 to 8 in.) high, are popular again. Leading varieties are the yellow *A. squarrosa* 'Louisae' and the *A. squarrosa* hybrids 'Brockfeld', 'Dania' and 'Fritz Prinsler'; the scarlet *A. aurantiaca* and the orange-scarlet *A. aurantiaca* var. *roezlii*. All blossom for about six weeks in autumn, occasionally at other seasons. They are normally pruned to stay 30 to 45 cm (12 to 18 in.) tall.

HOW TO GROW. Aphelandras do best in bright indirect or curtain-filtered sunlight, night temperatures of 16° to 18°C (60° to 65°F) and day temperatures of 21°C (70°F) or higher. Pot in 2 parts moss peat, 1 part packaged potting

FLAMINGO FLOWER
Anthurium scherzerianum

ZEBRA PLANT
Aphelandra squarrosa 'Louisae'

soil and 1 part sharp sand. Place the pot on a humidifying tray (*page 43*). Keep moist from March until October, give less water the rest of the year. Fertilize every two weeks during flowering. In March cut back half of the previous season's growth, and repot. Propagate from stem cuttings in spring.

ARDISIA

A. crenata, also called *A. crispa*; *A. japonica* (coral berry)

Massive clusters of pea-sized red berries give ardisias special appeal at Christmas, when the fruit is mature. The berries often cling to plants for a year, even after the next season's tiny, fragrant flowers appear in midwinter or early spring. *A. crenata* may grow 90 cm (3 ft) tall with reddish flowers; *A. japonica* 60 cm (2 ft) tall with white flowers. After the plants reach 45 to 60 cm (18 to 24 in.), they lose their lower leaves and appear tree-like.

HOW TO GROW. Ardisias do best in bright indirect or curtain-filtered sunlight, night temperatures of 10° to 13°C (50° to 55°F) and day temperatures of 20° to 22°C (68° to 72°F). Avoid draughts. Keep soil moist and fertilize every two weeks. To keep the plants bushy, cut them down to 5 cm (2 in.) in early spring; keep the soil quite dry until new shoots appear, then remove all but the three strongest shoots. Repot in fresh soil. Propagate in spring from seeds, stem cuttings or air layers (*page 94*).

CORAL BERRY
Ardisia crenata

ASTER See *Felicia*

ASTILBE

A. x *arendsii* hybrids (commonly but erroneously known as spiraeas)

These hardy herbaceous perennials make excellent, long-lasting pot plants, particularly for cool rooms. They have handsome, deeply cut, fern-like leaves and 60 to 90 cm (2 to 3 ft) stems with compact plumes of myriads of tiny flowers in spring. These may be white, pink, red or fuchsia-pink.

HOW TO GROW. Indoors astilbes do best in bright indirect or curtain-filtered light and night temperatures of 10° to 16°C (50° to 60°F) and day temperatures of 16°C (60°F) or higher. They need plenty of water during the growing season and must never dry out at the roots. After blooming, the plants can be planted out in the garden, and lifted and potted again, if desired, in late summer for spring flowering the following year. Feed every month during the growing season. Propagate by division in spring.

AZALEA See *Rhododendron*

B

BEGONIA

B. rex (rex begonia); *B. semperflorens* hybrids; *B. tuberhybrida* (tuberous-rooted begonia); *B.* 'Gloire de Lorraine'

Begonias make up the largest genus of plants suitable for indoor culture. The popular *B. semperflorens* has satiny flowers less than 2.5 cm (1 in.) across. They come in white, salmon-pink or rose-red with oval, waxy, green or reddish leaves as large as 10 cm (4 in.). The cultivars bloom profusely and continuously, growing 15 to 35 cm (6 to 14 in.) tall. The blossoms of the summer-flowering tuberous-rooted begonia are usually 7.5 to 10 cm (3 to 4 in.) across and come in white, pink, rose-red, deep red, yellow and orange. There are also 7.5 to 15 cm (3 to 6 in.) tall

ASTILBE
Astilbe x *arendsii* hybrid

double-flowered types which bloom on and on from summer until early autumn; the pendulous kinds have slender drooping stems and single or semi-double, 5 to 7.5 cm (2 to 3 in.) flowers. Rex begonias bear 2.5 to 5 cm (1 to 2 in.) pink or white flowers usually in spring, but are prized most for their large, often hairy leaves, which are shaped like elephant ears and come in striking shades of green, red, bronze, silver or rose. *B.* 'Gloire de Lorraine' is an exceptional long-flowering, winter-blooming group derived from *B. socotrana*, with rich pink flowers. It has the same cultural needs as *B. semperflorens*.

HOW TO GROW. *B. semperflorens* and tuberous-rooted begonias require at least four hours of direct sunlight a day from November until March, but should be given bright indirect or curtain-filtered light the rest of the year; rex begonias need to be protected from direct sunlight at all times. All these begonias do best in night temperatures of 10° to 13°C (50° to 55°F), day temperatures of 20° to 22°C (68° to 72°F). Pot in a highly organic soil mixture (up to 1 part moss peat to 1 part packaged potting soil). During the growing season, let *B. semperflorens* dry slightly between thorough waterings, but let the others remain barely damp; withhold moisture from the tuberous-rooted varieties when the plants are dormant. Fertilize every two weeks during the growing season. The species can be grown from seeds. *B. semperflorens* and *B.* 'Gloire de Lorraine' can be propagated from stem cuttings at any time; tuberous-rooted begonias can be grown from stem cuttings in early spring or by division of tubers; rex begonias can be grown very easily from leaf cuttings or by division in summer or autumn.

BELOPERONE
B. comosa; *B. guttata* (both called shrimp plant)

The shrimp plant is named for the appearance of its hanging 7.5 to 10 cm (3 to 4 in.) long formations of petal-like bracts from which the tiny white true flowers protrude. The bracts come in yellow, yellow and red, or solid red, depending on the cultivar. The oval hairy leaves, often as long as the bracts, are pea-green, and in the case of *B. comosa* are sometimes bordered in brick-red. Both species bloom throughout the year. Pinch off the tips of stems to keep plants at a height of 30 to 45 cm (12 to 18 in.).

HOW TO GROW. Shrimp plants do best in at least four hours of direct sunlight a day, night temperatures of 10° to 13°C (50° to 55°F) and day temperatures of 20° to 22°C (68° to 72°F). Allow the soil to become slightly dry between waterings. Fertilize every two weeks. Propagate from pinched-off tips.

BILLBERGIA
B. 'Fantasia'; *B. horrida* var. *tigrina*; *B. leptopoda* (permanent wave plant); *B. nutans* (queen's tears); *B. pyramidalis* (summer torch). See also *Aechmea*

Billbergias are bromeliads that bear petal-like bracts and tubular flowers on stalks 30 to 60 cm (1 to 2 ft) long, each stalk surrounded by strap-like leaves that form a water-holding cup. 'Fantasia', a *B. pyramidalis* hybrid, produces white-marbled leaves and rose-coloured bracts with blue-tipped rose flowers in summer; *B. horrida* var. *tigrina* has reddish-brown leaves with narrow silver bars and rose-coloured bracts with violet-tipped green flowers in late winter; *B. leptopoda* has curly-tipped cream-mottled leaves and rosy-red bracts with green-tipped blue flowers in early spring; *B. nutans* has grey-green leaves and rose-coloured bracts with blue-edged green flowers in winter and is the best for room cultivation; *B. pyramidalis*

BEGONIA
Begonia semperflorens

SHRIMP PLANT
Beloperone guttata 'Yellow Queen'

BILLBERGIA
Billbergia 'Fantasia'

has grey-barred green leaves and scarlet bracts with blue-tipped crimson flowers in winter.

HOW TO GROW. Billbergias do best in at least four hours of direct sunlight a day, but should be given indirect or curtain-filtered sunlight at midday in summer. Night temperatures of 16° to 18°C (60° to 65°F), day temperatures of 21°C (70°F) or higher are ideal. Use a lime-free mixture of equal parts coarse sand and moss peat. Keep moist; fertilize every two weeks. Keep the cup at the base of the leaves full of tepid, soft water. Propagate by division or from offsets that appear at the base after flowering. Detach these and pot them up separately.

BOUGAINVILLEA
B. x buttiana

Bougainvilleas are fast-spreading tropical vines noted for their spectacular clusters of papery 2.5 cm (1 in.) petal-like bracts, which range in colour from bright purple through shades of red and pink to copper, yellow and white. A brilliant red cultivar, 'Barbara Karst'—as well as other cultivars, if given ample sun and high temperatures—will blossom almost continuously. But under less than optimum conditions most cultivars bloom between early spring and late summer, and enter a rest phase in autumn and early winter.

HOW TO GROW. Bougainvilleas do best in at least four hours of direct sunlight a day, night temperatures of 16°C to 18°C (60° to 65°F) and day temperatures of 21°C (70°F) or higher. Allow the soil to become moderately dry between thorough waterings and fertilize every two weeks during the growing season; omit fertilizer and reduce water while the plants are resting. Repot in very early spring, but do not disturb the roots. Bougainvilleas can be pruned to bush form or trained to a trellis, and can be kept small by growing less vigorous strains and training these along wire fixed in the pot. Propagate from stem cuttings in summer, rooted in considerable heat.

BRASSAVOLA
B. nodosa (lady-of-the-night orchid)

Delightfully fragrant from early evening until the middle of the night, B. nodosa blooms for most of the year, bearing long-lasting 7.5 to 10 cm (3 to 4 in.) blossoms in white, yellow or pale green, with white flaring lips (*photograph, page 57*), as many as 50 flowers may be in bloom simultaneously. Plants, which have pencil-shaped leaves, rarely grow taller than 30 cm (12 in.).

HOW TO GROW. B. nodosa does best in bright indirect sunlight, night temperatures of 13° to 18°C (55° to 65°F) and day temperatures of 20°C (68°F) or higher. It can be grown in a mixture of 2 parts fir bark or shredded tree-fern fibre and 1 part coarse moss peat, or simply on a slab of tree fern. Place the pot on a humidifying tray (*page 82*) and let the potting medium become moderately dry between thorough waterings. Fertilize monthly with a high-nitrogen formula, diluting $\frac{1}{4}$ teaspoon in 1 litre (2 pt) of water.

BRASSIA
B. caudata

These orchids have fragrant, waxy, long-lasting blooms (*photograph, page 59*) with 6 cm ($2\frac{1}{2}$ in.) greenish-yellow petals with brown spots and leaf-like outer petals or sepals which grow 12.5 to 20 cm (5 to 8 in.) long. Flower spikes 37.5 cm (15 in.) or more in length bear up to 12 flowers each, in autumn and winter. The arching leaves, 20 to 25 cm (8 to 10 in.) long, are green with reddish-brown spots.

BOUGAINVILLEA
Bougainvillea x *buttiana* 'Barbara Karst'

HOW TO GROW. *B. caudata* does best in at least four hours of direct sunlight a day, night temperatures of 18° to 21°C (65° to 70°F) and day temperatures of 24°C (75°F) or higher. Pot in a mixture of 2 parts fir bark or shredded tree-fern fibre and 1 part coarse moss peat, or mount on a slab of tree fern. Place the pot on a humidifying tray (*page 82*). Keep moist; fertilize monthly with a high-nitrogen formula, diluting ¼ teaspoon in 1 litre (2 pt) of water.

BROWALLIA
B. hybrids; *B. speciosa* 'Major'; *B. viscosa*

Bushy annual plants with thin stems that grow up to 60 cm (2 ft) long, browallias bear masses of satiny 2.5 to 5 cm (1 to 2 in.) trumpet-shaped blossoms all the year. The cultivar 'Ultramarine', a rich deep blue, and 'Sapphire', blue and only 15 to 22.5 cm (6 to 9 in.) high, are derived from *B. viscosa. B. speciosa* 'Major' bears blue or white flowers; the cultivar 'Silver Bells' has white flowers.

HOW TO GROW. Browallias flower according to when they were sown. Early spring sowings flower in summer; summer sowings bloom in winter. Browallias need at least four hours of direct sunlight a day from November through to February, but should have morning sun only and no direct rays the rest of the year. They do best in night temperatures of 13° to 16°C (55° to 60°F) and day temperatures of 20° to 22°C (68° to 72°F). Grow in a loam-based proprietary compost and keep moist; fertilize every two weeks, monthly in winter. Propagate from seeds.

BRUNFELSIA
B. pauciflora var. *calycina*, also called *B. calycina* and *B. calycina* var. *eximea* (yesterday, today and tomorrow; chameleon plant)

A slow-growing evergreen, named for the changing colours of its sweetly scented, 5 cm (2 in.) flowers, which are dark purple with white eyes the first day they appear, become lavender on the second day and by the third day have turned white. Under ideal conditions Brunfelsias bloom abundantly all year, but they generally rest for a few weeks in late spring.

HOW TO GROW. Brunfelsias do best in at least four hours of direct sunlight a day from November until February, with indirect or curtain-filtered sunlight the rest of the year. Night temperatures of 10° to 13°C (50° to 55°F) and day temperatures of 20° to 22°C (68° to 72°F) are ideal. Keep the soil moist and fertilize every two weeks while the plants are actively growing; use less water and no fertilizer when they are resting. To keep plants compact and bushy, pinch off the ends of the stems periodically; these tips may be rooted in spring.

C

CALCEOLARIA
C. x *herbeohybrida*, also called *C.* hybrids; *C. integrifolia*, also called *C. rugosa* (both called slipper flower)

Calceolarias have large leaves up to 15 cm (6 in.) long and sac-like two-lipped blossoms up to 5 cm (2 in.) across; the lower lip is enormously inflated, the upper one much less so. The flowers, which bloom profusely in spring, come in red, pink, maroon, bronze or yellow, usually with brown or purple markings. Many strains of *C.* x *herbeohybrida* are available commercially, ranging from 15 to 30 cm (6 to 12 in.) in height. *C. integrifolia*, a shrubby tree, grows 30 to 60 cm (1 to 2 ft) tall and blooms from spring to autumn. Calceolarias are difficult to bring to flowering size and are generally bought from florists at blooming time, then

BROWALLIA
Browallia speciosa 'Major'

YESTERDAY, TODAY AND TOMORROW
Brunfelsia pauciflora var. *calycina*

SLIPPER FLOWER
Calceolaria x *herbeohybrida* 'Multiflora Nana'

RED POWDER-PUFF TREE
Calliandra haematocephala

COMMON CAMELLIA
Camellia japonica 'Debutante'

discarded a month or so later when flowering has ceased.

HOW TO GROW. Calceolarias do best in bright indirect or curtain-filtered sunlight, night temperatures of 4° to 7°C (40° to 45°F) and day temperatures of 13° to 16°C (55° to 60°F). Avoid wetting the crowns of thick foliage at soil level; keep the soil barely moist so that it dries by nightfall. Do not fertilize when plants are blossoming. Propagate from seeds in summer to flower in spring. *C. integrifolia* can also be propagated from stem cuttings in autumn.

CALLIANDRA
C. haematocephala, also called *C. inequilatera* (red powderpuff tree); *C. tweedyi*

Calliandras are rare in Europe, although frequently grown as house plants in America. They have deeply cut leaves and 5 to 7.5 cm (2 to 3 in.) fluffy flower heads with hundreds of delicate, bright red, pink or purplish-red stamens. The plants blossom for many weeks during the winter and spring from the time they are about 30 cm (12 in.) tall; their foliage, bronzy when new, is attractive all the year round. They grow into bushy mounds and are usually kept 60 to 90 cm (2 to 3 ft) tall by trimming.

HOW TO GROW. Calliandras do best in at least four hours of direct sunlight a day, with night temperatures of 16° to 18°C (60° to 65°F) and day temperatures of 21°C (70°F) or higher. Keep the soil barely moist. Fertilize monthly from March until September. To shape plants or restrict growth, prune in late spring or early summer, after flowering has ended. Propagate from cuttings of newly grown stems in spring or by air layering at any time (*page 94*).

CAMELLIA
C. japonica (common camellia); *C. reticulata* (net-vein camellia); *C. sasanqua*

Camellias are renowned for the perfection of their white, pink, red or multi-coloured flowers, up to 7.5 cm (3 in.) across. They bloom profusely for several weeks—*C. sasanqua* usually between autumn and spring, *C. japonica* and *C. reticulata* from late winter to late spring, depending upon the variety. The plants have glossy, dark green leaves up to 10 cm (4 in.) long, and are usually pruned back to keep their height at about 75 to 90 cm (2½ to 3 ft).

HOW TO GROW. Camellias do best in bright indirect or curtain-filtered sunlight, night temperatures of 4° to 7°C (40° to 45°F) and day temperatures of 16°C (60°F) or lower. Pot in a mixture composed of 2 parts moss peat, 1 part packaged potting soil and 1 part sharp sand; do not add lime. Keep the potting medium well moistened at all times and feed with an acid-type fertilizer in early spring and summer. To produce large blossoms, snap off all but one bud in each cluster. Avoid sudden changes of temperature or light conditions, or irregular watering alternating between very moist and very dry soil; any of these can cause bud drop. During the summer months, after flowering, bury the pots to their rims in cool shade outdoors and topdress them with moist peat. Always use soft water at room temperature for indoor plants. To restrict the size of the plant, prune after all flowering has stopped. Propagate from stem cuttings.

CAMPANULA
C. elatines; *C. fragilis*; *C. isophylla* (trailing campanula)

All these campanulas bear an abundance of 2.5 to 4 cm (1 to 1½ in.) flowers from midsummer until late autumn, deep violet-blue in *C. elatines*, mid-blue in *C. fragilis*, pale blue in *C. isophylla* and white in *C. isophylla* 'Alba'.

Another form, in which the foliage has cream variegations, is known as *C. isophylla* 'Mayi'. All have trailing 15 to 30 cm (6 to 12 in.) stems that make them ideal for hanging containers.

HOW TO GROW. These campanulas do best in plenty of sunlight, except in midsummer, when they should be given bright indirect or curtain-filtered sunlight. Night temperatures of 10° to 13°C (50° to 55°F) and day temperatures of 20° to 22°C (68° to 72°F) are ideal. Plant in a potting mixture composed of 2 parts moss peat and 1 part packaged potting soil and 1 part sharp sand. Keep the mixture evenly moist and fertilize monthly during the growing season; leave the mixture slightly dry, without any fertilizer, during the rest of the year. Campanulas can be propagated from stem cuttings in spring.

CAPSICUM
C. annuum (red pepper)
This species is notable not for its tiny white flowers, but for its masses of colourful, pungent fruit. The 5 to 7.5 cm (2 to 3 in.) long peppers, a form of chili pepper, appear in summer and autumn, and change colours as they ripen. Green, white, yellow, red or purple fruits sometimes appear simultaneously on a single plant. The plants, which begin to bear fruit when they are six to eight months old, grow about 30 cm (12 in.) high.

HOW TO GROW. Ornamental pepper plants do best in at least four hours of direct sunlight a day, night temperatures of 16° to 18°C (60° to 65°F) and day temperatures of 21°C (70°F) or higher. Keep the soil moist, but do not fertilize. Plants are treated as annuals and should be discarded when they are no longer attractive; propagate from seeds in early spring.

CARISSA
C. macrocarpa (Natal plum)
The Natal plum is a spiny evergreen plant with rich green, closely set 2.5 cm (1 in.) long oval leaves and fragrant flowers, 4 to 5 cm (1½ to 2 in.) across, which are followed by 4 to 5 cm (1½ to 2 in.) scarlet fruits that look like plums but taste like cranberries. The flowers are apt to bloom at any time of the year, often when ripe fruit is still clinging to the branches. Low growing or prostrate varieties have been raised in America, but are not generally available in Europe. These are kept dwarf by regular pruning. *C. macrocarpa* 'Nana Compacta' rarely grows more than 45 to 60 cm (1½ to 2 ft) tall.

HOW TO GROW. Natal plums do best in at least four hours of direct sunlight a day, night temperatures of 10° to 18°C (50° to 65°F) and day temperatures of 20°C (68°F) or higher. Keep moist; fertilize every three or four months. Propagation is by means of seed (if available) or air layering.

CATTLEYA
C. gaskelliana; *C. labiata*; *C. mossiae*; *C. trianae*
The most familiar of all orchids, commonly used in corsages, cattleyas are showy plants with 12.5 to 17.5 cm (5 to 7 in.) flowers on top of 30 to 45 cm (12 to 18 in.) stems. *C. labiata* (*photograph, page 57*) bears two to seven ruffle-lipped blossoms; the flowers vary from dark mauve and rose to pure white, or white with a rosy lip, often with yellow throats. *C. trianae* produces light pink to deep lavender flowers, singly or in clusters of up to five. *C. mossiae* bears two to five rosy-lavender flowers on each stalk in spring. *C. gaskelliana*, a fragrant, slightly shorter species, bears 25 to 35 cm (10 to 14 in.) high spikes each of

TRAILING CAMPANULA
Campanula isophylla 'Alba'

RED PEPPER
Capsicum annuum

NATAL PLUM
Carissa macrocarpa 'Nana Compacta'

NIGHT JESSAMINE
Cestrum nocturnum

HINDUSTAN GENTIAN
Chirita lavandulacea

up to five medium to dark lavender flowers.

HOW TO GROW. Cattleyas are plants needing high temperatures and plenty of humidity during the growing season and cool dryish conditions during dormancy. They are therefore difficult to cultivate indoors and are better in a warm greenhouse where such conditions are possible. They flourish in night temperatures of 13° to 18°C (55° to 65°F) and day temperatures of 20°C (68°F) or higher. The compost should consist of 3 parts chopped osmunda fibre to 1 part sphagnum moss and 1 part polystyrene granules. The pots must have good drainage. Propagate by division of the rhizomes in spring.

CESTRUM
C. diurnum (day jessamine); *C. nocturnum* (night jessamine); *C. parqui*; *C. purpureum*

Like the plants called jasmines, cestrums are extremely fragrant. Their white to greenish-yellow blossoms, about 2.5 cm (1 in.) long, bloom in clusters intermittently all year, usually followed by black berries. *C. diurnum*, fragrant by day, has glossy 7.5 to 10 cm (3 to 4 in.) long leaves. *C. nocturnum* is fragrant by night; the berries are white, the thin oval leaves may grow up to 20 cm (8 in.) long. *C. parqui*, also fragrant at night, has willow-like leaves 5 to 12.5 cm (2 to 5 in.) long. There are also kinds with pink or red flowers, including *C. purpureum*, one of the best with bunches of scarlet, tubular flowers. All species are gangling but can be kept under 60 cm (2 ft) tall by periodically pinching off the stem tips.

HOW TO GROW. Cestrums do best in at least four hours of direct sunlight a day, night temperatures of 16° to 18°C (60° to 65°F) and day temperatures of 21°C (70°F) or higher. Keep the soil moist; fertilize every three to four months. To encourage branching, prune old growth after flowers fade. Propagate by stem cuttings at any time.

CHIRITA
C. lavandulacea (Hindustan gentian); *C. sinensis* (silver chirita)

The most common of these gesneriads, *C. lavandulacea*, bears flowers about 3 cm (1¼ in.) across, with flaring lavender lobes and white throats, from late summer through most of the following year, but each plant lasts only a year. The soft, hairy leaves may be up to 20 cm (8 in.) long, and plants grow 30 to 60 cm (12 to 24 in.) tall. *C. sinensis*, a tuberous-rooted summer-flowering species bearing clusters of tiny lavender flowers, grows only 15 cm (6 in.) tall and forms a rosette of elliptical, dark green, hairy leaves blotched with silver.

HOW TO GROW. Chiritas make good house and greenhouse plants given warmth, humidity and shade from direct sunlight. *C. sinensis* can also be grown under 14 to 16 hours a day of artificial light. Night temperatures of 18° to 21°C (65° to 70°F) and day temperatures of 24°C (75°F) or higher are ideal. Keep moist; place the pot on a humidifying tray (*page 43*). Fertilize monthly during the growing season. Propagate chiritas from leaf cuttings taken in summer, or from seeds.

CHRYSANTHEMUM
C. frutescens (marguerite); *C. indicum* hybrids, also called *C.* x *hortorum* (florists' chrysanthemum)

Marguerites produce great numbers of daisy-like white, yellow or pink flowers, 5 to 7.5 cm (2 to 3 in.) across, that bloom intermittently throughout the year; their grey-green, lacy leaves are 7.5 to 15 cm (3 to 6 in.) long. Plants start to blossom when 15 cm (6 in.) tall and can be kept to less than 45 cm (18 in.) by pinching off the tips of stems. Florists' chrysanthemums, on the other hand, blossom for only two or three weeks and are prized for their quantities of white, golden-yellow, bronze, maroon, pink or lavender flowers, which come in many shapes and sizes. Growers use controlled flowering techniques so that these chrysanthemums can be bought, usually in bud, at any time of year. Unlike the marguerites, they can be planted out in the garden after they have finished flowering indoors.

HOW TO GROW. Marguerites need at least four hours of direct sunlight a day. They do best in night temperatures of 4° to 13°C (40° to 55°F) and day temperatures of 20°C (68°F) or lower. Keep the soil moist; fertilize every two weeks. Propagate at any time from stem cuttings. Treat florists' chrysanthemums the same as marguerites, but keep them out of direct sun when flowering. They may be planted in the garden when the flowers fade; if they survive, they will revert to their normal autumn flowering. All through the year florists sell dwarf pot chrysanthemums which are only 30 to 37.5 cm (12 to 15 in.) high. This dwarfing is achieved by special techniques by which the amount of light or darkness is controlled in an electrically lit greenhouse. Periods of darkness exceeding 9½ hours cause bud initiation to take place, so light is controlled by the use of blinds in summer and 100 watt lamps set at 1.2 metres (4 ft) above the plants in winter. In later years the plants will revert to their normal height and time of flowering. Propagate by stem cuttings or by division of the roots in early spring.

CINERARIA See *Senecio*

CITRUS

C. limon (lemon); *C. microcarpa*, also called *C. mitis* (calamondin); *C. reticulata* (mandarine, tangerine); *C. sinensis* (sweet orange); *C. taitensis* (orange)

The fragrant blossoms of citrus plants bloom intermittently throughout the year, but most profusely in spring and autumn; the fruit follows the flowers and often stays on the plants for many months. Most plants started from cuttings begin to flower and fruit in their first year and may be kept under 120 cm (4 ft) in height indefinitely by pinching off the tips of stems. Among the best cultivars for indoor gardeners are *C. limon* 'Meyeri', whose fruits are somewhat less acid than ordinary lemons; *C. microcarpa*, which generally grows less than 60 cm (2 ft) high indoors and produces tart oranges 2.5 cm (1 in.) or less in diameter; *C. reticulata*, whose cultivars produce tangerines, mandarines and Satsuma oranges; *C. sinensis*, which bears full-sized oranges that make delicious eating; and *C. taitensis*, which produces a heavy crop of tart oranges, each only 2.5 cm (1 in.) or so in diameter.

HOW TO GROW. Citrus plants need at least four hours of direct sunlight a day, night temperatures of 10° to 13°C (50° to 55°F) and day temperatures of 20° to 22°C (68° to 72°F). Grow in large pots or small tubs of loamy compost and set these outdoors in summer if possible or by an open window. Keep in a good light, but cool, not more than 4° to 6°C (40° to 43°F) in winter. They must have plenty of water during the growing season, or the fruits will drop off. Fertilize in very early spring, early summer and late summer. To control size, pinch off new growth at any time. Propagate from stem cuttings or, more satisfactorily, by grafting named cultivars on to seedling rootstocks. This is not easy for amateurs, who will probably prefer to purchase their plants from florists.

TOP: MARGUERITE
Chrysanthemum frutescens

BOTTOM: FLORISTS' CHRYSANTHEMUM
Chrysanthemum indicum hybrid

ORANGE
Citrus taitensis

BLEEDING HEART VINE
Clerodendrum thomsoniae

KAFFIR LILY
Clivia miniata

ARABIAN COFFEE
Coffea arabica

CLERODENDRUM, also called CLERODENDRON

C. speciosissimum, also called *C. fallax*; *C. philippinum* 'Pleniflorum', also called *C. fragrans*; *C. thomsoniae* (bleeding heart vine)

Clerodendrums are large plants well suited to big pots and tubs, but they may be kept at a height of 60 to 90 cm (2 to 3 ft) by pinching off the tips of stems. All species bear large clusters of 2.5 to 5 cm (1 to 2 in.) flowers and beautiful heart-shaped leaves. *C. speciosissimum* blooms in summer, bearing scarlet blossoms. *C. philippinum* 'Pleniflorum', with hyacinth-scented blush-white blossoms, blooms intermittently throughout the year. *C. thomsoniae* trails beautifully from hanging baskets. It bears snow-white flowers, balloon-like at the base, with flaring scarlet petals; the flowers bloom in spring and summer, sometimes into winter if given enough warmth.

HOW TO GROW. Clerodendrums do best in bright indirect or curtain-filtered sunlight, night temperatures of 16° to 18°C (60° to 65°F) and day temperatures of 21°C (70°F) or higher. Keep the potting mixture well moistened while the plants are growing, and on the dry side while they are resting. Fertilize every two weeks during the growing season only. To produce more flowers, which are borne only on new growth, prune the plants after they have stopped blooming; *C. speciosissimum* and *C. philippinum* 'Pleniflorum' should be cut hard back, but on the trailing *C. thomsoniae* cut out completely any untidy shoots and shorten the side-shoots by half. Propagate from stem cuttings in spring or early summer, in gentle heat.

CLIVIA also called IMANTOPHYLLUM

C. miniata; *C. x cyrtanthiflora*, (both called Kaffir lily)

Kaffir lilies bloom in winter, bearing clusters of 12 to 20 brilliantly coloured lily-like flowers, up to 7.5 cm (3 in.) across, on top of 30 to 37.5 cm (12 to 15 in.) stalks that rise from waxy, dark green, strap-like leaves 45 to 60 cm (18 to 24 in.) long. *C. miniata* bears orange to scarlet blossoms with yellow throats; the hybrid *C.x cyrtanthiflora* has salmon-pink flowers, and there are also numerous other cultivars with blooms in shades of scarlet, salmon, yellow and white as well as blends of these colours. If you can bring yourself to do it, they make fine cut flowers.

HOW TO GROW. Kaffir lilies do best in bright indirect or curtain-filtered sunlight, night temperatures of 10° to 13°C (50° to 55°F) and day temperatures of 20° to 22°C (68° to 72°F). From midwinter until late summer let the soil become slightly dry between thorough waterings and fertilize every month or two. In the autumn let the plants rest without fertilizer and with only enough moisture to keep them from wilting. Propagate in late spring by dividing the fleshy roots. Since Kaffir lilies bloom more abundantly if their roots are not disturbed, repot them only when the plants become extremely overcrowded (about every three or four years).

COFFEA

C. arabica (Arabian coffee)

At the bases of their 10 to 15 cm (4 to 6 in.) long, glossy green leaves, Arabian coffee plants bear clusters of sweetly scented, 18 mm (¾ in.) white flowers intermittently throughout the year; these mature into pulpy, glistening red, 12 mm (½ in.) berries. Within each berry are two seeds, the "beans" from which coffee is made. Plants, which do not begin to blossom or bear fruit until they are three or four years old, grow upright to a height of 120 cm (4 ft) or more unless the tips of stems are pinched out.

HOW TO GROW. The Arabian coffee plant does best in

curtain-filtered sunlight, night temperatures of 16° to 18°C (60° to 65°F) and day temperatures of 21°C (70°F) or higher. Keep the soil evenly moist; fertilize every two weeks from spring to autumn, monthly for the rest of the year. Try to avoid touching the leaves, which are thin and tender. Propagate from fresh seeds at any time or from cuttings of upright-growing tips (not from cuttings of side branches, which generally develop into poorly shaped plants).

COLUMNEA
C. affinis; *C. gloriosa*; *C. linearis*; *C.* hybrids

Ablaze with tubular 5 to 10 cm (2 to 4 in.) flowers through the year, columneas make stunning plants for hanging containers. The leaves of these gesneriads, set in pairs and often hairy, grow 2.5 to 12.5 cm (1 to 5 in.) long, and stems reach 120 cm (4 ft) in length if the tips of stems are not pinched out. *C. affinis* has yellow flowers covered with orange hairs; *C. gloriosa*, red blossoms with yellow throats; *C. linearis*, rosy-pink flowers with white hairs. Three excellent hybrids are *C.x banksii*, vermilion; *C. gloriosa* 'Purpurea' with purplish leaves; and 'Yellow Dragon', bright yellow blossoms. The strain of hybrids called 'Stavanger' are easier to grow and less temperamental than the species.

HOW TO GROW. Columneas do best in bright indirect or curtain-filtered sunlight, but they also grow well in 14 to 16 hours of artificial light a day. Night temperatures of 18° to 21°C (65° to 70°F) and day temperatures over 24°C (75°F) are ideal. (Columnea species should be given night temperatures of 10° to 16°C (50° to 60°F) in winter to assure full flowering.) Plant in a mixture of 2 parts moss peat to 1 part packaged potting soil and 1 part sharp sand; keep the mixture moist and fertilize monthly. To encourage new branches, prune the plants after a period of flowering. Propagate in early summer from stem cuttings or root divisions which should be given heat until rooted.

x CRINDONNA
x *C. memoria-corsii*, also called x *Amarcrinum memoria-corsii*

Crindonnas are bigeneric hybrids between *Amaryllis belladonna* and *Crinum moorei*. They have great clusters of fragrant pink flowers, some as large as 10 cm (4 in.) in diameter, in late summer and early autumn. The blossoms appear on top of 90 cm (3 ft) high stalks that are surrounded by dark green strap-like leaves 4 to 7.5 cm (1½ to 3 in.) wide and up to 60 cm (2 ft) long.

HOW TO GROW. Crindonnas do best in at least four hours of direct sunlight a day, with night temperatures of 10° to 13°C (50° to 55°F) and day temperatures of 20° to 22°C (68° to 72°F). Keep the soil moist and fertilize monthly during the growing season; reduce moisture and do not feed while plants are dormant over the winter. Plant in a greenhouse bed or in tubs; they are too large for most pots. Leave the top third of the bulb out of the soil. Crindonnas bloom best when their roots are undisturbed, so repot only after three or four years. Propagate from the small bulbs that develop alongside larger ones.

CRINUM
C. bulbispermum, also called *C. capense*; *C.* hybrids; *C. moorei* (all called crinum)

Crinums are majestic bulb plants whose fragrant clusters of 7.5 to 15 cm (3 to 6 in.) lily-like flowers bloom at the top of 60 to 90 cm (2 to 3 ft) stalks in late summer; arching out from the base of the stalks are strap-like leaves,

COLUMNEA
Columnea 'Yellow Dragon'

CRINDONNA
x *Crindonna memoria-corsii*

CRINUM
Crinum hybrid

60 to 120 cm (2 to 4 ft) long. *C. bulbispermum* bears rosy-red blossoms with white inside. Crinum hybrids, particularly of *C.*x *powellii*, are available in white, deep pink and rosy-red or deeper shades; *C. moorei* bears blush-pink flowers; they have wide-open trumpets with prominent stamens, and each stem may carry as many as ten individual blooms.

HOW TO GROW. Crinums do best in at least four hours of direct sunlight a day (curtain-filtered sunlight during the hottest part of the summer), night temperatures of 10° to 13°C (50° to 55°F) and day temperatures of 20° to 22°C (68° to 72°F). Keep the soil moist and fertilize during the growing season, from late spring until early autumn. Let the soil become slightly dry and do not fertilize when the plants are resting. Grow crinums in tubs, deep soil beds or very large containers. Propagate in early spring from the small bulbs that develop beside larger ones; they will usually reach flowering size after three years if kept growing under the same conditions as mature plants. Seedlings take one or two years longer.

CROCUS
Crocus 'Pickwick'

CROCUS
Many species and cultivars known as crocus

Harbingers of spring, the many species and cultivars of crocuses make fine midwinter pot plants, growing 10 to 12.5 cm (4 to 5 in.) high and sending up 5 cm (2 in.) cup-shaped blossoms just as the slender, grass-like leaves begin to emerge from the corms. Among the particularly attractive types available are 'Pickwick' (with blossoms striped pale and deep lilac), 'Jeanne d'Arc' (white), 'Little Dorrit' (amethyst-blue), 'Remembrance' (purple) and 'E. P. Bowles' (buttercup-yellow).

HOW TO GROW. Crocuses do best in at least four hours of direct sunlight a day, night temperatures of 4° to 7°C (40° to 45°F) and day temperatures of about 16°C (60°F). If they are too hot the flower buds fail to develop satisfactorily. Keep the soil well moistened as long as the foliage is green; do not fertilize at any time. Crocuses are often bought as fully blossoming plants from florists or nurseries in the midwinter months, but they may also be started from large-sized dormant corms; plant the corms in pots in early autumn and keep them in a cold frame until mid-January or later, at which time they may be brought indoors. When they have finished blooming and the foliage has withered, knock the crocuses out of the pot, and plant the new corms in the garden in late summer.

CROSSANDRA
Crossandra infundibuliformis

CROSSANDRA
C. infundibuliformis, also called *C. undulifolia*

House plants with pastel, salmon-orange flowers that bloom all the year round are rare—a fact that makes crossandras interesting as well as beautiful selections for indoor gardens. Their overlapping blossoms appear above dark green leaves, 5 to 7.5 cm (2 to 3 in.) long. The plants begin to bloom seven to nine months after they are started from seed, and grow about 30 cm (12 in.) tall. A Swedish cultivar called 'Mona Wallhed' is a more vigorous form and makes a better house plant.

HOW TO GROW. Crossandras do best in at least four hours of direct sunlight a day except during the hottest part of the year, when they should be protected by a sheer curtain or blind. Night temperatures of 16° to 18°C (60° to 65°F) and day temperatures of 21°C (70°F) or higher are ideal. Plant in a mixture of 2 parts moss peat to 1 part packaged potting soil and 1 part sharp sand; keep the potting medium well moistened at all times and fertilize every two weeks all the year round. Propagate from seeds in spring or from stem cuttings from cut-back plants in summer.

CRYPTANTHUS

C. bivittatus, also called *C. rosea picta*; *C. bromelioides* 'Tricolor' (rainbow star); *C. fosterianus*; *C. zonatus* (zebra plant); (all called earth star)

The bromeliads known as earth stars derive their name from the star-like spread of their flat, oddly marked leaves, which surround clusters of tiny flowers. The plants listed here bear white blossoms in summer and differ mainly in foliage. *C. bivittatus* has bronze-green leaves with lengthways white stripes; *C. fosterianus* has chocolate-brown leaves with zebra-like grey stripes; *C. bromelioides* 'Tricolor', a variegated variety with rose-margined, green and cream leaves; and *C. zonatus*, reddish-brown leaves with zig-zag silvery bands. All of them spread about 30 cm (12 in.) or more except *C. bivittatus*, which grows only 10 to 15 cm (4 to 6 in.) across.

HOW TO GROW. Earth stars do best in bright indirect or curtain-filtered sunlight, night temperatures of 16° to 18°C (60° to 65°F) and day temperatures of 21°C (70°F) or higher. Plant in a mixture of 2 parts moss peat to 1 part packaged potting soil and 1 part sharp sand; do not add lime. Allow the mixture to dry slightly between waterings and fertilize monthly from mid-spring until early autumn. Propagate from shoots that appear at the base of the plant between the leaves.

CUPHEA

C. hyssopifolia; *C. ignea*, also called *C. platycentra* (cigar plant); *C. llavea* var. *miniata* 'Firefly'

Cupheas are low bushy plants that grow 15 to 60 cm (6 to 24 in.) high and bloom abundantly all the year round. A favourite for generations has been the cigar plant (*C. ignea*) which gets its name from its 18 mm ($\frac{3}{4}$ in.) long, cigar-shaped scarlet flowers, complete with ash-grey tips; varieties of the plant are available in lavender, pink, rose, purple and white. Two other species produce tiny bell-like flowers—*C. hyssopifolia*, with lavender blooms, and *C. llavea* var. *miniata* 'Firefly' with bright red blooms. All have 2.5 cm (1 in.) long green leaves that turn red at the edges in the sun and are oval in shape, except for *C. hyssopifolia*, which has needle-like leaves.

HOW TO GROW. Cupheas do best in at least four hours of direct sunlight a day, night temperatures of 10° to 13°C (50° to 55°F) and day temperatures of 20° to 22°C (68° to 72°F). Keep the soil moist; fertilize every two weeks. Propagate at any time from stem cuttings or seeds. Cupheas started from seeds begin to flower when they are about four or five months old.

CYCLAMEN

C. persicum

Among the loveliest of house plants, cyclamens bear 5 to 7.5 cm (2 to 3 in.) flowers whose petals sweep up like the wings of butterflies. The flowers bloom in shades of pink, red, purple and white above thick, dark green leaves that often have silvery markings. Plants blossom profusely from mid-autumn until mid-spring and grow about 30 cm (12 in.) tall.

HOW TO GROW. Cyclamens do best in bright indirect or curtain-filtered sunlight, night temperatures of 4° to 13°C (40° to 55°F) and day temperatures of 18°C (65°F) or lower. Plant in a mixture of 2 parts moss peat to 1 part packaged potting soil and 1 part sharp sand; leave half the corm exposed above the soil surface. Keep the mixture moist; fertilize every two weeks during the growing season. When the leaves start to turn yellow, gradually withhold water until the corm is dormant. Store until late summer (August

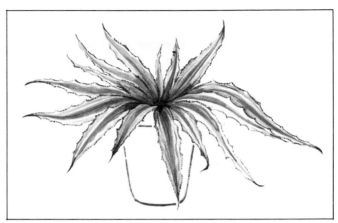

RAINBOW STAR
Cryptanthus bromelioides 'Tricolor'

CIGAR PLANT
Cuphea ignea

113

CYCLAMEN
Cyclamen persicum

Illustration by Pamela Freeman

GENISTA
Cytisus x *racemosus*

WINTER DAPHNE
Daphne odora

or September) by laying the pot on its side, then repot and start into growth. Use lime-free water for cyclamens and keep the buds and corm dry. Plants may be propagated from seeds in early spring, but most gardeners purchase these plants from florists when they are already in flower.

CYMBIDIUM
C. hybrid miniatures

Miniature cymbidium orchids rarely grow more than 30 cm (12 in.) high, but bear spikes of up to 30 flowers, 5 to 7.5 cm (2 to 3 in.) across, that range in colour from mahogany, bronze and maroon to green, yellow, pink and white. The blossoms open from autumn to spring, depending upon the variety, and often last for two to three months. The one shown in the photograph on page 57 is 'Minuet', a pinkish-brown cymbidium introduced in 1931 as the first hybrid miniature.

HOW TO GROW. Miniature cymbidiums do best in at least four hours of direct sunlight a day, but should be protected from hot midday sun to keep the leaves from turning brown. Night temperatures of 10° to 16°C (50° to 60°F) and day temperatures of 20°C (68°F) or higher are ideal. Keep the roots cool, but the tops of the plants warm, airy and in a light place. Plant in equal parts fibrous loam, peat, osmunda fibre and sand, or use peat fibre mixed with sphagnum moss. Place the pot on a humidifying tray (*page 82*). Keep the mixture damp and fertilize monthly with a high-nitrogen feed. Propagate by division when repotting in spring or early summer.

CYRTANTHERA See *Jacobinia*

CYTISUS
C. canariensis, *C.* x *racemosus* (both called genista and, by some botanists, *Teline canariensis*)

These are the florists' genistas, small shrubs which with pruning can be kept down to 60 to 90 cm (2 to 3 ft). In early spring and summer they are covered with small, pea-shaped, fragrant, golden-yellow flowers. The evergreen leaves are small and clover-shaped.

HOW TO GROW. Genistas appreciate a little lime in the soil, so can be watered with hard water without fear. Keep the soil moist; it must never dry out. Grow in a soil-based compost and feed during the growing season at three-week intervals. The plants benefit from being placed outside in summer. Overwinter in cool temperatures of 4° to 8°C (40° to 46°F), but move the plants into warmer conditions for flowering. Propagate by heel cuttings of young shoots, rooted with bottom heat by seed.

D

DAPHNE
D. odora, also called *D. indica* (winter daphne)

D. odora lives up to its botanical name with a notable sweet fragrance. Clusters of 12 mm ($\frac{1}{2}$ in.) wide, pink to reddish-purple flowers bloom indoors from November until March. The 5 to 7.5 cm (2 to 3 in.) long leaves are a shiny, leathery green and are edged with creamy-yellow in the cultivar *D. odora* 'Aureo-marginata', which often has almost white flowers with purple exteriors. Plants are usually kept to a height of 30 to 60 cm (1 to 2 ft) by pruning them back.

HOW TO GROW. Winter daphne does best in bright indirect or curtain-filtered sunlight, night temperatures of 4° to 7°C (40° to 45°F) and day temperatures of 20°C

(68°F) or lower. Keep the soil barely damp. A single feeding of slow-acting acid-type fertilizer in early spring is sufficient for the year. Propagate in summer from stem cuttings or by air layering (*page 94*).

DENDROBIUM
D. loddigesii

Of the hundreds of orchids in the *Dendrobium* genus, one of the best for indoor culture is *D. loddigesii*, whose 4 to 5 cm (1½ to 2 in.) fragrant, long-lasting flowers bloom in late winter or early spring. The blossoms, lilac-pink with over-sized orange-centred lips, appear singly all along the trailing stems above 7.5 cm (3 in.) leaves (*photograph, page 59*).

HOW TO GROW. *D. loddigesii* does best in bright indirect or curtain-filtered sunlight, with night temperatures of 10° to 16°C (50° to 60°F) and day temperatures of 16° to 21°C (60° to 70°F). It can be grown on a slab of tree fern or in a mixture of 2 parts fir bark or shredded osmunda fibre and 1 part coarse moss peat. Keep the potting medium well moistened during the growing season and place the pot on a humidifying tray (*page 82*). Fertilize monthly from spring and through summer with a high-nitrogen formula, diluted at the rate of ¼ teaspoon to 1 litre (2 pt) of water. In late autumn and winter withhold fertilizer and provide only enough water to keep the plant from shrivelling.

DIPLADENIA
D. 'Amoena'; D. boliviensis; D. sanderi 'Rosea'; D. splendens, also known as Mandevilla splendens

These handsome vines bear masses of silky 6 to 7.5 cm (2½ to 3 in.) flowers, much like those of morning glories, among glossy 2.5 to 5 cm (1 to 2 in.) leaves. *D. 'Amoena'*, with rose-pink flowers, and *D. boliviensis*, with white flowers, usually blossom from March through to September; *D. sanderi* 'Rosea', with salmon-pink flowers, blooms continuously throughout the year. *D. splendens* bears pinkish-white flowers up to 10 cm (4 in.) across in summer. Plants begin to flower when they are less than 30 cm (12 in.) tall, and may easily be kept below 90 cm (3 ft) in height by pinching off the tips of the stems.

HOW TO GROW. Dipladenias do best in bright indirect or curtain-filtered sunlight, night temperatures of 16° to 18°C (60° to 65°F) and day temperatures of 21°C (70°F) or higher. Allow the soil to become slightly dry between thorough waterings; fertilize every two weeks except when the plants are resting. Propagate by stem cuttings in early spring, rooted with bottom heat.

DYCKIA
D. brevifolia; D. fosteriana 'Silver Queen'

In summer these bromeliads bear 15 to 20 waxy flowers, each 12 to 25 mm (½ to 1 in.) long, on a slender 30 to 60 cm (1 to 2 ft) branching stalk that rises above stiff rosettes of arching leaves. *D. brevifolia* has bright orange, tubular flowers above dark green leaves; *D. fosteriana* 'Silver Queen' has orange-red flowers set above scalloped, silvery-grey leaves.

HOW TO GROW. Dyckias do best in full sun or very light shade, night temperatures of 10° to 13°C (50° to 55°F) and day temperatures of 20° to 22°C (68° to 72°F). Pot in a mixture composed of 2 parts moss peat, 1 part packaged potting soil and 1 part sharp sand; do not add lime. Allow the potting medium to become moderately dry between thorough waterings; fertilize every two weeks. Propagate from the new shoots that appear at the base of the plants.

DIPLADENIA
Dipladenia 'Amoena'

DYCKIA
Dyckia fosteriana 'Silver Queen'

E

EPIDENDRUM

E. cochleatum (clamshell or cockleshell orchid)

This orchid is noted for the purplish-black and green, shell-shaped lip and slender 6 to 8.5 cm (2½ to 3½ in.) yellowish-green petals of its flowers, which hang gracefully upside down in clusters of three to seven from the top of 20 to 25 cm (8 to 10 in.) flower spikes (*photograph, page 60*). The faintly fragrant flowers may appear at any time of the year.

HOW TO GROW. *E. cochleatum* does best in bright indirect sunlight, night temperatures of 10° to 18°C (50° to 65°F) and day temperatures of 20°C (68°F) or higher. It is epiphytic, so can be grown on a slab of tree fern or potted in a mixture composed of 3 parts chopped osmunda fibre and 2 parts chopped sphagnum moss; good drainage is essential. Place the pot on a humidifying tray (*page 43*) and keep the potting medium abundantly moistened, using lime-free water. Fertilize monthly with a high-nitrogen formula, at the rate of ¼ teaspoon per 1 litre (2 pt) of water.

EPIPHYLLUM

E. ackermannii, also called *Nopalxochia ackermannii*; *E. oxypetalum*, also called *Phyllocactus grandis* (queen of the night); *E.* hybrids (all called orchid cactus). See also *Zygocactus*

Without spines or leaves but ornamented by richly coloured flowers, the orchid cactus is one of the most spectacular flowering plants in cultivation. Blossoms, which are often fragrant, appear directly from soft, waxy stems that consist of flattened or ribbed sections loosely joined together. Although orchid cacti usually bloom in the spring, a number of hybrids, such as *E.* 'Hermosissimum', are winter-flowering. There are also day-flowering and night-flowering types. Plants range from 30 cm (12 in.) window-sill specimens to giants 1.5 to 1.8 metres (5 to 6 ft) tall, and flowers vary in size from 6 to 25 cm (2½ to 10 in.) across. In addition to the hybrids, of which there are thousands, two good house-plant species are *E. ackermannii*, whose many 10 to 15 cm (4 to 6 in.) scarlet flowers open mainly in the daytime, and *E. oxypetalum*, sometimes called "queen of the night" because its waxy, white 10 to 15 cm (4 to 6 in.) flowers open in the evening.

HOW TO GROW. Orchid cacti do best in bright indirect or curtain-filtered sunlight, night temperatures of 10° to 13°C (50° to 55°F) and day temperatures of 20° to 22°C (68° to 72°F). (Higher night temperatures in winter cause stems rather than flower buds to grow.) Pot in a mixture of 2 parts moss peat to 1 part packaged potting soil and 1 part sharp sand. Keep the mixture moist, using soft water, and fertilize every two weeks from April to August with a low-nitrogen house-plant fertilizer; keep fairly dry and omit fertilizer for the rest of the year. Propagate from stem cuttings in summer.

EPISCIA

E. dianthiflora; *E.* hybrids; *E. lilacina*; *E. punctata* (all called episcia)

Episcias, gesneriads well suited to hanging containers, have handsome 5 to 7.5 cm (2 to 3 in.) leaves and dainty 12 mm to 4 cm (½ to 1½ in.) flowers that bloom continuously from early summer to early autumn. *E. dianthiflora* bears downy green leaves and white, fringed-petalled flowers; *E. lilacina* has dark bronze leaves and lavender flowers; its cultivar 'Ember Lace', a rare but beautiful form, has brown, pink and green quilted leaves. *E. punctata* has green leaves and purple-spotted white blossoms. Various

ORCHID CACTUS
Epiphyllum 'Hermosissimum'

EPISCIA
Episcia lilacina 'Ember Lace'

named cultivars have white, pink, yellow or reddish flowers.

HOW TO GROW. Episcias do best in bright indirect or curtain-filtered sunlight and will also grow well in 14 to 16 hours of artificial light a day. Night temperatures of 18° to 21°C (65° to 70°F) and day temperatures of 24°C (75°F) or higher are ideal. Pot in a mixture of 2 parts moss peat and 1 part packaged potting soil and 1 part sharp sand. Keep the potting medium moist at all times and place the pot on a humidifying tray (*page 43*). Fertilize once a month during the growing season. Pinch off the tips of the stems to encourage branching. For fresh growth, cut back the plants when they have stopped blooming. Propagate from runners (*page 93*) or from stem cuttings at any time.

ERANTHEMUM

E. nervosum, also called *E. pulchellum*; *E. wattii* (both called eranthemum, blue sage)

Spikes of handsome flowers about 2.5 cm (1 in.) across appear among the slender 7.5 cm (3 in.) green leaves of eranthemums throughout winter and early spring. *E. nervosum* bears blue flowers and grows 45 to 60 cm (18 to 24 in.) tall; *E. wattii* produces purple flowers and grows less than 30 cm (12 in.) high.

HOW TO GROW. Eranthemums do best in at least four hours of direct sunlight a day in winter and light shade in summer. Night temperatures of 16° to 18°C (60° to 65°F) and day temperatures of 21°C (70°F) or higher are ideal. Keep the soil moist and fertilize every two weeks during the growing season; reduce water and omit fertilizer in late spring and early summer. Prune to about 12.5 cm (5 in.) above the base after the resting period and pinch off the tips of stems during the summer to encourage branching and bushy growth. Propagate from stem cuttings of new growth in summer.

ERICA

E. gracilis (rose heath); *E. hiemalis*, also called *E. hyemalis*; *E. x willmorei* (all also called heathers)

Several South African heathers make popular pot plants around Christmas time, especially *E. gracilis* which has tiny pale green leaves and long spikes of tubular pink or pale purple flowers on 45 cm (18 in.) stems; 'Nivalis' is white-flowered. *E. hiemalis* grows to 60 cm (2 ft) and has white flowers with a rosy flush. The spring flowering *E.x willmorei* hybrids come in pink, lilac-red and white.

HOW TO GROW. Ericas appreciate plenty of light with about 4 hours' sunshine daily, night temperatures 8° to 10°C (46° to 50°F) and day temperatures of around 18°C (65°F). Use only soft water and spray over the foliage frequently, if the soil ball becomes dry or the atmosphere is too hot, the needle-like leaves fall off. Grow in a lime-free, humus-type compost. Feed in summer, after flowering, and pinch back the young growths to maintain a compact habit; keep the plants cool, setting them outside in the garden if possible. Bring them indoors again in late summer. Propagate by heel cuttings of young growth rooted in late summer.

ERVATAMIA

E. divaricata, also called *E. coronaria*, *Tabernaemontana coronaria* and *Nerium coronarium* (crape jasmine)

With its glossy, dark green 7.5 to 10 cm (3 to 4 in.) leaves and exquisitely fragrant 5 cm (2 in.) wide, white flowers, which bloom throughout the summer and intermittently through the rest of the year, *E. divaricata*—especially the many-petalled variety 'Plena'—might easily be mistaken

BLUE SAGE
Eranthemum nervosum

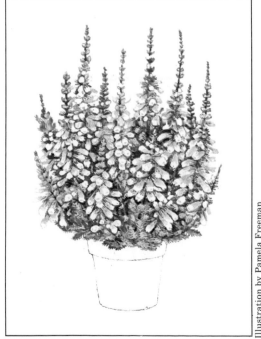

ROSE HEATH
Erica gracilis

Illustration by Pamela Freeman

117

CRAPE JASMINE
Ervatamia divaricata 'Plena'

AMAZON LILY
Eucharis grandiflora

POINSETTIA
Euphorbia pulcherrima

for true gardenia, except that the flowers are smaller and have frilly petals. ,Plants may grow to a height of 1.8 metres (6 ft) or more if not pruned.

HOW TO GROW. Crape jasmines do best in at least four hours of direct sunlight a day, night temperatures of 18° to 21°C (65° to 70°F) and day temperatures of 24°C (75°F) or higher. Keep the soil moist at all times; fertilize every two weeks from April to September, monthly during the rest of the year. Before new growth starts in early spring, prune back plants to keep them at the desired height, and repot them in fresh potting mixture in larger containers if needed. Propagate from heel cuttings of new growth in summer, rooted in gentle heat.

EUCHARIS
E. grandiflora, also called *E. amazonica* (Amazon lily)

A superb bulbous plant with white fragrant flowers that look something like white narcissi with spiky inner crowns or coronas. These appear irregularly in summer in clusters of three to six, each about 5 cm (2 in.) across on stalks 30 to 60 cm (12 to 24 in.) tall, which are set among shiny 20 cm (8 in.) long leaves.

HOW TO GROW. Amazon lilies do best in bright indirect or curtain-filtered sunlight, night temperatures of 18° to 21°C (65° to 70°F) and day temperatures of 24°C (75°F) or higher. Plant in a mixture composed of 2 parts moss peat, 1 part packaged potting soil and 1 part sharp sand. Keep the potting medium very moist and fertilize during the growing season; at other times keep the plants in light shade, water them less frequently and do not fertilize. Propagate at any time by separating the small bulbs that develop beside larger ones.

EUPHORBIA
E. pulcherrima (poinsettia); *E. fulgens*, also called *E. jacquiniiflora* (scarlet plume)

Poinsettias, whose bright red petal-like bracts appear in late autumn, have long been esteemed as Christmas plants. The true flowers are tiny greenish yellow nubs in the centres of the bracts, which may be white or pink as well as red. Most florists' plants are 30 to 60 cm (1 to 2 ft) tall, but 90 to 120 cm (3 to 4 ft) plants are not uncommon. The bracts—some as much as 30 cm (12 in.) across—may stay colourful for six months or more. A lesser-known relative is the scarlet plume, so named because its 60 cm (2 ft) arching stems with narrow willow-like leaves are studded with waxy, orange-scarlet flowers, 12 mm ($\frac{1}{2}$ in.) in diameter, in winter.

HOW TO GROW. Both species do best in at least four hours of direct sunlight a day in a draught-free position. Night temperatures of 10° to 18°C (50° to 65°F) and day temperatures of 20°C (68°F) or higher are ideal. Soil should be allowed to dry slightly between thorough waterings. Cut back plants in late spring after flowering and repot in fresh potting soil. Cuttings from the tips of new growth can be rooted in summer. Fertilize every two weeks in spring and summer; do not fertilize for the rest of the year. In the case of poinsettias, flowers will develop only on plants that have had an alternation of a light period and at least 14 hours of uninterrupted darkness each day for approximately 40 days. Chemical dwarfing compounds are commonly used by commercial growers to obtain short-stemmed plants with several large flower heads. Without special treatment, however, these revert to tall, rather lanky plants the following season, and it is usually easier to purchase new plants each year. If properly looked after, these remain colourful for six to eight months.

EXACUM
E. affine (Persian violet)

Masses of fragrant 12 mm (½ in.) blue flowers with prominent yellow pollen-bearing stamens appear among the shiny 12 to 25 mm (½ to 1 in.) heart-shaped leaves of *Exacum affine*. This charming 15 to 20 cm (6 to 8 in.) high plant, unlike the more familiar African violet, blooms profusely for about four months or so in summer and should then be discarded. *E. affine* 'Atrocaeruleum' has dark lavender flowers; 'Blithe Spirit' bears white blossoms; 'Midget' produces blue flowers.

HOW TO GROW. Exacums do best in bright indirect or curtain-filtered sunlight, with night temperatures of 16° to 18°C (60° to 65°F) and day temperatures of 21°C (70°F) or less. Pot in a proprietary peat-based or loam compost. Keep the potting medium moist at all times and fertilize every two weeks. Sow the dust-like seeds, which germinate readily, in spring for flowering plants during autumn and winter. The seeds can also be sown in late summer and will then produce sturdier, larger plants to bloom in the following year. To ensure germination, raise the seedlings in a temperature of 18°C (65°F).

PERSIAN VIOLET
Exacum affine 'Midget'

F
FELICIA
F. amelloides, also called *F. capensis*, *Agathaea coelestis*, *Aster rotundifolius* (blue daisy); *F. bergeriana* (kingfisher daisy)

These sky-blue, yellow-centred daisies, which bloom almost continuously all the year round, make unusual additions to house-plant collections. The flowers grow on wiry stems above pebbly-textured, 12 mm (½ in.) oval leaves. *F. amelloides*, which can be kept about 30 cm (12 in.) tall by pinching out leggy stems, has 2.5 to 4 cm (1 to 1½ in.) blossoms. The diminutive *F. bergeriana*, an annual, bears blue, yellow-centred flowers on dainty 15 cm (6 in.) plants. Flowers of both species open only in sunshine.

HOW TO GROW. Felicias do best in at least four hours of direct sunlight a day, night temperatures of 10° to 13°C (50° to 55°F) and day temperatures of 20° to 22°C (68° to 72°F). Keep the soil damp and fertilize every two weeks. Both species can be propagated from seeds (sown in midsummer, they produce fine flowering plants by late autumn). *F. amelloides* can also be grown from stem cuttings; root them in gentle heat and move gradually into larger pots. Pinch off the main growing tip to encourage bushy and branching plants to flower in late autumn.

FORTUNELLA
F. hindsii (dwarf kumquat); *F. margarita* (oval kumquat)

Both these species are small spiny trees bearing small fragrant white flowers in spring, followed by highly decorative fruit in autumn. *F. margarita*, generally kept to about 60 cm (2 ft) high indoors, has shiny dark green leaves about 4 cm (1½ in.) long; its 4 cm (1½ in.) golden-orange fruits remain on the plant from October to January or later, and may be made into preserves. *F. hindsii*, which grows about 30 cm (12 in.) high, bears decorative cherry-sized, scarlet-orange fruit.

HOW TO GROW. Fortunellas do best in at least four hours of direct sunlight a day, night temperatures of 10° to 13°C (50° to 55°F) and day temperatures of 20° to 22°C (68° to 72°F). Allow the soil to dry slightly between thorough waterings. Fertilize three times a year, in very early spring, early summer and late summer. Propagate from stem cuttings in late spring, or from seeds sown at any time and germinated in gentle heat.

BLUE DAISY
Felicia amelloides

OVAL KUMQUAT
Fortunella margarita

FUCHSIA
F. magellanica hybrids; *F. triphylla* (honeysuckle fuchsia) (all called fuchsia)

Fuchsias have delicate hoopskirt-shaped flowers, 4 to 7.5 cm (1½ to 3 in.) long, set among crisp oval leaves on 30 to 90 cm (1 to 3 ft) stems. Although most fuchsias bloom in spring and summer, many blossom throughout the year. Countless cultivars and hybrids are in cultivation with pink, red, purple, magenta and white coloration and blendings; they have single or double flowers of various shapes and sizes. Some are pendulous and suitable for hanging baskets or for trailing over the sides of pedestal containers; others can be trained as tall standards for well-lit corners. Outstanding among the hybrids are 'Abundance' (a trailing plant with light pink double flowers), 'Cascade' (trailing, with pink and red single blooms), 'Mrs. Victor Reiter' (trailing, with crimson and white single flowers) and 'Pink Cloud' (upright and arching, with pink single flowers). The so-called honeysuckle fuchsia, *F. triphylla*, which grows about 45 cm (18 in.) high, bears clusters of 2.5 cm (1 in.) tubular flowers throughout the year; the variety 'Gartenmeister Bonstedt' has salmon-orange flowers among reddish leaves, and 'Swanley Yellow', despite its name, has orange blossoms in thick clusters.

HOW TO GROW. Fuchsias do best in at least four hours of direct sunlight a day, but should be protected from midday sun in summer. Night temperatures of 10° to 13°C (50° to 55°F) and day temperatures of 20° to 22°C (68° to 72°F) are ideal. Keep the soil moist when plants are flowering and fertilize every two weeks; fertilize monthly and keep the soil drier for those plants that rest in autumn and winter. Prune summer-flowering plants to about 15 cm (6 in.) from soil level, but shorten only side laterals on standards when plants are resting in autumn to early winter. Propagate named varieties from stem cuttings of new non-flowering growth in late spring.

G

GARDENIA
G. jasminoides, also called *G. florida* (gardenia, Cape jasmine)

The goal of many a gardener is to grow a richly fragrant gardenia in the house. Of the many varieties in cultivation, *G. jasminoides* 'Veitchii' is the one most often grown indoors; its waxy, snow-white flowers, about 7.5 cm (3 in.) across, normally appear in winter and spring among shiny, dark green 10 to 15 cm (4 to 6 in.) leaves on bushes 30 to 90 cm (1 to 3 ft) tall. Varieties that bear the larger flowers—up to 12.5 cm (5 in.)—familiar in corsages and buttonholes are also sometimes grown in pots. Among them are 'Belmont' and 'Fortuniana'.

HOW TO GROW. Gardenias do best in at least four hours of direct sunlight a day. Most will blossom continuously if they have night temperatures of 16° to 18°C (60° to 65°F), but will not set new flower buds if night temperatures rise above 18°C (65°F). Day temperatures of 20° to 22°C (68° to 72°F) are ideal. Pot in 2 parts moss peat to 1 part packaged potting soil and 1 part sharp sand; do not add lime. Keep the mixture moist and well drained. Fertilize monthly. Bud drop, common among plants newly brought indoors from a greenhouse, is usually caused by a too-dry atmosphere; it can be prevented by syringing buds with tepid water and by setting plants on a humidifying tray (*page 45*). Propagate at any time from stem cuttings of new growth, making sure to cover the pot with a clear plastic bag to conserve moisture; when established, pinch out the growing tip to encourage side-branching.

GAZANIA
G. hybrids (gazania, treasure flower)

The daisy-like gazania, most varieties of which are hybrids of *G. longiscapa*, bears long-lasting 7.5 to 10 cm (3 to 4 in.) dark-centred flowers in yellow, gold, cream, yellow-orange, pink or bronze-red. The blossoms open only in sunshine, closing at night and on cloudy days. The plants, which bloom through the summer, grow 15 to 30 cm (6 to 12 in.) tall with the blossoms arching over clumps of slender, irregularly lobed leaves that are dark green above and felty-white underneath.

HOW TO GROW. Gazanias do best in direct sunlight which is the only time they open properly; they appreciate night temperatures of 10° to 13°C (50° to 55°F) and day temperatures of 20° to 22°C (68° to 72°F). Soil should be light and well drained, and allowed to become nearly dry between thorough waterings. Fertilize monthly throughout the growing season. Propagate from seeds in late winter or early spring, germinating at a temperature of 16°C (60°F); pot the seedlings up when they are large enough to handle, usually in June. New plants can also be raised from cuttings taken in mid to late summer for blooms the next year.

GELSEMIUM
G. sempervirens (false jasmine)

Clouds of fragrant, yellow 2.5 cm (1 in.) flowers adorn this vine in winter and early spring, appearing among gleaming 4 to 7.5 cm (1½ to 3 in.) willow-like leaves. Plants can be allowed to trail from hanging containers or can be trained to trellis up to 120 cm (4 ft) high, through which the slender canes of the vine should be interwoven.

HOW TO GROW. False jasmine does best in full sun or very light shade, night temperatures of 10° to 13°C (50° to 55°F) and day temperatures of 20° to 22°C (68° to 72°F). Keep the soil moist and fertilize monthly except when plants are resting in the autumn. Plants may be easily propagated by air layering (*page 94*), from stem cuttings taken in spring from established new growth, or from seeds in spring. Prune after flowering in spring to keep plants to the desired size and to encourage side-shoots.

GLORIOSA
G. rothschildiana; *G. superba* (both called glory lily)

This graceful, tuberous-rooted ornamental vine, which bears impressive 7.5 to 10 cm (3 to 4 in.) lily-like flowers, climbs to a height of 90 to 120 cm (3 to 4 ft), clinging to supports by means of tendrils at the tips of its lance-like leaves. *G. rothschildiana* has scarlet and yellow flowers, *G. superba* yellow-green to orange and red flowers; the narrow petals of both curve sharply back and are wavy-edged or crimped, most conspicuously in *G. superba*. Because glory lilies go through alternate periods of growth and dormancy, they can be brought into blossom at any season if they are planted at different times of the year. Most gardeners plant them in April to flower in mid-summer, the normal blooming season (late summer to autumn for *G. superba*).

HOW TO GROW. Glory lilies do best in at least four hours of direct sunlight a day, night temperatures of 18° to 21°C (65° to 70°F) and day temperatures of 24°C (75°F) or higher. Keep the soil moist and fertilize every two weeks until the flowers fade; withhold moisture and food during the dormant season, normally from October to January. Propagate by dividing tubers (a risky procedure) during the dormant period, or by seeds; it is easier to remove and grow on the small offsets when repotting.

GAZANIA
Gazania hybrid

FALSE JASMINE
Gelsemium sempervirens

GLORY LILY
Gloriosa rothschildiana

GUZMANIA
Guzmania monostachya

SALMON BLOOD LILY
Haemanthus multiflorus

CHERRY PIE
Heliotropium arborescens

GLOXINIA See *Sinningia*

GUZMANIA
G. lingulata; *G. monostachya*, also called *G. tricolor*

Guzmanias have long been favoured by bromeliad enthusiasts because their spikes of bright petal-like bracts stay colourful for months. The smooth-edged, glossy leaves, which form a water-holding rosette, are often colourful too, with delicate brown, purple or maroon lines running lengthways. *G. lingulata* 'Cardinalis' has red bracts with yellowish-white flowers rising from a rosette, 45 cm (18 in.) or more across, formed by slender purplish-green leaves. *G. lingulata* 'Minor' bears scarlet, yellow or orange bracts, with yellowish-white flowers, above 20 to 30 cm (8 to 12 in.) rosettes formed by strap-like leathery leaves with purple markings. *G. monostachya* has 30 to 45 cm (12 to 18 in.) rosettes composed of bayonet-like yellow-green leaves around a stout stem bearing salmon-red bracts set with white flowers.

HOW TO GROW. Guzmanias do best in bright indirect or curtain-filtered sunlight, but can take direct sun in winter. Night temperatures of 16° to 18°C (60° to 65°F) and day temperatures of 21°C (70°F) or higher are ideal. Pot in a mixture of 2 parts moss peat to 1 part packaged potting soil and 1 part sharp sand; do not add lime. Keep moist; fertilize monthly. Keep soft water in the cup formed by the leaf rosette. Propagate from shoots that appear at the base of plants and pot up separately in spring.

H
HAEMANTHUS
H. coccineus (ox-tongue lily); *H. x hybridus*; *H. katharinae* (blood flower); *H. multiflorus* (salmon blood lily). (All called blood lily)

Blood lilies, so called because of the colour of their globular flower clusters, make spectacular pot plants. Each flower cluster, 15 to 30 cm (6 to 12 in.) across, is composed of many 2 to 5 cm (¾ to 2 in.) tubular blossoms—each with six protruding pollen-bearing stamens which are usually yellow—and is set on an upright stem 20 to 50 cm (8 to 20 in.) high. Plants bear two or more huge leaves up to 45 cm (18 in.) long and 15 cm (6 in.) wide. *H. coccineus* produces coral-red flowers in autumn; *H. katharinae* (pink blooms) and salmon-pink or scarlet hybrids flower in late spring or early summer; *H. multiflorus* bears red flowers in summer, on very tall stems.

HOW TO GROW. Blood lilies do best in at least four hours of direct sunlight a day, night temperatures of 10° to 13°C (50° to 55°F) and day temperatures of 20° to 22°C (68° to 72°F). Keep moist and fertilize monthly during the growing season; keep nearly dry and omit fertilizer during late autumn and winter. Propagate while the plants are resting by removing the small bulbs that develop beside the larger ones. Plant one bulb to a pot, setting the tip just above the soil. The pot should be 5 cm (2 in.) larger in diameter than the bulb. Plants flower more profusely if the roots are crowded and should be repotted only every three to five years. Each spring wash out part of the old soil without disturbing the roots and replace with fresh soil.

HEERIA See *Schizocentron*

HELIOTROPIUM
H. arborescens, also called *H. peruvianum* (cherry pie); *H. x hybridum* (all called heliotrope)

The delightful fragrance of heliotropes is so pervasive that a single cluster will perfume a whole room. Many modern varieties are hybrids of the vanilla-scented *H. arborescens*, which bears large clusters of minute, soft-textured purple flowerlets all the year round. The hybrids come in shades of lavender, purple, blue and white, and produce clusters of flowers 7.5 to 15 cm (3 to 6 in.) across. Heliotropes can be grown as bushy plants 15 to 30 cm (6 to 12 in.) or more tall, or they can be trained to single stems 90 to 120 cm (3 to 4 ft) tall.

HOW TO GROW. Heliotropes do best in at least four hours of direct sunlight a day, night temperatures of 10° to 13°C (50° to 55°F) and day temperatures of 20° to 22°C (68° to 72°F). Keep moist; fertilize every two weeks. Propagate from seeds; good colour forms are better increased from stem cuttings in late spring or summer. Some gardeners let plants rest in autumn, pruning them to keep the desired height and to force branching and abundant flowers in late winter and spring.

HETEROCENTRON See *Schizocentron*

HIBISCUS

H. rosa-sinensis (Chinese hibiscus, Chinese rose); *H. schizopetalus* (Japanese lantern)

The fragile beauty of hibiscus flowers, which bloom all the year round, belies the ease with which these plants are grown and their remarkable longevity of 25 years or more. The papery blossoms of *H. rosa-sinensis* grow up to 12.5 cm (5 in.) across and range from snowy white through cream to yellow, salmon, orange and scarlet. A notable cultivar called 'Cooperi' has 6 cm (2½ in.) scarlet flowers and narrow, 5 cm (2 in.) leaves marked with olive green, pink, crimson and white. *H. schizopetalus* has pendulous 6 cm (2½ in.) orange-red flowers with lacy-edged petals. Plants can be kept under 90 cm (3 ft) tall by pruning.

HOW TO GROW. Hibiscuses do best in at least four hours of direct sun a day, night temperatures of 16° to 18°C (60° to 65°F), day temperatures of 21°C (70°F) or higher. Keep moist; fertilize monthly. Propagate from stem cuttings of new growth in late spring.

HIPPEASTRUM

H. hybrids, also called *H.* x *hortorum* (amaryllis)

Known to most gardeners as amaryllis, *Hippeastrum* hybrids have smooth-textured lily-like flowers, sometimes 20 to 25 cm (8 to 10 in.) across. They bloom in winter or spring in clusters of three or four blossoms on top of 30 to 60 cm (12 to 24 in.) stems just as the dark green strap-shaped leaves arise from the bulbs. Most bulbs send up a second flower stalk when the first one begins to fade. Seed-grown bulbs are sold by colour; superior cultivars that have been propagated vegetatively are sold by name. Among the latter are 'Appleblossom' (blush-pink), 'Fire Dance' (bright red), 'Minerva' (white and red with red veining), 'Parsifal' (orange-scarlet) and 'Mont Blanc' (snowy-white).

HOW TO GROW. Amaryllises do best in at least four hours of direct sunlight a day, night temperatures of 16° to 18°C (60° to 65°F) and day temperatures of 21°C (70°F) or higher. Keep plants cool and out of direct sun while in bloom. Plant one bulb to a pot, allowing 5 cm (2 in.) of space between bulb and pot. Water well once, then wait for the stalk to appear before watering again. Keep moist and fertilize monthly until leaves turn yellow in late summer, then reduce water and omit fertilizer until about a month before flowers are wanted. Before plants start new

CHINESE HIBISCUS
Hibiscus rosa-sinensis

AMARYLLIS
Hippeastrum 'Fire Dance'

growth, wash away some of the old soil and replace with fresh soil. Repot every three to four years. Propagate from the small bulbs that develop beside the large ones. Plants propagated from seeds require three to four years to reach flowering size.

HOYA
H. australis; *H. bella*, also called *H. páxtonii*; *H. carnosa*; *H. cinnamomifolia*; *H. coronaria*, also called *H. grandi-flora*; *H. purpureo-fusca* (all called wax plant)

Vines with 5 to 10 cm (2 to 4 in.) leaves, hoyas take their common name from their long-lasting clusters of 12 to 25 mm (½ to 1 in.) star-shaped flowers, which are sweetly fragrant and so shiny they appear to be made of wax. Recommended species are *H. australis*, whose red-centred blush-white flowers appear in late summer; *H. bella*, a bushy plant with pendulous branches that bear white flowers with rosy-violet centres in summer; *H. carnosa*, which bears pinkish-white flowers with red centres in summer and has foliage that is sometimes edged with pink and cream; *H. cinnamomifolia*, which bears yellowish-green flowers with purple-red centres in the summer; *H. coronaria*, whose summer-blooming yellow flowers have five red dots at the base of each blossom; and *H. purpureo-fusca*, whose autumn-blooming brownish-red flowers have white hairs in a purple centre. It is also known as 'Silver Pink' because of the silvery pink blotches on its leaves.

HOW TO GROW. Hoyas do best in at least four hours of direct sunlight a day, but can also be grown in bright indirect or curtain-filtered sunlight. Night temperatures of 16° to 18°C (60° to 65°F) and day temperatures of 21°C (70°F) or higher are ideal. Water freely during flowering, but allow the soil to become almost dry between waterings when the plants are resting. Fertilize every two months in spring and summer. Train the vines on a 60 to 120 cm (2 to 4 ft) trellis. Do not remove the leafless spurs or stubs, on which new flowers appear every year. New plants may be started at any time by air layering (*page 94*) or from stem cuttings.

HYACINTHUS
H. orientalis (hyacinth); *H. orientalis* var. *albulus* (Roman hyacinth)

Hyacinths, which bear their waxy, bell-shaped flowers in clusters 15 to 25 cm (6 to 10 in.) high, bring winter-weary indoor gardeners one of the first sweet scents of spring. The most popular are the large-flowered cultivars of *H. orientalis*, which include 'Amsterdam' (salmon-pink), 'Bismarck' (pale blue), 'City of Haarlem' (primrose-yellow), 'L'Innocence' (white), 'King of the Blues' (indigo-blue) and 'Pink Pearl' (deep pink). The so-called Roman hyacinths, derived from a strain known as *H. orientalis* var. *albulus*, bear blue, pink, or white flowers. Fairy hyacinths, a cross of large-flowered hyacinths with Roman hyacinths, produce several flower clusters from each bulb.

HOW TO GROW. Hyacinths should be started in September or October. Plant them in bulb fibre or a peat-based potting compost leaving the noses exposed. Plunge the containers outdoors under 15 cm (6 in.) of light soil, leaves or ashes, for eight or nine weeks in a cool place, then gradually bring into light and temperatures around 10°C (50°F). When leaves are well developed and buds are showing, take them into a temperature of 16°C (60°F) to flower. They need plenty of light at this stage and moist soil. If the dormant bulbs cannot be placed outside, wrap the bowls in black polythene and store in a cool room at 4°C (40°F). Do not try to propagate hyacinth bulbs.

WAX PLANT
Hoya carnosa

HYACINTH
Hyacinthus orientalis
'King of the Blues'

HYDRANGEA

H. macrophylla, also called *Hortensia* (common hydrangea, house hydrangea)

One of the unforgettable joys of spring is the sight of hydrangeas, whose enormous clusters of soft-textured flowers come in pink, red, lavender, blue and purple as well as white. Each cluster, which may be 20 to 25 cm (8 to 10 in.) in diameter, is composed of a mass of 2.5 to 4 cm (1 to 1½ in.) sterile flowers set among shiny, oval 5 to 15 cm (2 to 6 in.) dark green leaves. Hydrangeas purchased in bloom are usually 45 to 60 cm (18 to 24 in.) tall and bloom for six weeks or more with proper care.

HOW TO GROW. Hydrangeas do best in bright indirect or curtain-filtered sunlight, night temperatures of 13° to 16°C (55° to 60°F) and day temperatures of 16° to 18°C (60° to 65°F). Keep the soil very wet; do not fertilize. Water with soft water, especially the blue-flowered varieties. Special blue colorants (basically aluminium sulphate) can be used to make the flowers blue. Make this up according to the manufacturer's instructions and give at weekly intervals when watering. Cut out the flowering branches after blooming and repot annually in a peat-based compost. Plunge outside, to the pot rim, for the summer in a place where it will not dry out; bring indoors in late autumn. If relegated permanently to the garden, in near frost-free climates remove them from the pots before planting.

▮ IMPATIENS

I. walleriana, also called *I. holstii*; *I. sultani* (busy Lizzie)

Busy Lizzie, beloved for its ability to bloom all year round in dim light even for inexperienced gardeners, is a name that suits this charming species far better than the genus name *Impatiens*, which refers to the manner in which the plants' seed pods explode when ripe, catapulting seeds in all directions. A favourite for generations it grows 15 to 30 cm (6 to 12 in.) tall, bearing soft, flat flowers 2.5 to 5 cm (1 to 2 in.) across in pink, red, orange-scarlet, purple, gold, white or red and white. The shiny 2.5 to 5 cm (1 to 2 in.) leaves may be green, maroon or a variegated green and white.

HOW TO GROW. Busy Lizzie does equally well in bright indirect or curtain-filtered sunlight, in light shade or in 14 to 16 hours of artificial light a day. Night temperatures of 16° to 18°C (60° to 65°F) and day temperatures of 21°C (70°F) or higher are ideal. Pot in 2 parts moss peat to 1 part packaged potting soil and 1 part sharp sand. Keep moist; fertilize every two weeks during the growing period. Propagate at any time from stem cuttings or seeds.

IPOMOEA, also called PHARBITIS

I. purpurea; *I. violacea*, also called *I. tricolor* and *I. rubro-caerulea* (both also called morning glory)

Although morning glories are usually considered to be summer-flowering garden plants, these decorative vines with their trumpet-shaped 6 to 20 cm (2½ to 8 in.) flowers and 5 to 7.5 cm (2 to 3 in.) heart-shaped leaves make handsome, easy-to-grow additions to indoor gardens. *I. purpurea* and *I. violacea* bear blossoms up to 10 cm (4 in.) across in blue, purple, scarlet, pink, white or multi-colours. 'Early Call' has rose-red blooms 7.5 cm (3 in.) or more across in late summer.

HOW TO GROW. Morning glories do best in at least four hours of direct sunlight a day and plenty of light for the rest of the day, night temperatures of 16° to 18°C (60° to 65°F) and day temperatures of 21°C (70°F) or higher. Keep the soil barely moist and feed monthly with a half-strength

COMMON HYDRANGEA
Hydrangea macrophylla

BUSY LIZZIE
Impatiens 'Scarlet Baby'

fertilizer beginning when the plants are 10 cm (4 in.) tall. Propagate from seeds in early spring for summer flowers. Nick the seeds with a knife or sandpaper to aid water absorption and plant six to eight seeds to a 25 cm (10 in.) flowerpot. When the seedlings are 5 cm (2 in.) high, thin them out, leaving the three strongest plants. Give these a light trellis or thin stakes for the stems to twine on. Discard plants when flowering is over.

ISOLOMA See *Kohleria*

IXORA
I. chinensis; *I. coccinea*; *I. hybrids*; *I. javanica* (all called ixora, flame-of-the-woods)

Ixoras are compact plants that bloom primarily in summer and intermittently for the rest of the year with proper care, in colours ranging from bright red through orange, yellow, pink and white. The species most often cultivated is *I. coccinea*, whose four-petalled red flowers, 2.5 cm (1 in.) across, grow in clusters 10 to 15 cm (4 to 6 in.) or more in diameter; the leaves, bronze toned when new, mature to a dark, shiny green. Together with the light orange *I. chinensis*, it is a parent of many of the hybrids. *I. javanica* bears slightly larger, salmon-red flowers. Many hybrid varieties are also suitable for house culture. Plants can easily be kept below 90 cm (3 ft) by pruning.

HOW TO GROW. Ixoras do best in at least four hours of direct sunlight a day, night temperatures of 16° to 18°C (60° to 65°F) and day temperatures of 21°C (70°F) or higher. Pot in a mixture of 2 parts moss peat to 1 part packaged potting soil and 1 part sharp sand; do not add lime. Keep moist; fertilize every two weeks in spring and summer, monthly for the rest of the year. Plants occasionally suffer from bud drop, especially if moved about, so they should be left in a position where they are doing well. Propagate from stem cuttings in spring.

J
JACOBINIA
J. carnea, also called *Justicia carnea* and *Cyrtanthera carnea* (king's-crown, Brazilian plume); *J. pauciflora*, also called *Libonia floribunda* and *Sericographis pauciflora*; *J. suberecta*

These tropical plants bear slender two-lipped flowers, often in pompom-like spikes at the ends of the branches. *J. carnea* has fluffy 7.5 to 15 cm (3 to 6 in.) spikes of rosy-pink 5 cm (2 in.) long flowers, which bloom among coarse 10 to 20 cm (4 to 8 in.) oval leaves in late summer; plants reach a height of 30 to 90 cm (1 to 3 ft). *J. suberecta* grows about 30 cm (12 in.) tall and in spring produces orange-scarlet flowers about 2.5 cm (1 in.) long in clusters above velvety 6 cm (2½ in.) leaves. *J. pauciflora*, also about 30 cm (12 in.) tall, is a winter-blooming species that bears many solitary 2.5 cm (1 in.) long tubular scarlet flowers with yellow tips among 2 cm (¾ in.) leaves.

HOW TO GROW. Jacobinias do best in at least four hours of direct sunlight a day in winter and bright indirect or curtain-filtered sunlight for the rest of the year. Night temperatures of 10° to 13°C (50° to 55°F) and day temperatures of 18°C (65°F) or higher are ideal. Keep the soil moist and place the pot on a humidifying tray (*page 45*), or spray over the foliage occasionally. Fertilize every two weeks during the growing season. Since old plants are apt to be straggly, they should be cut back and repotted after flowering to force new growth. Propagate from stem cuttings each spring, rooted with bottom heat.

MORNING GLORY
Ipomoea 'Early Call'

IXORA
Ixora coccinea

JACOBINIA
Jacobinia suberecta

JASMINUM

J. volubile, also called *J. simplicifolium*; *J. humile* 'Revolutum'; *J. mesnyi*, also called *J. primulinum* (primrose jasmine); *J. officinale*, also called *J. officinale affine*, *J. grandiflorum* (white jasmine); *J. parkeri*; *J. polyanthum* (Chinese jasmine); *J. sambac* (Arabian jasmine)

Sweet fragrance is the hallmark of most jasmines. *J. volubile* bears clusters of star-shaped 2.5 cm (1 in.) white flowers in winter and has 5 cm (2 in.) waxy, oval leaves. *J. humile* 'Revolutum' has clusters of 5 cm (2 in.) lemon-yellow flowers among feathery leaves from June to September. *J. mesnyi* bears round 5 cm (2 in.) yellow flowers in spring. From June to October *J. officinale* bears clusters of star-shaped, 2 cm (¾ in.) white flowers. *J. parkeri*, only 20 to 30 cm (8 to 12 in.) tall, has star-shaped 6 to 12 mm (¼ to ½ in.) yellow flowers in summer. *J. polyanthum* produces springtime clusters of star-shaped, 2 cm (¾ in.) white, pink-budded flowers. *J. sambac*, which blooms from early spring to late autumn, bears clusters of rosette-shaped 2.5 cm (1 in.) flowers that are gardenia-white at first and gradually turn purple as they fade. The variety 'Plena' has double flowers.

HOW TO GROW. Jasmines thrive in at least four hours of direct sunlight a day. *J. humile* 'Revolutum' does best in night temperatures of 4° to 7°C (40° to 45°F) and day temperatures of 20°C (68°F) or lower; *J. sambac* and its varieties in night temperatures of 16° to 18°C (60° to 65°F) and day temperatures of 22°C (72°F) or higher; the other jasmines flourish in night temperatures of 10° to 13°C (50° to 55°F) and day temperatures of 20° to 22°C (68° to 72°F). Keep the soil moist at all times and fertilize every two weeks except when plants are resting. Propagate at any time from stem cuttings. Prune all species except *J. parkeri* after the blooming period to keep plants under 90 cm (3 ft) tall; cut flowered shoots back to a strong bud about 5 cm (2 in.) from the base and remove entirely old stems. The height of jasmine plants can also be controlled by weaving their branches through a low trellis. In summer stand the plants outdoors in full sun.

JUSTICIA See *Jacobinia*

K

KALANCHOË

K. blossfeldiana

Colourful, winter-blooming house plants whose flowers last for many weeks, *K. blossfeldiana* cultivars grow 20 to 30 cm (8 to 12 in.) high with an equal spread and bear masses of 6 to 12 mm (¼ to ½ in.) four-petalled red or yellow blossoms that may nearly cover the waxy, thick, 2.5 to 5 cm (1 to 2 in.) leaves. Excellent red cultivars of these succulents include 'Vulcan', 'Scarlet Gnome', 'Tom Thumb' and 'Brilliant Star'; a bright yellow cultivar is 'Tom Thumb Golden' and a strain with flowers of various colours is Hummel's Hybrids.

HOW TO GROW. Kalanchoës do best in at least four hours of direct sunlight a day, night temperatures of 10° to 16°C (50° to 60°F) and day temperatures of 20° to 22°C (68° to 72°F). Allow the soil to become nearly dry between thorough waterings and fertilize every two weeks until the plants come into flower. Propagate from stem cuttings in early autumn, or, for finer plants, sow seeds at any time from January to July (the later the sowing, the smaller the plants will be when they begin to blossom). To ensure blooms for the Christmas season, give plants at least 14 hours a day of uninterrupted darkness from about September 1 until early October.

CHINESE JASMINE
Jasminum polyanthum

KALANCHOË
Kalanchoë blossfeldiana 'Vulcan'

KOHLERIA

K. amabilis; *K. bogotensis*; *K. eriantha*, also called *Isoloma erianthum*; *K. lindeniana*

Kohlerias are easily cultivated, 20 to 75 cm (8 to 30 in.) plants with conspicuous hairy leaves and tubular five-petalled flowers that occur in a variety of colours, often spotted with contrasting hues. Some of these gesneriads grow upright, but most have trailing stems that make them suitable for hanging containers. *K. amabilis* bears abundant 5 cm (2 in.) rose-pink flowers with red dots from late winter and through spring and summer; *K. bogotensis*, 2.5 cm (1 in.) long red-spotted yellow flowers, and *K. eriantha*, 2.5 cm (1 in.) red-orange flowers with red spots, bloom in winter and spring; *K. lindeniana* has 12 mm ($\frac{1}{2}$ in.) fragrant, lavender and white flowers with yellow throats in late autumn and spring.

HOW TO GROW. Kohlerias do best in bright indirect or curtain-filtered sunlight, and also grow well in 14 to 16 hours of artificial light a day. Night temperatures of 18° to 21°C (65° to 70°F) and day temperatures of 24°C (75°F) or higher are ideal. Pot in 2 parts moss peat to 1 part packaged potting soil and 1 part sharp sand. Keep moist and fertilize monthly while the plants are growing. The species listed above go into a semi-dormant period between blooming periods and can be cut back to encourage fresh growth while resting; keep the plants on the dry side and do not fertilize during this time. Propagate from stem cuttings of new growth, making sure to cover the pot with a clear plastic bag to conserve moisture.

KOHLERIA
Kohleria amabilis

L

LACHENALIA

L. aloides, also called *L. tricolor*; *L. bulbifera*, also called *L. pendula* (both called Cape cowslip)

Cape cowslips are easy-to-grow 22.5 to 30 cm (9 to 12 in.) tall bulbous plants for pots or hanging baskets. They bear spikes of waxy, 2.5 cm (1 in.) long flowers in winter and early spring. The 15 to 20 cm (6 to 8 in.) leaves are often purple spotted. Outstanding are *L. aloides* (green banded with red and yellow). *L. aloides* 'Lutea' (yellow flowers); *L. aloides* 'Nelsonii' (gold tinged with green); *L. bulbifera* (multicoloured coral, yellow and purple).

HOW TO GROW. Cape cowslips do best in at least four hours of direct sunlight a day, night temperatures of 4° to 7°C (40° to 45°F) and day temperatures of 20°C (68°F) or lower. Keep the soil moist and fertilize monthly during the growing season. Keep dry during the dormant period. Propagate by separating new bulbs from the old ones.

LAELIA

L. flava; *L. lundii* var. *regnellii*

One of the finest orchids for growing indoors is *L. flava*, whose golden-yellow 5 to 6 cm (2 to $2\frac{1}{2}$ in.) blossoms are borne in clusters of four to ten on wiry, 45 cm (18 in.) spikes (*photograph, page 58*). The long-lasting flowers bloom in midwinter. *L. lundii* var. *regnellii* rarely grows more than 10 to 12.5 cm (4 to 5 in.) tall, bearing one or two pale pink flowers 2.5 to 4 cm (1 to $1\frac{1}{2}$ in.) across, with ruffled lips delicately veined in red.

HOW TO GROW. Laelias do best in at least four hours of direct sunlight a day, but should be shielded with a light curtain or blinds during the hottest part of the day. Night temperatures of 13° to 18°C (55° to 65°F) and day temperatures of 20°C (68°F) or higher are ideal. Pot in a mixture of 2 parts fir bark or shredded osmunda-fern fibre and 1 part coarse moss peat. Place the pot on a humidifying tray (*page 82*) or spray over frequently, and let the

CAPE COWSLIP
Lachenalia bulbifera

potting medium become moderately dry between thorough waterings. Fertilize monthly with a high-nitrogen formula, diluted at the rate of ¼ teaspoon to 1 litre (2 pt) of water.

x LAELIOCATTLEYA
Hybrids derived from *Cattleya* and *Laelia*

Laeliocattleyas, which bloom at various times of the year, are among the most colourful orchids suitable for indoor culture. Most of the varieties being bred today are large-flowering but compact plants that produce clusters of long-lasting 7.5 to 10 cm (3 to 4 in.) blossoms in shades of greenish-yellow, golden-yellow, orange and pink, often with vivid rose-to-purple lips. One superb yellow variety is 'El Cerrito' (*photograph, page 59*).

HOW TO GROW. Laeliocattleyas do best in bright indirect or curtain-filtered sunlight, night temperatures of 13° to 18°C (55° to 65°F) and day temperatures of 20°C (68°F) or higher. Plant in a mixture of 2 parts fir bark or shredded osmunda-fern fibre and 1 part coarse moss peat. Place the pot on a humidifying tray (*page 82*) or spray the foliage frequently; water freely, but let the potting medium become moderately dry between thorough waterings when they are dormant. Fertilize monthly with a high-nitrogen formula, diluting ¼ teaspoon in 1 litre (2 pt) of water.

LANTANA
L. camara (common lantana); *L.* hybrids; *L. montevidensis*, also called *L. sellowiana* and *L. delicatissima* (trailing lantana)

Lantanas bear abundant 2.5 cm (1 in.) clusters of tiny fragrant flowers, mainly in spring and summer and intermittently in autumn and winter, among pungent, 2.5 cm (1 in.) long, rough green leaves. The blossoms of common and hybrid lantanas come in white, yellow, pink, red, orange and bicoloured combinations. The plants can be kept 20 to 30 cm (8 to 12 in.) tall by pinching back stem tips or they can be trained to grow in a tree shape with great heads of foliage and flowers above a single stem 60 to 90 cm (2 to 3 ft) tall. Trailing lantanas, which have rosy-lilac flowers, grow up to 120 cm (4 ft) long and bloom most heavily in summer; they are especially graceful in hanging baskets.

HOW TO GROW. Lantanas do best in at least four hours of direct sunlight a day, night temperatures of 13° to 16°C (55° to 60°F) and day temperatures of 20°C (68°F) or higher. Allow the soil to dry out slightly between thorough waterings. Fertilize every two weeks. Propagate from stem cuttings at any time.

LIBONIA See *Jacobinia*

LILIUM
L. longiflorum (Easter lily)

Easter lilies, famed for their snow-white flowers and sweet fragrance, are grown by the millions each year, timed to open their blossoms for the Easter season. The flowers 15 to 20 cm (6 to 8 in.) long with a 10 to 12.5 cm (4 to 5 in.) spread, bloom for about a week; the leaves are up to 15 cm (6 in.) long. Among the most popular varieties, because of their comparatively low stature, are 'Croft', which grows about 60 cm (2 ft) tall; 'Ace', 30 to 60 cm (1 to 2 ft); and 'Estate', about 90 cm (3 ft).

HOW TO GROW. Easter lilies do best in bright indirect or curtain-filtered sunlight when in flower, with night temperatures of 4° to 13°C (40° to 55°F) and day temperatures

TOP: COMMON LANTANA
Lantana camara

BOTTOM: TRAILING LANTANA
Lantana montevidensis

EASTER LILY
Lilium longiflorum 'Croft'

of 20°C (68°F) or lower. Keep the soil moist while the plants are in blossom, but do not fertilize. After the flowers fade, set the plants in the sun and water until the foliage matures. The culture of Easter lily bulbs indoors is difficult for the average house-plant gardener, and the resulting plants will rarely be as satisfactory as professionally grown plants bought from florists. You can plant the bulbs in pots, where they will flower without forcing in summer, indoors and in the garden.

M

MALPIGHIA
M. coccigera (holly malpighia); *M. glabra* (Barbados cherry)

These are small trees, rarely obtainable in Europe. *M. coccigera*, with spiny-edged, holly-like leaves, begins to produce 12 mm (½ in.) pink flowers with fringed petals when it is only 7.5 to 10 cm (3 to 4 in.) tall. The flowers bloom profusely in summer and are followed by 12 mm (½ in.) red fruit. Plants grow slowly to a height of about 30 cm (12 in.) and are often used as Japanese miniature bonsai plants. *M. glabra* grows 90 cm (3 ft) or more tall and in summer produces a scattering of 2 cm (¾ in.) rose-red flowers, followed by cherry-sized red fruit.

HOW TO GROW. Both species do best in direct sunlight or very light shade, night temperatures of 13° to 16°C (55° to 60°F) and day temperatures of 20° to 22°C (68° to 72°F). Allow the soil to become slightly dry between thorough waterings; fertilize twice a year, in early spring and early summer. Propagate in spring or summer from stem cuttings or seeds.

MALVAVISCUS
M. arboreus (sleeping hibiscus)

An upright, bushy species with 5 to 7.5 cm (2 to 3 in.) long, heart-shaped leaves, this shrub produces 4 to 6 cm (1½ to 2½ in.) red blossoms from the time it is about 25 cm (10 in.) tall. The flowers bloom all year round, but they never fully open, which accounts for the plant's common name. Indoors, plants are generally pruned back to a height of about 60 cm (2 ft). Cultivars with white or pink flowers exist, but are not widely available. The type, too, is uncommon in Europe.

HOW TO GROW. Sleeping hibiscus does best in at least four hours of direct sunlight a day, night temperatures of 16° to 18°C (60° to 65°F) and day temperatures of 21°C (70°F) or higher. Keep the soil moist at all times and fertilize every two weeks. Old plants may be cut back to a height of 15 to 30 cm (6 to 12 in.) and repotted in fresh potting mixture in early spring. Propagate from stem cuttings at any time.

MANDEVILLA See *Dipladenia*

MANETTIA
M. bicolor (firecracker vine); *M. inflata*

M. bicolor takes its common name from its hairy, 2 cm (¾ in.) long, tubular scarlet flowers tipped with yellow that bloom continuously throughout the year. Slender oval leaves, about 5 cm (2 in.) long, seem almost to smother the plant's thread-like, twining stems, which may be trained on a 60 to 120 cm (2 to 4 ft) high trellis. *M. inflata* is similar, but with the red parts of the flower inflated.

HOW TO GROW. *M. bicolor* does best in very light shade, night temperatures of 13° to 16°C (55° to 60°F) and day

HOLLY MALPIGHIA
Malpighia coccigera

SLEEPING HIBISCUS
Malvaviscus arboreus

temperatures of 20° to 22°C (68° to 72°F); *M. inflata* prefers cooler winter temperatures. Keep the soil moist at all times and fertilize every two weeks. Propagate from stem cuttings at any time of year.

MAXILLARIA
M. tenuifolia

One of the easiest-to-grow orchids, this plant bears long-lasting coconut-scented blossoms, only about 4 cm (1½ in.) across, which are dark red with yellow speckles (*photograph, page 60*). They bloom in summer, appearing singly on low stems above grass-like leaves. Plants normally grow to a height of 25 to 30 cm (10 to 12 in.).

HOW TO GROW. *M. tenuifolia* does best in bright indirect or curtain-filtered sunlight, night temperatures of 13° to 21°C (55° to 70°F) and day temperatures of 20°C (68°F) or higher. Plant on a slab of tree fern or in a mixture of 2 parts sphagnum moss or shredded osmunda-fern fibre and 1 part coarse moss peat. Place the pot on a humidifying tray (*page 82*) or spray over the foliage from time to time; keep the potting medium moist at all times. Fertilize monthly with a high-nitrogen formula, diluted at the rate of ¼ teaspoon per 1 litre (2 pt) of water.

MUSCARI
M. armeniacum; M. aucheri, also called *M. tubergenianum; M. botryoides,* (all called grape hyacinth)

Muscaris are bulbous plants that bear fragrant 15 to 20 cm (6 to 8 in.) spikes of tiny bell-shaped blossoms in midwinter or early spring. Three species—*M. armeniacum* (and its excellent cultivar 'Heavenly Blue'), *M. aucheri* and *M. botryoides*—have deep blue flowers; the variety *M. botryoides album* (pearls of Spain) has white blooms. Plants grow 22.5 to 30 cm (9 to 12 in.) tall and have grass-like, blue-green leaves 15 to 20 cm (6 to 8 in.) long.

HOW TO GROW. Grape hyacinths do best in at least four hours of direct sunlight a day, night temperatures of 4° to 7°C (40° to 45°F) and day temperatures of 20°C (68°F) or lower. Plants are often purchased at florists when already blooming in midwinter, but may also be grown from bulbs planted in pots in early autumn for winter flowering. In both cases, grow the plants at cool temperatures and keep the soil moist until the foliage withers; do not fertilize. During the spring and summer dormancy let the bulbs remain dry; you can then start growth in the pots again or plant them outdoors in the garden during the autumn. Propagate from the small bulbs that develop next to the larger ones.

MYSTACIDIUM See *Angraecum*

N

NAEGELIA See *Smithiantha*

NARCISSUS

Although botanically both are narcissi, the large trumpet-flowered types are commonly called daffodils and the bunch-flowered tazettas, narcissi.

Two kinds of narcissus are of special interest as house plants: the large trumpet-flowered varieties, whose blossoms are often 10 cm (4 in.) or more across and rise above lance-like, grey-green leaves 25 to 30 cm (10 to 12 in.) long; and the tazetta varieties, which bear four to eight fragrant, 2.5 to 5 cm (1 to 2 in.) trumpet-shaped flowers on each stem.

FIRECRACKER VINE
Manettia bicolor

GRAPE HYACINTH
Muscari armeniacum

TOP: DAFFODIL
Narcissus 'King Alfred'   BOTTOM: NARCISSUS
Narcissus tazetta 'Soleil d'Or'

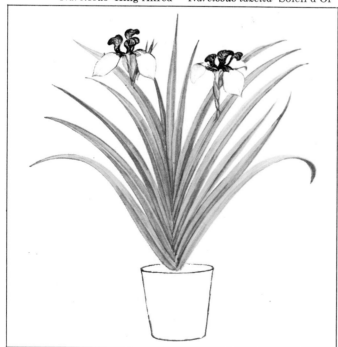

APOSTLE PLANT
Neomarica gracilis

Both kinds are usually brought into flower in winter and spring; individual blossoms often remain colourful for seven to ten days. Large-flowered hybrids are 'King Alfred' (golden-yellow flowers), 'Celebrity' (white flowers with soft yellow trumpets), and 'Mount Hood' (white flowers). Among the tazettas are hardy types like 'Geranium', whose white flowers have orange-scarlet centres, and 'Cheerfulness', a creamy-yellow, double variety. Fragrant, tender tazettas include 'Paper White' (white flowers), 'Soleil d'Or' (yellow with orange cups), and 'Chinese Sacred Lily' (white with golden-yellow cups).

HOW TO GROW. Narcissi do best in bright indirect or curtain-filtered sunlight when blooming, night temperatures of 4° to 7°C (40° to 45°F) and day temperatures of around 16°C (60°F) or lower. Tender tazettas will grow well in night temperatures of 13° to 16°C (55° to 60°F). These can be set in any material that supports them, such as pebbles, chips, sand, moss peat or bulb fibre; plant them shallowly, so that only the bases are anchored. Keep the growing medium wet; do not fertilize. Set the bulbs in a cool dark place until new growth is about 10 cm (4 in.) tall, then bring them out to bloom. Discard tender tazettas after flowering. Hardy narcissi are usually planted in deep pots or bowls for indoor flowering and grown in soil-based compost or bulb fibre. Keep them cool at a temperature of 4°C (40°F) and in darkness for nine weeks before bringing them into light and temperatures around 10°C (50°F) for the foliage to develop, and then into 16°C (60°F) for flowering. Later the bulbs can be saved for garden planting. Propagation of narcissi is best left to professional growers.

NEOFINETIA
N. falcata, also called *Angraecum falcatum*

This summer-flowering miniature orchid, which grows only 7.5 to 15 cm (3 to 6 in.) tall, bears spikes of five to seven long-spurred, 2.5 cm (1 in.) white blossoms (*photograph, page 59*). The flowers are especially fragrant at night.

HOW TO GROW. *N. falcata* does best in bright indirect or curtain-filtered sunlight, night temperatures of 13° to 18°C (55° to 65°F) and day temperatures of 20°C (68°F) or higher. Plant on a slab of tree fern or in 2 parts fir bark or shredded osmunda fibre and 1 part coarse moss peat. Place the pot on a humidifying tray (*page 82*) or spray over the foliage frequently; keep the potting medium moist. Fertilize monthly from spring until mid-autumn with a high-nitrogen formula, diluting $\frac{1}{4}$ teaspoon in 1 litre (2 pt) of water. Do not feed in late autumn and winter; water only enough to keep the plant from shrivelling.

NEOMARICA
N. caerulea, *N. gracilis*, *N. northiana* (all called Apostle plant, walking iris)

An iris-like plant that grows 30 to 45 cm (12 to 18 in.) tall, *N. gracilis* bears sword-shaped leaves and fragrant flowers whose three outer petals are white with yellow and brown markings at the base, and whose three inner petals are blue. Each 5 cm (2 in.) flower lasts a day, but plants bloom for long periods in summer. *N. caerulea* grows 60 to 90 cm (2 to 3 ft) tall; its 5 to 10 cm (2 to 4 in.) flowers have sky-blue outer petals, paler blue inner petals marked yellow and brown; *N. northiana* has white outer petals, violet-tipped inner petals.

HOW TO GROW. These rare but attractive plants do best in bright indirect or curtain-filtered sunlight, night temperatures of 10° to 13°C (50° to 55°F) and day temperatures of 20° to 22°C (68° to 72°F). Keep the soil wet; fertilize monthly. To propagate, use new plants at the tops of flower stems as you would runners (*page 93*).

NERIUM CORONARIUM See *Ervatamia*

NICOTIANA
N. alata 'Grandiflora', also called *N. affinis* (flowering tobacco)

Varieties of nicotiana—usually grown outdoors as summer annuals—also make delightful winter house plants. They range in height from 30 to 120 cm (1 to 4 ft), the dwarf kinds being particularly useful. Their trumpet-shaped flowers, each about 5 cm (2 in.) across, range from white and pink to scarlet and include such unusual shades as lime-green, chartreuse, wine-red, and chocolate-brown. The flowers, especially fragrant in the evening, rise above soft, hairy, oval leaves 10 to 15 cm (4 to 6 in.) long.

HOW TO GROW. Flowering tobacco plants do best in at least four hours of direct sunlight a day, night temperatures of 10° to 16°C (50° to 60°F) and day temperatures of 20° to 22°C (68° to 72°F). Keep the soil moist and fertilize every two weeks. Start plants from seeds in midsummer for midwinter flowering indoors, or dig plants from the garden in autumn and cut them back to 15 to 20 cm (6 to 8 in.) before potting; they will branch freely and blossom in midwinter. Discard after flowering.

NIDULARIUM
N. fulgens; *N. innocentii*

Nidularium, a Latin word meaning "little bird nest", describes the way the flowers of this bromeliad are borne deep within the nest-like centres of rosette-shaped leaf clusters that measure from 45 to 60 cm (18 to 24 in.) across. Weeks before the flowers appear, which may be at any time of the year, the centres of the rosettes become brightly coloured, usually red. The flowers remain colourful for months. *N. fulgens* bears violet blooms among bright red, green-tipped petal-like bracts, and pale green spiny-edged leaves with dark green spots; *N. innocentii* 'Striatum' has white flowers and broad, ivory-striped, spiny-edged leaves.

HOW TO GROW. Nidulariums do best in bright indirect or curtain-filtered sunlight, night temperatures of 16° to 18°C (60° to 65°F) and day temperatures of 21°C (70°F) or higher. Pot in 2 parts moss peat, 1 part packaged potting soil and 1 part sharp sand; do not add lime. Keep moist; keep water in the cup formed by the leaf rosette and feed monthly with a quarter-strength house-plant fertilizer. Propagate from new shoots that appear at the base of plants after flowering.

NOPALXOCHIA See *Epiphyllum*

O
ODONTOGLOSSUM
O. pulchellum (lily-of-the-valley orchid)

The nearly 30 cm (12 in.) high flower spikes of this orchid bear five to ten waxy 4 cm (1½ in.) flowers (*photograph, page 60*). The blossoms, white with yellow lips, bloom in winter and early spring, lasting as long as six or seven weeks, and have a strong lily-of-the-valley fragrance.

HOW TO GROW. *O. pulchellum* does best in at least four hours of direct sunlight a day, but should be shielded from sun at midday. Night temperatures of 13° to 18°C (55° to

FLOWERING TOBACCO
Nicotiana alata 'Grandiflora'

NIDULARIUM
Nidularium fulgens

133

65°F) and day temperatures of 20°C (68°F) or higher are ideal. Plant in 2 parts fir bark or shredded osmunda-fern fibre and 1 part coarse moss peat. Place the pot on a humidifying tray (*page 82*) in summer or spray over the foliage frequently. Let the mixture dry moderately between thorough waterings. Fertilize monthly with a high-nitrogen formula, diluted at the rate of ¼ teaspoon per 1 litre (2 pt) of water.

OLEA See *Osmanthus*

ONCIDIUM
O. varicosum var. *rogersii* (dancing lady orchid)

Oncidiums bear great clusters of long-lasting delicate flowers, sometimes with 100 or more in bloom at once. *O. varicosum* var. *rogersii*, which blossoms in autumn and winter, has bright yellow flowers up to 5 cm (2 in.) across with wide, flaring, skirt-shaped lips (*photograph, page 58*).

HOW TO GROW. Oncidiums do best in at least four hours of direct sunlight a day but should be shaded from hot mid-day rays by curtains or blinds. Night temperatures of 13° to 18°C (55° to 65°F) and day temperatures of 20°C (68°F) or higher are ideal. Pot in a mixture of 2 parts fir bark or osmunda-fern fibre and 1 part coarse moss peat. Place the pot on a humidifying tray (*page 82*). Allow the potting medium to become moderately dry between thorough waterings during the growing season, from winter until late summer; while the plant is dormant in the autumn, water only enough to keep from shrivelling. Fertilize monthly during the growing season with a high-nitrogen formula, diluted at ¼ teaspoon per 1 litre (2 pt) of water.

FALSE SEA ONION
Ornithogalum caudatum

ORNITHOGALUM
O. arabicum; *O. caudatum* (false sea onion); *O. thyrsoides* (chincherinchee)

These bulbous plants are notable for their long-lasting clusters of fragrant, star-shaped flowers, which appear on a central stalk in winter and spring. *O. arabicum* produces six to twelve white 5 cm (2 in.) flowers with conspicuous black, pollen-receiving pistils on a 30 to 60 cm (1 to 2 ft) stalk among slender 45 cm (18 in.) green leaves. *O. caudatum* bears a mass of 50 to 100 small white flowers with a green centre line on each petal; the 45 to 90 cm (1½ to 3 ft) flower stalk grows from a 7.5 to 10 cm (3 to 4 in.) bulb that is almost entirely out of the soil. *O. thyrsoides* has white or yellow 5 cm (2 in.) flowers on a 15 to 45 cm (6 to 18 in.) stalk; blossoms often last six weeks or more.

HOW TO GROW. These species do best in at least four hours of direct sunlight a day, night temperatures of 10° to 16°C (50° to 60°F) and day temperatures of 20° to 22°C (68° to 72°F). Allow the soil to become slightly dry between thorough waterings and fertilize monthly during the growing season; do not water or fertilize while the bulbs are dormant. Pot or repot bulbs in a loam-based compost in early autumn. Propagate during dormancy from the small bulbs that develop beside larger ones.

SWEET OLIVE
Osmanthus fragrans

OSMANTHUS
O. fragrans, also called *Olea fragrans* (sweet olive)

The orange-blossom fragrance of this shrubby plant comes from clusters of almost unnoticeable four-petalled greenish-white flowers, each less than 6 mm (¼ in.) across, set among handsome leathery dark green leaves 7.5 cm (3 in.) long. Plants, which grow 60 to 90 cm (2 to 3 ft) tall in pots but up to 9 metres (30 ft) in nature, bloom continuously all the year.

HOW TO GROW. *O. fragrans* thrives in bright sun or very light shade, night temperatures of 10° to 13°C (50° to 55°F) and day temperatures of 20° to 22°C (68° to 72°F). Keep the soil moist and fertilize monthly. Propagate in summer from stem cuttings.

OXALIS

O. bowiei, also called *O. bowieana* and *O. purpurata* var. *bowiei*; *O. brasiliensis*; *O. pes-caprae*, also called *O. cernua* (Bermuda buttercup); *O. purpurea* 'Grand Duchess', also called *O. variabilis* 'Grand Duchess'

These charming bulbous plants, which grow only 10 to 15 cm (4 to 6 in.) high, bear many satiny 2.5 to 4 cm (1 to 1½ in.) flowers among 5 to 10 cm (2 to 4 in.) clover-like leaves during spring and summer. The flowers of *O. bowiei* are purplish-pink; *O. brasiliensis*, rosy-red; *O. pes-caprae*, yellow, single or double; 'Grand Duchess', bright pink or white. Blossoms open only on sunny days and close at night and in cloudy weather.

HOW TO GROW. Oxalis needs a sunny position or very bright light, otherwise the flowers do not open properly; it prefers night temperatures of 10° to 16°C (50° to 60°F) and day temperatures of 20° to 22°C (68° to 72°F). Keep moist; fertilize monthly while the plants are growing. Do not keep the plants too hot or overwater them, or the stems may collapse. After the foliage withers, keep the bulbs dry until autumn. Propagate in autumn from the small bulbs that develop beside larger ones.

P
PACHYSTACHYS

P. lutea (lollipop plant)

P. lutea is a comparative newcomer to the house plant scene, but is becoming popular on account of its long flowering season, which spans from spring until winter. It has a shrubby habit and grows about 60 cm (2 ft) tall, with long, oval and pointed leaves and showy terminal spikes of white flowers set off by brilliant orange bracts.

HOW TO GROW. Plants do best in night temperatures of 10° to 13°C (50° to 55°F), and a day temperature of 18°C (65°F) or higher. Water as required, letting the soil become fairly dry between watering. Feed at three-week intervals during the growing season. Propagate from soft tip cuttings, rooted with bottom heat, in spring or early summer.

PAPHIOPEDILUM, formerly called CYPRIPEDIUM

P. callosum, *P. hybrids* (lady's slipper orchid)

Paphiopedilums have strap-shaped leathery leaves, sometimes heavily mottled with light and dark patches, sometimes plain green. The former are the easier to grow in the warmth of centrally heated houses or greenhouses; those with clear green foliage require temperatures too cool for easy indoor culture. *P. callosum*, an outstanding species that blooms in spring and summer, bears single 10 cm (4 in.) blossoms on 25 to 37.5 cm (10 to 15 in.) tall stalks. Their pale green petals have rosy-purple tips and are warted and hairy along their upper edges; the pouch-shaped lip is brownish-purple, and the large, leaf-like outer sepals are white with purple lines. Hybrids usually grow less than 37.5 cm (15 in.) tall. They bear 7.5 to 12.5 cm (3 to 5 in.) flowers in colours ranging from white and yellow to rose, pink, green and brown, usually with several colours in one blossom (*photograph*, *page 57*); individual flowers often last more than a month.

OXALIS
Oxalis purpurea 'Grand Duchess'

LOLLIPOP PLANT
Pachystachys lutea

Illustration by Pamela Freeman

135

HOW TO GROW. Mottled-leaved paphiopedilums do best in partial shade; too much light produces yellowish leaves and fewer blossoms. Night temperatures of 18° to 21°C (65° to 70°F) and day temperatures of 24°C (75°F) or higher are ideal. Plant in a compost made up of equal parts osmunda fibre, sphagnum moss and sifted loam. Where the atmosphere is dry, place the pot on a humidifying tray (*page 82*). Fertilize monthly with a high-nitrogen formula, diluted at the rate of $\frac{1}{4}$ teaspoon in 1 litre (2 pt) of water. Propagate by division of pot-bound plants.

PASSIFLORA

P. x *alato-caerulea*; *P. caerulea*; *P. coccinea*; *P. edulis* (granadilla); *P. trifasciata* (all called passion flower)

Clinging by tendrils to trellis or stakes, or trained to string around a window, passion flower vines display intriguing blossoms of 10 outer petals and an intricate inner crown among deeply lobed leaves. *P. caerulea* is the easiest and most adaptable with fragrant, 10 cm (4 in.) blue and white flowers and five to seven lobed leaves. Warmer conditions are necessary for *P.* x *alato-caerulea*, a hybrid of this species, with fragrant purple, pink and white 10 cm (4 in.) flowers and smooth 10 to 15 cm (4 to 6 in.) leaves; *P. coccinea*, with 10 to 12.5 cm (4 to 5 in.) scarlet flowers and coarse, oval 7.5 to 15 cm (3 to 6 in.) leaves; *P. edulis*, with 6 cm ($2\frac{1}{2}$ in.) purple and white flowers, followed by purple or yellow egg-like fruits, and shiny 10 to 15 cm (4 to 6 in.) leaves; and *P. trifasciata*, with fragrant 2.5 to 4 cm (1 to $1\frac{1}{2}$ in.) yellow-white flowers and 10 to 15 cm (4 to 6 in.) leaves, purple below and olive to bronze-green with silvery-pink markings above.

HOW TO GROW. Passion flowers do best in soil borders in cool or heated greenhouses, but can also be grown in tubs or large pots of loam based compost in warm sun lounges and similar light situations. They need at least four hours of direct sunlight a day, night temperatures of 13° to 18°C (55° to 65°F) and day temperatures of 20°C (68°F) or higher. However, *P. caerulea* can be grown in cooler conditions and is hardy outdoors in many areas. Keep the soil moist; fertilize every two weeks during the growing season. When plants are resting, keep the soil slightly dry. Cut plants back to 15 cm (6 in.) in January to force branching. Propagate from stem cuttings or seeds at any time.

PELARGONIUM

P. crispum; *P. denticulatum*; *P. graveolens*; *P. odoratissimum*; *P. tomentosum* (all called scented-leaf geranium); *P.* x *hortorum*, also called *P. zonale* hybrids (zonal pelargoniums, geraniums); *P.* x *domesticum*, also called *P. grandiflorum* hybrids (Martha Washington or regal pelargoniums); *P. peltatum* (ivy geranium)

Geraniums are among the most widely grown flowering pot plants in the world. The best strains for indoor gardens are varieties of *P.* x *hortorum*, which vary from 7.5 to 90 cm (3 to 36 in.) in height and bear flower clusters up to 10 cm (4 in.) across in red, white, pink or lavender; most bloom from spring to late autumn. The soft plush leaves are horseshoe-shaped with conspicuous bronze or maroon zonal markings; others have pink, red or white leaf markings or borders. Also widely grown indoors are the spring-blooming scented-leaved geraniums such as *P. crispum* (lemon-scented, violet-coloured flowers); *P. denticulatum* (pine-scented, lavender flowers); *P. graveolens* (rose-scented, pinkish-purple flowers); *P. odoratissimum* (apple-scented, white flowers); and *P. tomentosum* (peppermint-scented, white flowers). All of them grow 30 to 90 cm (1 to 3 ft) tall. *P.* x *domesticum* comes mainly in pink, white

PASSION FLOWER
Passiflora x *alato-caerulea*

GERANIUM
Pelargonium x *hortorum* 'Skies of Italy'

and purple shades, usually veined or striated with other shades and sometimes white-margined. They grow 37.5 to 60 cm (15 to 24 in.) tall, with a branching habit, large flower heads and plain green, toothed, palmate leaves. Varieties of the trailing ivy geranium, *P. peltatum*, bear 5 to 7.5 cm (2 to 3 in.) clusters of white, pink, red or lavender flowers from late spring to autumn.

HOW TO GROW. Geraniums do best in at least four hours of direct sunlight a day, night temperatures of 10° to 13°C (50° to 55°F) and day temperatures of 20° to 22°C (68° to 72°F), although night temperatures may go up to 18°C (65°F). Allow the soil to become moderately dry between thorough waterings. Fertilize every two weeks from March until October, monthly for the rest of the year. Propagate from stem cuttings in spring or summer.

PENTAS
P. lanceolata, also called *P. carnea* (Egyptian star cluster)

These plants bear 10 cm (4 in.) clusters of 12 mm ($\frac{1}{2}$ in.) flowers; the hairy oval leaves 7.5 to 10 cm (3 to 4 in.) long, are often deeply veined. The cultivar 'Orchid Star' has rosy-lavender flowers, and pink, rose and white forms also exist. The upright, bushy plants, usually kept 30 to 45 cm (12 to 18 in.) tall by pinching off the tips, bloom all year.

HOW TO GROW. Pentas does best in at least four hours of direct sunlight a day, night temperatures of 10° to 18°C (50° to 65°F) and day temperatures of 20°C (68°F) or higher. Keep soil moist and fertilize every two weeks. Propagate from stem cuttings in spring.

PETUNIA
P. x *hybrida*, also called *P.* hybrids

Petunias make fine indoor plants, even though they last but a single season. The blossoms, up to 10 cm (4 in.) across, are often fringed, and come in colours ranging from white and pale yellow through pink and red to blue and deep purple, with some varieties multicoloured. There are both single and double kinds. Plants grow up to 15 or 30 cm (6 to 12 in.) or taller.

HOW TO GROW. Petunias do best in at least four hours of direct sunlight a day, and day temperatures around 16°C (60°F). Night temperatures during the winter must be 10° to 13°C (50° to 55°F); if higher, flower buds will not form. Let the soil become slightly dry between thorough waterings. Fertilize every two weeks. The best winter-flowering plants come from seedlings started in mid-summer and grown cool to start with, preferably outdoors. To induce bushy plants, pinch out the growing tips when the plants are 7.5 to 10 cm (3 to 4 in.) high; garden plants, cut back and potted in September, sometimes flower all winter indoors.

PHALAENOPSIS
P. amabilis, *P.* hybrids (all called moth orchids)

Widely used in bridal bouquets, these orchids bear flat, 8.5 to 10 cm ($3\frac{1}{2}$ to 4 in.) blossoms in white, pink, yellow or purple, often with spots or bars of contrasting colours. Dozens of flowers may bloom at a time on arching, often branching, flower stalks 60 to 120 cm (2 to 4 ft) long. The foliage—five or six lustrous leaves up to 30 cm (12 in.) long and 5 to 7.5 cm (2 to 3 in.) wide—is rarely more than 30 cm (12 in.) high. Most of the modern white cultivars are derived from *P. amabilis*, whose lips are tinged with yellow and spotted with red (*photograph, page 59*). Most species bloom in spring, although cultivars may blossom at any season and some bloom all the year round.

EGYPTIAN STAR CLUSTER
Pentas lanceolata 'Orchid Star'

PETUNIA
Petunia hybrid

FAIRY PRIMROSE
Primula malacoides

DWARF POMEGRANATE
Punica granatum 'Nana'

HOW TO GROW. Phalaenopsis does best in bright indirect or curtain-filtered sunlight, night temperatures of 18° to 24°C (65° to 75°F) and day temperatures of 24°C (75°F) or higher. Plant in a mixture of equal parts sphagnum moss and osmunda fibre with a little leaf-mould. Place the pot on a humidifying tray (*page 82*) and keep the planting medium moist. Fertilize monthly with a high-nitrogen formula, diluted at the rate of ¼ teaspoon per 1 litre (2 pt) of water. To encourage branching and further flowers, cut off the flower stalks just below the bottom flower when the blooms have faded.

PHARBITIS See *Ipomoea*
PHYLLOCACTUS See *Epiphyllum*

PRIMULA
P. malacoides (fairy primrose); *P. obconica*; *P. elatior* hybrids (polyanthus)

Three kinds of primroses bring a touch of spring to homes in winter. The daintiest, *P. malacoides*, bears clouds of pink, red or white flowers, 2.5 cm (1 in.) or less across, arranged in tiers on slender 20 to 25 cm (8 to 10 in.) stalks. Clusters of fragrant, rather larger blossoms, up to 5 cm (2 in.) across, adorn the other two; *P. obconica*, which comes in red, pink, lavender and white (and has rough hairy leaves that may cause a skin rash), and the polyanthus, which is shorter and bears white, yellow, pink, red, lavender, blue or purple, single or double flowers. Blossoming plants of all three kinds are usually bought from florists and discarded when flowering ends. Polyanthus, derived from the crossing of *P. vulgaris* and *P. veris*, however, can be transplanted into a shady garden to grow on in future years as hardy perennials.

HOW TO GROW. Primroses do best in bright indirect or curtain-filtered sunlight, night temperatures of 4° to 10°C (40° to 50°F) and day temperatures of 20°C (68°F) or lower. Keep slightly moist; fertilize every two weeks. Plants can be started from seeds sown outside or in pans in a cold frame as soon as ripe, and grown on under cool conditions. Bring indoors when flower buds appear.

PUNICA
P. granatum 'Nana' (dwarf pomegranate)

One of the oldest of cultivated fruits, the pomegranate was known to the Romans as the apple of Carthage. *P. granatum* 'Nana', a dwarf cultivar, grows no more than 37.5 cm (15 in.) tall. Its 2.5 cm (1 in.) bell-shaped, orange-red flowers blossom all the year round, most profusely in spring and summer, and are occasionally followed by 5 cm (2 in.) edible reddish fruit. There is also a cultivar with double flowers called 'Pleniflora'.

HOW TO GROW. Pomegranates do best in at least four hours of direct sunlight a day, night temperatures of 13° to 16°C (55° to 60°F) and day temperatures of 20° to 22°C (68° to 72°F). Keep the soil moist and fertilize every three or four months. Propagate from stem cuttings in summer.

R

RECHSTEINERIA
R. cardinalis (cardinal flower); *R. leucotricha* (Brazilian edelweiss); *R. verticillata* (double decker plant)

These tuberous-rooted gesneriads, which grow 30 to 45 cm (12 to 18 in.) tall, make excellent long-blooming house plants, bearing 2.5 to 5 cm (1 to 2 in.) tubular flowers above hairy 10 to 15 cm (4 to 6 in.), usually heart-shaped leaves. The bright red *R. cardinalis* blooms for most of the year if old stems are removed. *R. leucotricha* has salmon-rose flowers; it may blossom for one month at any time from December until May. *R. verticillata*, with tiers of pink-spotted purple flowers above its foliage, usually produces its flowers in spring.

HOW TO GROW. Rechsteinerias do best in bright indirect or curtain-filtered sunlight, but can take direct sun in winter; *R. cardinalis* and *R. leucotricha* also thrive under 14 to 16 hours a day of artificial light. Night temperatures of 18° to 21°C (65° to 70°F) and day temperatures of 24°C (75°F) or higher are ideal. Pot in 2 parts moss peat to 1 part packaged potting soil and 1 part sharp sand, and place pots on a humidifying tray (*page 43*). Water from the bottom so that moisture does not touch the leaves or flowers. Allow the soil to become very slightly dry between thorough waterings and fertilize monthly during the growing season; reduce water and omit fertilizer for the rest of the year. Propagate plants from basal cuttings, leaving part of the old tuber attached, and root in equal parts sand and peat in a propagating frame with bottom heat in early spring; all three species can be started from seeds.

CARDINAL FLOWER
Rechsteineria cardinalis

RHIPSALIDOPSIS
R. gaertneri, also called *Schlumbergera gaertneri* (Easter cactus); *R. x graeseri*; *R. rosea*

R. gaertneri is often confused with *Zygocactus truncatus* (*page 151*), but requires more warmth and humidity than that species and flowers at a later season, from April onwards. It has flat, leaf-like stems about 5 cm (2 in.) long, arranged in series; these are slightly notched along their edges. The star-like flowers, 4 cm (1½ in.) long, last about eight weeks and are scarlet. *R. rosea* is pink and *R. x graeseri*, orange-red and carmine. All grow 30 to 45 cm (12 to 18 in.) high.

HOW TO GROW. These cacti do best in bright indirect or curtain-filtered sunlight and night temperatures around 10° to 13°C (50° to 55°F) until the buds appear when the temperature should be 16° to 18°C (60° to 65°F). Day temperatures of 21°C (70°F) or higher are ideal. Grow in a lime-free, peat-based compost. Feed occasionally during the growing season with a special cactus fertilizer. *R. gaertneri* can be propagated from seeds or tip joints rooted in summer with bottom heat.

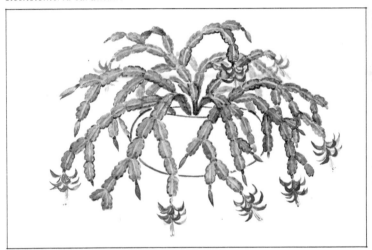

EASTER CACTUS
Rhipsalidopsis gaertneri hybrid

RHODODENDRON
R. simsii (Indian azalea)

This is a well-known pot plant with neat, small evergreen leaves and masses of red, pink, white or multi-coloured 2.5 to 10 cm (1 to 4 in.) blossoms for two to four weeks in late winter or early spring. Plants grow from 15 to 60 cm (6 to 24 in.) tall.

HOW TO GROW. *R. simsii* thrives in at least four hours of direct or very bright indirect sunlight a day, with night temperatures of 4° to 13°C (40° to 55°F) and day temperatures of 20°C (68°F) or lower. Pot in a mixture of 2 parts moss peat to 1 part packaged potting soil and 1 part sharp sand; do not add lime. Keep the potting medium moist. Fertilize with an acid-type fertilizer every two weeks from the time the flowers fade in spring until new buds form during the late summer; do not fertilize in autumn, winter or while plants are flowering. If the leaves lose their rich green colour, moisten the soil monthly with a solution of 25 grams (1 oz.) iron sulphate to 8 litres (2 gal) of water, or iron chelate mixed and applied according to the instructions on the label. Propagate from stem cuttings of new growth in early summer and root in gentle heat.

INDIAN AZALEA
Rhododendron simsii cultivar

MINIATURE ROSE
Rosa chinensis 'Minima'

ROSEMARY
Rosmarinus lavandulaceus

RHYNCHOSPERMUM See *Trachelospermum*
RICHARDIA See *Zantedeschia*

RODRIGUEZIA

R. venusta

These miniature orchids bear arching 15 cm (6 in.) stalks of fragrant 4 cm (1½ in.) blossoms in white or blush-pink, each with a yellow oblong blotch on its lip (*photograph, page 60*). The flowers bloom at different times of the year, usually in summer and autumn, amid slender 10 to 12.5 cm (4 to 5 in.) leaves.

HOW TO GROW. Rodriguezias do best in bright indirect or curtain-filtered sunlight, night temperatures of 13° to 18°C (55° to 65°F) and day temperatures of 20°C (68°F) or higher. Plant in a mixture of 2 parts fir bark or shredded osmunda fibre and 1 part coarse moss peat, or mount vertically on a slab of tree fern. Place the pot on a humidifying tray (*page 82*) and keep the potting medium moist at all times. Fertilize monthly with a high-nitrogen formula, diluted at the rate of ¼ teaspoon per 1 litre (2 pt) of water.

ROSA

R. chinensis 'Minima', also called *R.* 'Roulettii' (miniature roses)

Miniature roses grow well indoors, blooming abundantly all the year. Their fragrant, 2 to 4 cm (¾ to 1½ in.) flowers come in white and shades of pink, red and yellow, as well as blends, and are borne among tiny, five-leaflet leaves. The many cultivars available range in height from 15 to 30 cm (6 to 12 in.) at maturity; some bloom when only 7.5 to 10 cm (3 to 4 in.) high.

HOW TO GROW. Miniature roses do best in at least four hours of direct sunlight a day, night temperatures of 10° to 18°C (50° to 65°F) and day temperatures of 20°C (68°F) or higher. Keep moist and fertilize every two weeks. To keep red spider mites from sapping strength from the plants, wash the leaves—especially the undersides—forcefully with clear water occasionally. Propagate from stem cuttings in midsummer or by seed, although these do not come true from named varieties.

ROSMARINUS

R. officinalis (rosemary); *R. lavandulaceus*, also called *R. officinalis prostratus*

Rosemary, used for centuries in cooking, also makes a splendid window-sill plant. Its two-lipped violet-blue fragrant flowers, 12 to 20 mm (½ to ¾ in.) across, bloom in spring and summer; the aromatic leaves, 2 to 5 cm (¾ to 2 in.) long, are dark green above and fuzzy white beneath. A more tender, prostrate kind, *R. lavandulaceus*, can be kept under 37.5 cm (15 in.) tall by pinching off the tips of stems (the pinched-off tips can be used for seasoning).

HOW TO GROW. Rosemary does best in plenty of direct sunlight, night temperatures of 10° to 13°C (50° to 55°F) and day temperatures of 20° to 22°C (68° to 72°F). Let the soil become moderately dry between thorough waterings; fertilize every two or three months. Propagate from heel cuttings with a sliver of the old wood attached in midsummer; root the cuttings in a cold frame.

RUELLIA

R. graecizans, also called *R. amoena*; *R. macrantha*

Perhaps the finest ruellia for growing indoors is *R. macrantha*, a 60 to 90 cm (2 to 3 ft) plant that bears rosy-pink, bell-shaped 5 cm (2 in.) blossoms in winter and spring among 10 to 15 cm (4 to 6 in.) oval leaves. *R. graecizans*, bears 5 cm (2 in.) tubular blossoms of crimson through winter and spring on top of wiry stems 45 to 60 cm (18 to 24 in.) tall.

HOW TO GROW. Ruellias do best in bright indirect or curtain-filtered sunlight, night temperatures of 13° to 18°C (55° to 65°F) and day temperatures of 20°C (68°F) or higher. Pot in a mixture of 2 parts moss peat to 1 part packaged potting soil and 1 part sharp sand. Keep the soil moist and fertilize every month during the growing season; reduce water and omit fertilizer while plants are resting. Old plants tend to become straggly, so many gardeners grow new ones from stem cuttings each spring or summer.

RUSSELIA
R. equisetiformis, also called *R. juncea* (coral plant, fountain plant)

The bright green, arching branches of *R. equisetiformis*, which bear 2.5 to 5 cm (1 to 2 in.) long, tubular, scarlet flowers, may cascade out 90 cm (3 ft) or more across, making it a stunning choice for hanging containers. Plants bloom abundantly in summer if given optimum growing conditions. The finely divided branches appear leafless at first glance, but are actually covered with tiny scale-like leaves.

HOW TO GROW. Russelias do best in at least four hours of direct sunlight a day, night temperatures of 10° to 13°C (50° to 55°F) and day temperatures of 20° to 22°C (68° to 72°F). Let the soil become moderately dry between thorough waterings and fertilize with a diluted liquid feed every two weeks all the year round. Propagate from stem cuttings taken during the summer.

S
SAINTPAULIA
S. ionantha (African violet)

African violets are among the most popular flowering house plants. Many varieties of *S. ionantha* exist, and new hybrids are constantly being developed, one of the best strains being the 'Diana' group. Given proper care, these gesneriads blossom almost continuously, bearing clusters of velvety 2.5 to 4 cm (1 to 1½ in.) flowers in pink, blue or purple, as well as white and bicolors, all accented by conspicuous yellow pollen-bearing stamens. Flowers come in five-petalled single forms and many-petalled double forms; petal edges may be smooth, ruffled or frilled. Plants usually grow 10 to 15 cm (4 to 6 in.) tall, bearing flowers above rosettes of hairy 5 to 10 cm (2 to 4 in.) leaves, often deeply corrugated, that range from green to bronze, with some varieties mottled pink or white.

HOW TO GROW. African violets do best in bright indirect or curtain-filtered sunlight, or in 14 to 16 hours of artificial light a day. Temperatures of 16° to 18°C (60° to 65°F) or higher are ideal. They dislike hot dry air and direct sunlight. Pot in 2 parts moss peat to 1 part packaged potting soil and 1 part sharp sand and place the pot on a humidifying tray (*page 43*). Water with soft water, preferably from below the pot; if the foliage or crowns become wet, brown spots appear on the leaves and they collapse. Fertilize monthly with a weak liquid house-plant fertilizer, except during the resting period, when the soil should be kept barely moist and no fertilizer given. Propagate from seeds sown in gentle heat in spring. Seedlings seldom come true, and the named cultivars are better raised from leaf cuttings taken during the summer and rooted in water or in a sand and peat compost. Transfer the young plants to pots of the recommended growing medium.

RUELLIA
Ruellia macrantha

CORAL PLANT
Russelia equisetiformis

AFRICAN VIOLET
Saintpaulia ionantha hybrid

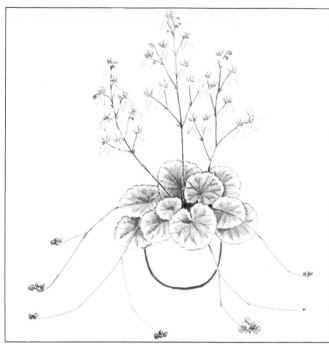

MOTHER-OF-THOUSANDS
Saxifraga stolonifera 'Tricolor'

Schizocentron elegans

SIBERIAN SQUILL
Scilla siberica 'Spring Beauty'

SAXIFRAGA

S. stolonifera, also called *S. sarmentosa* (mother-of-thousands)

S. stolonifera is a tufted plant with 2.5 to 4 cm (1 to 1½ in.) round, hairy mid-green leaves, flushed red beneath and with silvery veining. Many red, thread-like runners trail down to 45 cm (18 in.) lengths and bear young plantlets at their tips, a feature which makes them attractive for hanging baskets and as pedestal pot plants. The white flowers, in summer, come in loose racemes of 22.5 to 30 cm (9 to 12 in.), with one or two petals on each bloom larger than the rest. *S. stolonifera* 'Tricolor' is slightly smaller; its green and cream leaves have traces of pink and purplish-rose undersides.

HOW TO GROW. These plants do best in light shade, night temperatures of 4° to 7°C (40° to 45°F), although they will tolerate up to 16°C (60°F), and day temperatures of 20°C (68°F) or lower. Let the soil dry slightly between thorough waterings. To encourage colourful foliage, fertilize sparingly, every three to four months. Propagate from runners (*page 93*).

SCHIZOCENTRON

S. elegans, also called *Heeria elegans, Heterocentron elegans*

This is a charming creeping plant particularly suited to hanging containers; it sends out an abundance of satiny, rosy-purple 2.5 cm (1 in.) flowers in late spring or early summer. Its dark green leaves are 12 mm (½ in.) long and diamond shaped.

HOW TO GROW. The plant grows best in partial shade, night temperatures of 10° to 13°C (50° to 55°F) and day temperatures of 20° to 22°C (68° to 72°F). Keep the soil moist and fertilize monthly. Propagate by division or by separating the rooted shoots.

SCILLA

S. siberica (Siberian squill); *S. mischtschenkoana*, also called *S. tubergeniana*

Scillas, familiar as early spring-flowering bulbs outdoors, are equally lovely as midwinter-blooming house plants, producing waxy bell-shaped flowers surrounded by smooth strap-like green leaves. *S. siberica* bears 12 to 25 mm (½ to 1 in.) deep blue flowers on 15 cm (6 in.) spikes amid 12 mm (½ in.) wide leaves that are 20 to 30 cm (8 to 12 in.) tall; the variety 'Spring Beauty', which grows about 25 cm (10 in.) tall, has 2.5 to 4 cm (1 to 1½ in.) blue blossoms. *S. mischtschenkoana* bears 4 cm (1½ in.) pale blue flowers that fade to white; it grows about 15 cm (6 in.) high.

HOW TO GROW. Scillas do best in full sun or light shade, night temperatures of 4° to 7°C (40° to 45°F) and day temperatures of 20°C (68°F) or lower. Pot new bulbs in early autumn and put them in a cool dark place for eight to ten weeks before bringing them into the light. Keep the soil moist during active growth. Do not fertilize. After flowers fade and foliage withers, save the bulbs for planting out in the garden.

SENECIO

S. confusus (Mexican flame vine); *S. cruentus*, also called *Cineraria cruenta* and *Cineraria* hybrids (cineraria); *S. mikanioides*

These plants offer vivid colour for indoor gardens, especially in winter and spring. *S. confusus* is an uncommon vine bearing clusters of brilliant orange-red, daisy-like flowers 4 cm (1½ in.) across which may bloom occasionally throughout the year. *S. mikanioides* bears yellow flowers, only 8 mm (⅓ in.) across, in fragrant 2.5 to 7.5 cm (1 to 3 in.) clusters. Both can be kept small for use in hanging containers by pinching off the tips of stems. *S. confusus* can be trained on a 90 to 120 cm (3 to 4 ft) trellis. *S. cruentus* is the parent of the well-known florists' cinerarias. These are excellent plants for late winter-flowering with immense clusters of velvety daisy-like flowers that crown a dense growth of 7.5 to 10 cm (3 to 4 in.) leaves, green on top and purplish underneath. The blossoms, up to 10 cm (4 in.) or more across, may be white, pink, red, blue or purple with blue or white centres; some of them have concentric rings of varying colours.

HOW TO GROW. *S. confusus* and *S. mikanioides* do best in a greenhouse or must have at least four hours of direct sunlight a day in winter and curtain-filtered sunlight for the rest of the year; night temperatures of 10° to 13°C (50° to 55°F) and day temperatures of 20° to 22°C (68° to 72°F) are ideal. Keep moist and fertilize monthly. Cut back straggly plants after flowering to promote new growth. Propagate from stem cuttings. *S. cruentus* should be bought from florists and discarded after flowers fade. While in bloom, it does best in bright indirect or curtain-filtered sunlight, night temperatures of 4° to 7°C (40° to 45°F) and day temperatures of 20°C (68°F) or lower. Keep moist; do not fertilize and take care not to subject the leaves to dry heat, strong sunlight or rough handling.

SERICOGRAPHIS See *Jacobinia*

SINNINGIA
S. pusilla; *S. speciosa* (both called gloxinia)

The highly popular plants generally thought of as gloxinias are cultivars of *S. speciosa*, a tuberous-rooted Brazilian wild flower. The velvety, bell-shaped blossoms of these free-flowering gesneriads are very large—from 7.5 to 15 cm (3 to 6 in.) across—and may be single, with five petal-like lobes, or double, with many lobes. They come in white, pink, deep red, lavender and purple, often edged or spotted with contrasting hues, and are held slightly above the compact growth of velvety oval 12.5 cm (5 in.) leaves. The plants blossom in summer and autumn and go through periods of dormancy. An intriguing miniature gloxinia, *S. pusilla*, bears 12 mm (½ in.) violet flowers.

HOW TO GROW. Sinningias do best in bright indirect or curtain-filtered sunlight and can also be grown in 14 to 16 hours of artificial light a day. Night temperatures of 18° to 21° C (65° to 70°F) and day temperatures of 24°C (75°F) or higher are ideal. Set *S. pusilla* on a humidifying tray (*page 43*). Pot both types in 2 parts moss peat, 1 part packaged potting soil and 1 part sharp sand. Keep moist and fertilize monthly when the plants are growing. After flowering, sinningias should gradually be given less and less water until the leaves die down. The tubers should then be stored dry. In early spring they may be repotted in fresh compost and started again at a temperature of 21°C (70°F). Propagate both species from leaf cuttings or seeds.

SMITHIANTHA, formerly known as NAEGELIA
S. cinnabarina; *S. zebrina*; *S.* hybrids, also called *S.* x *hybrida* (all called temple bells)

The bell-shaped 4 cm (1½ in.) long flowers of these gesneriads come in white, pink, red, orange or yellow, often streaked or spotted inside with contrasting hues. They flower from midsummer well into autumn. The heart-shaped, deep green leaves are often marbled red and

TOP: MEXICAN FLAME VINE
Senecio confusus

BOTTOM: CINERARIA
Senecio cruentus

GLOXINIA
Sinningia speciosa hybrid

143

purple and covered with a mat of red hairs. *S. cinnabarina* bears red, rose or orange-red flowers. *S. zebrina* hybrids are bushy plants, with yellow, pink and red-spotted blossoms. Among hundreds of Smithiantha hybrids raised by hybridists in recent years are two exceptional strains: the British 'Butcher's Hybrids' and the American 'Cornell Hybrids'. The red-flowered 'Carmel' belongs to the latter. All grow about 30 cm (1 ft) tall.

HOW TO GROW. Smithianthas do best in bright indirect or curtain-filtered sunlight and can be grown under 14 to 16 hours of artificial light a day. Night temperatures of 18° to 21°C (64° to 70°F) and day temperatures of 24°C (75°F) or higher are ideal. Pot in 2 parts moss peat, 1 part packaged potting soil and 1 part sharp sand or vermiculite. Keep moist; fertilize monthly during the growing season. While the plants are dormant, moisten the soil just often enough to keep the scaly, thick underground stems (rhizomes) from dehydrating. Propagate by dividing the rhizomes when the plants are restarted into growth in spring; leaf cuttings can be taken in early summer and rooted in gentle heat before potting up in compost.

SOLANUM
S. capsicastrum (winter cherry); *S. pseudocapsicum* (Jerusalem cherry, Christmas cherry)

S. capsicastrum can be grown as an annual, biennial or perennial, its main attraction being not the summer blooming, 12 mm ($\frac{1}{2}$ in.) white starry flowers, but the round red, orange or yellow, marble-sized fruits which follow. These are at their best in midwinter. The leaves are narrowly oval and dark green, and there is also a variegated form. The very similar *S. pseudocapsicum* has larger fruits and is more robust. Both plants grow 25 to 30 cm (10 to 12 in.) high.

HOW TO GROW. Both plants do best in at least four hours of direct sunlight a day, night temperatures of 4°C (40°F) and day temperatures of 10°C (50°F) or higher. Allow the soil to become slightly dry between thorough soakings; fertilize monthly. Plants are usually grown as annuals from seeds sown in February or March. Those to be kept for a second season should be hard pruned in spring and, after growth restarts, repotted in a soil-based compost. They can be kept outdoors in summer in a sunny position, sheltered from winds. Spray the plants often to encourage fruits to set. A pinch of Epsom salts applied every three weeks after the berries have formed helps to prevent premature dropping of foliage and fruits. Pinch back the stem tips until late June to encourage bushy growth. Take the plants indoors again before the autumn.

x SOPHROLAELIOCATTLEYA
Hybrids derived from *Sophronitis*, *Laelia* and *Cattleya*

These compact plants rarely grow more than 30 cm (12 in.) high, but bear lavender to red flowers 10 to 17.5 cm (4 to 7 in.) across. Blossoms may appear at any season and the plants often bloom more than once a year. There are many varietal forms, including the American, scarlet-flowered 'Miami' (*photograph, page 58*).

HOW TO GROW. The hybrids do best in bright indirect or curtain-filtered sunlight, night temperatures of 13° to 18°C (55° to 65°F) and day temperatures of 20°C (68°F) or higher. Plant in 2 parts fir bark or shredded osmunda fibre and 1 part coarse moss peat. Place the pot on a humidifying tray (*page 82*); let the mixture dry slightly between thorough waterings. Fertilize monthly with a high-nitrogen formula, diluted at the rate of $\frac{1}{4}$ teaspoon per 1 litre (2 pt) of water.

TEMPLE BELLS
Smithiantha 'Carmel'

JERUSALEM CHERRY
Solanum pseudocapsicum

SPATHIPHYLLUM
S. wallisii (white sails); *S.* 'Mauna Loa'

Spathiphyllums bear handsome, long-lasting leaf-shaped white flowers called spathes, which turn apple-green with age and closely resemble the blossoms of calla lilies. The compact *S. wallisii* blooms in spring and again in autumn. The larger flowered and richly fragrant 'Mauna Loa' normally flowers only in spring, but under warm conditions may also bloom intermittently during the year. Both plants grow 30 to 45 cm (12 to 18 in.) tall and have shiny dark green leaves 20 to 25 cm (8 to 10 in.) long that rise on wiry stems and give the plants a striking appearance even when they are not flowering.

HOW TO GROW. Spathiphyllums do best in shade except in the winter, when they may receive curtain-filtered sunlight. Night temperatures of 16° to 18°C (60° to 65°F) and day temperatures of 21°C (70°F) or higher are ideal. Spathiphyllums are greedy plants which require plenty of water and feeding when in full growth, also annual repotting. Pot in a mixture of 2 parts moss peat, 1 part packaged potting soil and 1 part sharp sand. Keep the mixture moist and fertilize every two to three months. Propagate by division in spring.

SPREKELIA
S. formosissima, also called *Amaryllis formosissima* (Jacobean lily)

Each spring sprekelias send up single orchid-like flowers on top of pink 30 to 45 cm (12 to 18 in.) stalks; usually these bulbs send up only one stalk, but occasionally they send up two. The deep red 10 cm (4 in.) blossoms may appear before, with or after the narrow 20 to 30 cm (8 to 12 in.) green leaves.

HOW TO GROW. Sprekelias do best in at least four hours of direct sunlight a day, night temperatures of 16° to 18°C (60° to 65°F) and day temperatures of 21°C (70°F) or higher during their growing season from February to September, and 4° to 7°C (40° to 45°F) at night and 18°C (65°F) or lower when they are resting during the autumn and early winter. Keep the soil moist and fertilize monthly as long as the foliage is green; keep the soil dry and do not fertilize while the plants are dormant. Repot every three to four years, planting bulbs so that the necks are visible above the soil. New plants can be propagated from the small bulbs that develop next to the larger ones, but they will not reach flowering size for several years.

STEPHANOTIS
S. floribunda (stephanotis, Madagascar jasmine)

Stephanotis, a long-time favourite for bridal bouquets, bears its exceedingly fragrant white blooms on handsome vines between May and October. The waxy tubular flowers, about 2.5 cm (1 in.) across, bloom in 10 to 15 cm (4 to 6 in.) clusters among leathery dark green 7.5 to 10 cm (3 to 4 in.) leaves. This vine may be woven through a small trellis, trained around the top of a window or grown as a bush-type plant by pinching off the tips of new stems.

HOW TO GROW. Stephanotis does best in at least four hours of direct sunlight a day, with winter temperatures of 10° to 16°C (50° to 60°F) and summer temperatures of 21°C (70°F) or higher. This is warmer than many homes, but necessary if the plants are to flower well. If too cold the buds drop. A warm greenhouse gives the best results. Keep moist and fertilize monthly from March to October. The soil should be kept slightly on the dry side and fertilizer withheld from November until February. Propagate from stem cuttings rooted in temperatures around 29°C (85°F).

WHITE SAILS
Spathiphyllum wallisii

JACOBEAN LILY
Sprekelia formosissima

STEPHANOTIS
Stephanotis floribunda

BIRD-OF-PARADISE FLOWER
Strelitzia reginae

MARMALADE BUSH
Streptosolen jamesonii

STRELITZIA
S. reginae (bird-of-paradise flower)

Shaped like the heads of tropical birds, the multi-coloured 15 cm (6 in.) flowers of this exotic plant usually appear in summer and autumn, occasionally at other times, on stout stalks above spear-shaped leaves about 7.5 cm (3 in.) wide and 30 to 37.5 cm (12 to 15 in.) long. Plants are slow-growing, eventually reaching a height of 90 to 150 cm (3 to 5 ft).

HOW TO GROW. Strelitzias do best in at least four hours of direct sunlight a day, night temperatures of 10° to 13°C (50° to 55°F) and day temperatures of 20° to 22°C (68° to 72°F). Allow the soil to become slightly dry between thorough waterings and fertilize every two weeks. Plants should be grown in large tubs or soil borders in bright sun lounges or conservatories and divided only when it is absolutely necessary; divisions often require two or three years to reach flowering size. Strelitzias can also be propagated from seed in spring, but take five to ten years to produce any flowers.

STREPTOCARPUS
S. rexii and hybrids; *S.* x *hybridus* (Cape primrose); *S. saxorum*

Named for their primrose-like foliage and natural home near the Cape of Good Hope in South Africa, these gesneriads can be grown to blossom in spring, summer or autumn. Hybrids of *S. rexii* produce 5 to 12.5 cm (2 to 5 in.) trumpet-shaped blossoms in white, pink, rose, red, blue or purple, often with frilled edges and throats splashed with contrasting colours. Narrow stemless leaves, which are wrinkled and strap-shaped, form ground-hugging rosettes 25 to 50 cm (10 to 20 in.) in diameter. The English cultivar 'Constant Nymph' is outstanding with deep lavender-blue flowers, which bloom nearly all the year round, but set no seed. Another excellent strain is called 'Wiesmoor' hybrids. *S. saxorum*, a trailing species, bears 4 cm (1½ in.) wide, trumpet-like lavender-blue flowers.

HOW TO GROW. Streptocarpus does best in bright indirect or curtain-filtered sunlight and can be grown under 14 to 16 hours of artificial light a day. It thrives in night temperatures of 18° to 21°C (65° to 70°F) and day temperatures of 24°C (75°F) or higher. Pot in a mixture of 2 parts moss peat, 1 part packaged potting soil and 1 part sharp sand or vermiculite. Keep the mixture moist; fertilize monthly during the growing season—all the year round for *S. saxorum*, which does not rest. When *S. rexii* hybrids cease blooming, give them only enough water to prevent the leaves from wilting. Repot when new growth starts—plants are usually dormant for two to three months. Propagate the hybrids by division when dormant or from seeds or leaf cuttings at any time; propagate *S. saxorum* from stem cuttings or seeds.

STREPTOSOLEN
S. jamesonii (marmalade bush)

This is a rambling plant valued for its great clusters of bright orange, tubular flowers about 2.5 cm (1 in.) across, which appear in summer and intermittently through the year among 2.5 to 5 cm (1 to 2 in.) oval leaves. Plants are well suited to greenhouse or sun-lounge cultivation. If trained to a stake, they grow up to 90 cm (3 ft) tall in tree-like forms with the new growth trailing gracefully in the shape of an umbrella.

HOW TO GROW. Streptosolens do best in at least four hours of direct sunlight a day in winter, and in bright indirect or curtain-filtered sunlight in summer. Night temperatures of 10° to 13°C (50° to 55°F) and day temperatures of 20° to 22°C (68° to 72°F) are ideal. Keep the soil moist and fertilize monthly. Propagate from heel cuttings of young shoots in spring.

T

TABERNAEMONTANA See *Ervatamia*

TETRANEMA
T. mexicanum (Mexican foxglove)
   The Mexican foxglove bears 6 mm (¼ in.) pink to purple blossoms that look like small foxgloves. The dainty, nodding flowers bloom in summer, but spasmodically all the year round, on top of 15 to 20 cm (6 to 8 in.) flower stalks, which rise from the centre of a compact rosette of dark green, leathery leaves.
   HOW TO GROW. Tetranemas do best in partial shade, night temperatures of 10° to 13°C (50° to 55°F) and day temperatures of 20° to 22°C (68° to 72°F). Keep moist; fertilize every two weeks. Propagate by dividing old plants in spring or from seeds.

THUNBERGIA
T. alata (black-eyed-Susan vine, clock vine)
   Although perennial *T. alata* is usually grown as an annual in northern Europe. It makes a good pot plant, especially when grown up stakes or over a light wire-framework, but can also be allowed to cascade downwards from a hanging container. Its 2.5 to 5 cm (1 to 2 in.) wide flowers have black or dark purple centres and paper-thin white, buff, yellow or orange petals. The wiry stems grow about 60 to 120 cm (2 to 4 ft) long, bearing 2.5 to 5 cm (1 to 2 in.) long leaves.
   HOW TO GROW. Sow seed in March in small pots and pot up—three to a 15 cm (6 in.) pot—as soon as possible, using a soil-based compost with a little lime. Alternatively, buy young plants from florists. The plants do best in at least four hours of direct sunlight a day, night temperatures of 10° to 16°C (50° to 60°F) and day temperatures of 20° to 22°C (68° to 72°F). Keep moist and fertilize every two weeks during the growing season. When the vines become straggly, cut them off at the soil level and fresh growth will arise. Propagate from seeds.

TILLANDSIA
T. cyanea, also called *T. morreniana* (pink quill); *T. lindenii*, also called *T. lindeniana* (blue-flowered torch); *T. x duvalii*
   Most tillandsias grown as house plants have slender grey-green leaves that curve back at the ends and form loose rosettes; above the rosettes rise flower spikes that bear one or two blossoms at a time over a period of several weeks in spring. *T. cyanea* produces a flat diamond-shaped, pinkish-red spike with deep blue flowers; it grows 20 to 25 cm (8 to 10 in.) tall and has 15 cm (6 in.) long leaves. *T. lindenii* sends up a vivid pink, paddle-shaped bract, set with blue flowers; its rosette spreads 37.5 cm (15 in.) in diameter. *T. x duvalii* is a hybrid of the two other species and combines characteristics of both parents. Tillandsias comprise the largest genus of bromeliads, including the well-known air plant called Spanish moss.
   HOW TO GROW. Tillandsias do best in bright indirect or curtain-filtered sunlight, night temperatures of 16° to 18°C (60° to 65°F) and day temperatures of 21°C (70°F) or higher. Pot in a mixture of 2 parts moss peat to 1 part packaged

MEXICAN FOXGLOVE
Tetranema mexicanum

BLACK-EYED-SUSAN VINE
Thunbergia alata

PINK QUILL
Tillandsia cyanea

CONFEDERATE STAR JASMINE
Trachelospermum jasminoides

COMMON NASTURTIUM
Tropaeolum majus

potting soil and 1 part sharp sand or vermiculite set over a layer of coarse drainage material such as pieces of broken clay flowerpots. Do not add lime. Keep moist and feed monthly with a quarter-strength fertilizer during the growing season. Propagate from offsets that appear at the base of plants.

TRACHELOSPERMUM, also called RHYNCHOSPER-MUM
T. asiaticum (Japanese star jasmine, yellow star jasmine), *T. jasminoides* (Confederate star jasmine, Chinese star jasmine)

These slow-growing evergreen climbers, which have 4 to 6 cm (1½ to 2½ in.) long shiny green leaves, produce fragrant star-like, 12 to 25 mm (½ to 1 in.) flowers, generally in spring and summer. *T. asiaticum* has creamy-white flowers. *T. jasminoides* bears white flowers; a cultivar called 'Variegatum' has its leaves edged and mottled with white. Plants can be trained on low trellis or grown as bushes by pinching off the tips of stems.

HOW TO GROW. Trachelospermums do best in at least four hours of direct sunlight a day in winter, bright indirect or curtain-filtered sunlight for the rest of the year. Night temperatures of 10° to 13°C (50° to 55°F) and day temperatures of 20° to 22°C (68° to 72°F) are ideal. Allow the soil to become slightly dry between thorough waterings. Fertilize every two to three months. Propagate from stem cuttings in late summer.

TRICHOCENTRUM
T. tigrinum

These miniature orchids, which rarely reach 15 cm (6 in.) in height, bear sweetly fragrant, 5 cm (2 in.) flowers, one or two to a spike, in spring and early summer. The blossoms, yellow or yellow-green, are thickly covered with purplish-red spots, and have a widely flaring lip that is pure white except for a rosy-red base (*photograph, page 60*). The thick, 10 to 12.5 cm (4 to 5 in.) long leaves are green above and reddish underneath.

HOW TO GROW. Trichocentrum species do best in bright indirect or curtain-filtered sunlight, night temperatures of 13° to 21°C (55° to 70°F) and day temperatures of 20°C (68°F) or higher. They may be grown on a slab of tree fern or in a mixture of 2 parts fir bark or shredded osmunda fibre and 1 part coarse moss peat. Place the pot on a humidifying tray (*page 82*) and keep the potting medium constantly moist. Fertilize monthly with a high-nitrogen formula, diluted at the rate of ¼ teaspoon per 1 litre (2 pt) of water.

TRICHOSPORUM See *Aeschynanthus*

TROPAEOLUM
T. majus (common nasturtium)

These inexpensive annuals will blossom most of the summer and autumn on a sunny window sill. Their soft, faintly scented, single or double, 5 cm (2 in.) flowers, with few or many petals, come in white, yellow, orange, pink, scarlet, deep-red and mahogany-brown, often streaked and splashed with contrasting colours, appearing among shield-shaped, 4 to 6 cm (1½ to 2½ in.) leaves. Dwarf varieties grow 15 to 22.5 cm (6 to 9 in.) high; semi-tall 37.5 cm (15 in.) high; trailing or climbing types are attractive in hanging containers and may grow to 1.8 metres (6 ft).

HOW TO GROW. Tropaeolums do best in at least four hours

of direct sunlight a day, night temperatures of 4° to 13°C (40° to 55°F) and day temperatures of 20°C (68°F) or lower. Keep the soil moist and fertilize monthly. Protect against blackfly. Seeds sown in late summer will produce fine flowering plants for the winter; or sow in spring for summer flowering.

TULBAGHIA
T. fragrans (sweet garlic); *T. violacea* (society garlic, violet tulbaghia)

Tulbaghias are bulbous plants that bloom in summer. *T. fragrans* displays 20 to 30 sweetly scented lavender flowers in clusters at the tops of 30 to 37.5 cm (12 to 15 in.) tall stalks. The arching leaves of *T. violacea* give off a slight garlic-like odour when bruised; it has bright violet flowers.

HOW TO GROW. Tulbaghias do best in at least four hours of direct sunlight a day, night temperatures of 4° to 7°C (40° to 45°F) and day temperatures of 20°C (68°F) or lower. Keep the soil moist and fertilize monthly. Bulbs should be divided and repotted when they become overcrowded.

TULIPA
Several classes of large-flowered tulips

Familiar florists' flowers of winter and spring, tulips range in colour from white to cream, yellow, orange, pink, red, lavender-blue, purple, brown, nearly black and even green. Professional tulip growers recognize 15 categories in this genus, varying from 7.5 to nearly 90 cm (3 to 36 in.) in height, with blossoms 2.5 to 17.5 cm (1 to 7 in.) across when open, but most of these do not make satisfactory house plants. Although most tulips respond to cultivation as pot plants in conservatories, the best kinds for room culture are the single, early-flowered kinds like 'Keizerskroon', yellow, striped red, and 'Brilliant Star', scarlet; double earlies like the scarlet 'Scarlet Cardinal'; triumphs like 'Garden Party', white edged carmine, and 'Merry Widow', deep red, edged white. For later flowering a few Darwins may be tried, like 'Queen of Bartigons', pink and white; 'Sunkist', gold; and 'Bartigon', red; also the parrot 'Fantasy', which is pink and green.

HOW TO GROW. Tulips bought in bud and bloom, or planted in pots in autumn and grown cool as for narcissi, do best in bright indirect or curtain-filtered sunlight, night temperatures of 4° to 7°C (40° to 45°F) and day temperatures of 16°C (60°F) or lower. Keep the soil moist, but do not fertilize. Once forced by florists for indoor blooming, bulbs are useless for further forcing and are difficult to propagate, but they may be planted in the garden in cool climates if the foliage is allowed to mature normally and the bulbs are kept dry in an airy, dark place until planting time in the autumn.

V
VALLOTA
V. speciosa, also called *V. purpurea* (Scarborough lily)

This bulbous plant bears clusters of three to ten scarlet flowers, 7.5 to 10 cm (3 to 4 in.) in diameter, on 60 cm (2 ft) tall stalks in late summer; white and salmon-pink varieties are rarer but are sometimes available. The flower stalks are surrounded by smooth 30 to 45 cm (12 to 18 in.) long evergreen leaves.

HOW TO GROW. Scarborough lilies do best in at least four hours of direct sunlight a day, night temperatures of 10° to 13°C (50° to 55°F) and day temperatures of 20° to 22°C (68° to 72°F). Keep the soil well moistened and fertilize

SWEET GARLIC
Tulbaghia fragrans

PARROT TULIP
Tulipa 'Fantasy'

SCARBOROUGH LILY
Vallota speciosa

monthly from spring until autumn. After the flowers have faded, withhold fertilizer and water the plant sparingly so that the soil will stay slightly dry through the winter. Early each summer, wash away some of the old soil without disturbing the roots and replace it with fresh soil. Repot in fresh potting mixture every three or four years. Propagate in early summer from the small bulbs that develop beside the larger ones.

VELTHEIMIA
V. capensis, also called *V. glauca* (forest lily), often but erroneously offered for sale as *V. viridifolia*, a distinct plant rarely seen in Europe

V. capensis produces clusters of 50 to 60 tubular, 2.5 cm (1 in.) flowers that are deep pink or crushed strawberry, mottled white or green towards the mouth, but often a variable species. They bloom in winter at the top of flower stalks 30 to 60 cm (1 to 2 ft) tall. The leaves, which arch out attractively from the base of the plant, grow 30 to 35 cm (12 to 14 in.) long and are bright green above, glaucous beneath. They have wavy edges.

HOW TO GROW. Veltheimias do best in at least four hours of direct sunlight a day except when flowering, when they should have bright indirect or curtain-filtered sunlight. Night temperatures of 4° to 16°C (40° to 60°F) and day temperatures of 22°C (72°F) or lower are ideal. Pot so that the top third of the bulb is out of the soil. Keep the soil barely moist until growth starts in autumn, then keep constantly moist and fertilize monthly during the growing season. When the foliage dies down in the summer, keep the soil fairly dry and omit fertilizer. Propagate in spring from the small bulbs that develop beside the larger ones.

VRIESEA
V. guttata, *V.* x 'Mariae' (painted feather), *V. splendens* (flaming sword)

Vrieseas are popular bromeliads noted either for the exotic markings of their vase-shaped leaf rosettes or for their brilliantly coloured inflorescences. Two species combine both: *V. guttata* bears bright pink, paddle-shaped clusters of petal-like 2.5 to 5 cm (1 to 2 in.) bracts set with pale yellow flowers from late winter to early summer; grey-green leaves are covered with small maroon spots. *V. splendens*, which blooms in spring and summer, has sword-shaped clusters of 2.5 to 5 cm (1 to 2 in.) fiery red bracts with yellow flowers, and blue-green leaves with deep purplish crossbars. A summer-blooming variety with plain green leaves, but startling 2.5 to 5 cm (1 to 2 in.) orange-red and yellow bracts and yellow flowers, is the hybrid 'Mariae'. All grow about 30 cm (12 in.) tall.

HOW TO GROW. Vrieseas do best in bright indirect or curtain-filtered sunlight, night temperatures of 13° to 18°C (55° to 65°F) and day temperatures of 18°C (65°F) or higher. Pot in 2 parts moss peat to 1 part packaged potting soil and 1 part sharp sand or vermiculite. Set over a layer of drainage material, such as coarse gravel. Keep the mixture moist and the cup formed by the leaf rosette full of water; fertilize monthly. Propagate from the shoots that appear at the base.

Z
ZANTEDESCHIA
Z. aethiopica; *Z. elliottiana*, also called *Richardia elliottiana* (golden calla); *Z. rehmannii*, also called *Richardia rehmannii* (pink calla), (all called calla lily)

Calla lilies are easy-to-grow plants whose fragrant

FOREST LILY
Veltheimia capensis

PAINTED FEATHER
Vriesea x 'Mariae'

blooms flaunt rolled and flaring, 10 to 15 cm (4 to 6 in.) waxy single petals called spathes. Rising from the base of each spathe is a pencil-shaped spike, or spadix, bearing the plant's tiny true flowers. Thick leaves, up to 20 cm (8 in.) long and 12.5 cm (5 in.) wide, are shaped like arrowheads and frequently bear white markings. *Z. aethiopica* is pure white with a conspicuous golden spadix and has a very hardy, low-growing form, 60 cm (2 ft) high, called 'Crowborough'. This flowers intermittently from early summer until early autumn. Other types include *Z. elliottiana*, which grows up to 60 cm (2 ft) tall and bears 15 cm (6 in.) yellow flowers; and a 30 to 45 cm (12 to 18 in.) tall type, *Z. rehmannii*, with 10 cm (4 in.) pink flowers.

HOW TO GROW. Calla lilies do best in direct sunlight except at midday when they should be given bright indirect or curtain-filtered sunlight. Night temperatures of 10° to 18°C (50° to 65°F) and day temperatures of 20°C (68°F) or higher are ideal. Keep the soil thoroughly wet at all times; fertilize monthly during the growing season. Withhold moisture after the flowering stops. Propagate by division of tuberous roots in late summer or early autumn when the plants are repotted; the offsets may be detached at the same time and grown on in pots as new plants.

ZEPHYRANTHES
Z. candida (autumn zephyr lily); *Z. rosea* (zephyr lily)

Zephyr lilies are charming, easy-to-grow bulbous plants. *Z. candida* has white crocus-like flowers in late summer; *Z. rosea*, pink flowers between summer and early winter. In both cases each slender flower stalk bears a single upward-facing blossom about 5 cm (2 in.) across. It is not uncommon to have two or more crops of flowers during a year. The firm grass-like foliage grows 20 to 30 cm (8 to 12 in.) long.

HOW TO GROW. Zephyr lilies do best in at least four hours of direct sunlight a day, night temperatures of 4° to 7°C (40° to 45°F) and day temperatures of 20°C (68°F) or lower. Keep moist; fertilize monthly while plants are growing. After flowers and foliage wither, stop watering for about 10 weeks to let the plants rest, then renew watering and fertilizing. Propagate from the small bulbs that develop beside larger ones and repot every three or four years.

ZYGOCACTUS
Z. truncatus, also called *Epiphyllum truncatum* and *Schlumbergera truncata* (crab cactus, Christmas cactus)

This popular Christmas-flowering cactus is probably only represented in cultivation by hybrids and cultivars, of which there are many. The plant is epiphytic with flat, jointed stems; these are bright green with red markings, deeply notched and resemble crab's claws. The tubular flowers, which are borne at the tips of the stems, are 5 cm (2 in.) long and pink, red, carmine or white.

HOW TO GROW. Zygocactus does best in bright indirect or curtain-filtered sunlight, with minimum winter temperatures of 13°C (55°F) before flowering. To ensure bud formation, keep the plants in a cool position in the home or outdoors in July and withhold water and fertilizer at this time. In autumn, water the plants a little but spray over the foliage regularly until the buds appear. Once this happens, set the plant in its flowering position and do not move it again until it finishes blooming, or the buds will drop. When the buds have set, night temperatures of 16°C (60°F) and day temperatures of 21°C (70°F) are ideal. Propagate from cuttings. Purchased plants are often grafted on *Pereskia* or *Hylocereus* species of cacti.

GOLDEN CALLA LILY
Zantedeschia elliottiana

ZEPHYR LILY
Zephyranthes rosea

CRAB CACTUS
Zygocactus truncatus

Illustration by Pamela Freeman

Characteristics of 150 house plants

Listed below for quick references are the varieties illustrated in Chapter 6 and on pages 57-60.

Plant	White	Yellow-orange	Pink-red	Blue-purple	Multicolour	Fragrance	Colourful foliage	Decorative fruit	Climbing	Trailing	Under 30 cm (1 ft)	30 to 60 cm (1 to 2 ft)	Over 60 cm (2 ft)	Direct sun	Indirect or filtered sun	Shade	Artificial light	4° to 10°C (40° to 50°F)	10° to 16°C (50° to 60°F)	16° to 21°C (60° to 70°F)	Spring	Summer	Autumn	Winter
ABUTILON MEGAPOTAMICUM 'VARIEGATUM' (flowering maple)				●					●			●	●	●	●				●		●	●	●	
ACALYPHA HISPIDA (chenille plant)			●								●	●	●	●						●	●	●	●	●
ACHIMENES HYBRID (hot water plant)		●	●	●					●			●			●		●			●	●	●	●	
AECHMEA FASCIATA (urn plant)				●			●					●			●					●		●		
AESCHYNANTHUS LOBBIANUS (lipstick plant)				●					●				●		●					●		●		
AGAPANTHUS AFRICANUS (agapanthus)			●										●	●						●		●		
ALLAMANDA CATHARTICA 'WILLIAMSII' (allamanda)		●							●			●		●						●		●		
ANANAS COMOSUS 'VARIEGATUS' (pineapple)			●		●		●	●				●	●	●						●		●		
ANGRAECUM DISTICHUM (orchid)	●				●				●				●		●					●	●			
ANTHURIUM SCHERZERIANUM (flamingo flower)			●						●				●		●					●	●	●	●	●
APHELANDRA SQUARROSA 'LOUISAE' (zebra plant)		●					●					●			●					●		●		
ARDISIA CRENATA (coral berry)	●							●				●			●				●					●
ASTILBE X ARENDSII HYBRIDS	●		●									●			●			●	●		●	●		
BEGONIA SEMPERFLORENS (begonia)	●		●			●			●	●	●				●				●		●	●	●	
BELOPERONE GUTTATA 'YELLOW QUEEN' (shrimp plant)		●									●	●		●					●		●	●	●	●
BILLBERGIA 'FANTASIA' (billbergia)			●				●					●			●				●		●			●
BOUGAINVILLEA X BUTTIANA 'BARBARA KARST' (bougainvillea)			●					●				●			●				●		●	●	●	
BRASSAVOLA NODOSA (lady-of-the-night orchid)	●	●			●				●				●		●				●		●	●	●	●
BRASSIA CAUDATA			●	●	●						●		●		●							●	●	●
BROWALLIA SPECIOSA 'MAJOR' (browallia)				●						●	●	●		●	●				●		●	●	●	
BRUNFELSIA PAUCIFLORA var. CALYCINA (yesterday, today and tomorrow)			●	●							●	●			●				●		●	●	●	●
CALCEOLARIA X HERBEOHYBRIDA 'MULTIFLORA NANA' (slipper flower)		●								●		●			●		●		●		●			
CALLIANDRA HAEMATOCEPHALA (red powder-puff tree)			●				●				●		●		●					●	●	●		●
CAMELLIA JAPONICA 'DEBUTANTE' (common camellia)	●		●									●			●			●	●		●			●
CAMPANULA ISOPHYLLA 'ALBA' (trailing campanula)	●								●	●	●			●	●				●			●	●	
CAPSICUM ANNUUM (red pepper)	●						●		●		●			●					●		●	●	●	
CARISSA MACROCARPA 'NANA COMPACTA' (Natal plum)	●			●		●					●		●		●				●		●	●	●	●
CATTLEYA LABIATA	●		●	●							●		●		●				●		●	●	●	
CESTRUM NOCTURNUM (night jessamine)	●				●		●				●		●		●				●		●	●	●	
CHIRITA LAVANDULACEA (Hindustan gentian)				●							●				●				●		●	●	●	●
CHRYSANTHEMUM FRUTESCENS (marguerite)	●	●	●								●		●					●	●		●	●	●	
CHRYSANTHEMUM INDICUM HYBRIDEN (florists' chrysanthemum)	●	●	●								●			●				●	●		●	●	●	
CITRUS TAITENSIS (orange)	●				●	●	●					●	●						●		●	●	●	●
CLERODENDRUM THOMSONIAE (bleeding heart vine)	●								●			●			●				●		●	●		
CLIVIA MINIATA (Kaffir lily)		●									●			●					●		●	●		
COFFEA ARABICA (Arabian coffee)	●				●	●					●		●						●		●	●	●	●
COLUMNEA 'YELLOW DRAGON' (columnea)		●							●			●		●		●			●		●	●	●	●
X CRINDONNA MEMORIA-CORSII (crindonna)			●		●						●	●			●				●			●	●	
CRINUM HYBRID (crinum)			●		●						●	●	●		●				●			●	●	
CROCUS 'PICKWICK' (crocus)	●	●	●	●						●	●			●		●		●			●			●
CROSSANDRA INFUNDIBULIFORMIS (crossandra)		●								●	●	●		●						●	●	●	●	
CRYPTANTHUS BROMELIOIDES 'TRICOLOR' (rainbow star)	●						●			●	●		●						●		●			
CUPHEA IGNEA (cigar plant)	●		●	●						●	●		●						●		●	●	●	
CYCLAMEN PERSICUM (cyclamen)	●		●	●						●	●		●						●		●		●	●
CYMBIDIUM HYBRIDS (cymbidium orchid)	●	●	●							●		●		●				●			●			●
CYTISUS CANARIENSIS (genista)		●			●						●	●		●				●			●	●		
DAPHNE ODORA (winter daphne)	●		●			●					●		●					●			●			●
DENDROBIUM LODDIGESII (dendrobium orchid)			●	●					●		●			●					●		●	●		●
DIPLADENIA X AMOENA (dipladenia)			●						●			●		●					●		●	●	●	
DYCKIA FOSTERIANA 'SILVER QUEEN' (dyckia)		●				●	●				●		●	●	●				●		●			

Plant	White	Yellow-orange	Pink-red	Blue-purple	Multicolour	Fragrance	Colourful foliage	Decorative fruit	Climbing	Trailing	Under 30 cm (1 ft)	30 to 60 cm (1 to 2 ft)	Over 60 cm (2 ft)	Direct sun	Indirect or filtered sun	Shade	Artificial light	4° to 10°C (40° to 50°F)	10° to 16°C (50° to 60°F)	16° to 21°C (60° to 70°F)	Spring	Summer	Autumn	Winter
EPIDENDRUM COCHLEATUM (clamshell orchid)				•	•					•				•					•		•	•	•	•
EPIPHYLLUM 'HERMOSISSIMUM' (orchid cactus)			•		•						•	•		•					•					•
EPISCIA LILACINA 'EMBER LACE' (episcia)			•		•		•		•	•				•		•			•			•	•	
ERANTHEMUM NERVOSUM (blue sage)				•								•		•					•		•	•		
ERICA GRACILIS (rose heath)			•	•								•		•					•		•	•		
ERVATAMIA DIVARICATA 'PLENA' (crape jasmine)	•				•							•	•	•					•		•	•	•	
EUCHARIS GRANDIFLORA (Amazon lily)	•				•							•		•		•			•		•			
EUPHORBIA PULCHERRIMA (poinsettia)			•									•		•					•				•	•
EXACUM AFFINE 'MIDGET' (Persian violet)			•		•	•					•			•					•			•		
FELICIA AMELLOIDES (blue daisy)				•							•			•					•		•	•		
FORTUNELLA MARGARITA (oval kumquat)	•				•	•		•				•		•					•		•			
FUCHSIA 'PINK CLOUD' (fuchsia)			•									•	•	•					•		•	•		
GARDENIA JASMINOIDES 'VEITCHII' (gardenia)	•				•	•						•		•					•		•	•		
GAZANIA HYBRID (gazania)	•	•	•							•		•		•					•			•	•	
GELSEMIUM SEMPERVIRENS (false jasmine)		•			•			•	•			•	•	•		•			•		•			
GLORIOSA ROTHSCHILDIANA (glory lily)				•					•			•	•	•					•		•	•	•	
GUZMANIA MONOSTACHYA (guzmania)			•			•					•			•		•			•		•	•	•	•
HAEMANTHUS MULTIFLORUS (salmon blood lily)			•								•			•					•		•			
HELIOTROPIUM ARBORESCENS (cherry pie)				•		•					•	•		•					•		•	•	•	
HIBISCUS ROSA-SINENSIS (Chinese hibiscus)			•									•	•	•					•		•	•	•	•
HIPPEASTRUM 'FIRE DANCE' (amaryllis)	•		•	•								•		•					•		•	•		•
HOYA CARNOSA (wax plant)	•				•	•			•			•	•	•					•			•		
HYACINTHUS ORIENTALIS 'KING OF THE BLUES' (hyacinth)	•	•	•	•	•						•			•	•		•		•					•
HYDRANGEA MACROPHYLLA (common hydrangea)	•		•	•								•		•					•		•			
IMPATIENS WALLERIANA (busy Lizzie)	•	•	•	•							•			•	•	•			•		•	•	•	•
IPOMOEA 'EARLY CALL' (morning glory)			•					•				•	•	•					•		•			
IXORA COCCINEA (flame-of-the-woods)			•			•						•	•	•					•		•	•	•	•
JACOBINIA SUBERECTA (jacobinia)			•								•		•	•					•		•	•		
JASMINUM POLYANTHUM (Chinese jasmine)	•				•							•	•	•					•		•			
KALANCHOË BLOSSFELDIANA 'VULCAN' (kalanchoë)			•								•		•	•					•					•
KOHLERIA AMABILIS (kohleria)			•					•			•			•					•		•	•	•	
LACHENALIA BULBIFERA (Cape cowslip)				•							•		•	•		•		•	•		•			
LAELIA FLAVA (laelia orchid)		•									•			•				•	•		•			•
X LAELIOCATTLEYA 'EL CERRITO' (laeliocattleya orchid)		•									•			•					•		•			•
LANTANA CAMARA (common lantana)	•	•	•		•					•		•	•	•				•	•		•	•	•	•
LANTANA MONTEVIDENSIS (trailing lantana)			•		•					•		•	•	•					•		•	•		
LILIUM LONGIFLORUM 'CROFT' (Easter lily)	•				•						•			•				•	•		•			
MALPIGHIA COCCIGERA (holly malpighia)			•					•			•			•	•	•			•					
MALVAVISCUS ARBOREUS (sleeping hibiscus)			•										•	•					•		•	•	•	
MANETTIA BICOLOR (firecracker vine)				•					•		•			•		•			•		•	•	•	•
MAXILLARIA TENUIFOLIA (maxillaria orchid)				•	•						•			•					•		•	•		
MUSCARI ARMENIACUM (grape hyacinth)				•							•			•				•			•			•
NARCISSUS 'KING ALFRED' (daffodil)		•									•			•				•			•		•	•
NARCISSUS TAZETTA 'SOLEIL D'OR' (tazetta narcissus)		•			•						•			•				•	•					•
NEOFINETIA FALCATA (neofinetia orchid)	•										•			•					•			•		
NEOMARCIA GRACILIS (apostle plant)				•	•						•			•					•			•		
NICOTIANA ALATA 'GRANDIFLORA' (flowering tobacco)		•			•						•			•					•			•		
NIDULARIUM FULGENS (nidularium)		•	•				•				•			•					•		•	•	•	•
ODONTOGLOSSUM PULCHELLUM (lily-of-the-valley orchid)				•	•						•		•	•				•	•		•		•	•
ONCIDIUM VARICOSUM var. ROGERSII (dancing lady orchid)		•										•	•	•				•	•				•	•

Plant	White	Yellow-orange	Pink-red	Blue-purple	Multicolour	Fragrance	Colourful foliage	Decorative fruit	Climbing	Trailing	Under 30 cm (1 ft)	30 to 60 cm (1 to 2 ft)	Over 60 cm (2 ft)	Direct sun	Indirect or filtered sun	Shade	Artificial light	4° to 10°C (40° to 50°F)	10° to 16°C (50° to 60°F)	16° to 21°C (60° to 70°F)	Spring	Summer	Autumn	Winter
ORNITHOGALUM CAUDATUM (false sea onion)	●			●								●	●	●						●				●
OSMANTHUS FRAGRANS (sweet olive)	●			●								●	●	●	●					●	●	●	●	●
OXALIS PURPUREA 'GRAND DUCHESS' (oxalis)	●		●					●				●								●				●
PACHYSTACHYS LUTEA (lollipop plant)	●										●									●	●			
PAPHIOPEDILUM CALLOSUM 'BALINESE DANCER' (lady's slipper orchid)				●	●						●			●	●					●	●			
PASSIFLORA X ALATO-CAERULEA (passion flower)				●	●				●			●	●	●						●		●		
PELARGONIUM X HORTORUM 'SKIES OF ITALY' (geranium)			●				●					●		●						●		●		
PENTAS LANCEOLATA 'ORCHID STAR' (Egyptian star cluster)			●									●		●						●			●	
PETUNIA HYBRID (petunia)	●	●	●	●	●					●		●		●						●		●		
PHALAENOPSIS AMABILIS (moth orchid)	●	●	●	●									●		●					●	●	●		
PRIMULA MALACOIDES (fairy primrose)	●		●					●					●				●			●				●
PUNICA GRANATUM 'NANA' (dwarf pomegranate)			●					●				●		●						●		●		
RECHSTEINERIA CARDINALIS (cardinal flower)			●										●		●		●			●		●		
RHIPSALIDOPSIS GAERTNERI (Easter cactus)			●								●		●	●						●	●			
RHODODENDRON SIMSII (Indian azalea)	●		●	●								●	●		●	●				●				●
RODRIGUEZIA VENUSTA 'ANN' (rodriguezia orchid)				●	●				●			●			●					●			●	●
ROSA CHINENSIS 'MINIMA' (miniature rose)	●	●	●			●	●						●							●	●	●	●	●
ROSMARINUS LAVANDULACEUS (prostrate rosemary)			●		●	●						●		●						●		●	●	
RUELLIA MACRANTHA (ruellia)			●									●	●	●						●				●
RUSSELIA EQUISETIFORMIS (coral plant)			●							●		●	●	●						●		●		
SAINTPAULIA IONANTHA HYBRID (African violet)	●		●	●	●						●				●		●			●	●	●	●	●
SAXIFRAGA STOLONIFERA 'TRICOLOR' (mother of thousands)	●						●			●		●			●	●		●		●		●		
SCHIZOCENTRON ELEGANS (schizocentron)			●	●						●	●					●				●		●		
SCILLA SIBIRICA 'SPRING BEAUTY' (Siberian squill)				●							●			●	●			●	●		●			
SENECIO CONFUSUS (Mexican flame vine)			●						●	●		●	●	●						●		●		●
SENECIO CRUENTUS (cineraria)	●	●	●	●			●					●		●						●	●			●
SINNINGIA SPECIOSA HYBRID (gloxinia)	●		●	●	●						●				●		●			●		●		
SMITHIANTHA 'CARMEL' (temple bells)			●			●						●			●					●			●	
SOLANUM PSEUDOCAPSICUM (Jerusalem cherry)	●							●				●		●	●	●				●		●	●	●
X SOPHROLAELIOCATTLEYA 'MIAMI' (sophrolaeliocattleya orchid)			●									●		●						●	●		●	
SPATHIPHYLLUM WALLISII (white sails)	●				●							●			●	●				●	●	●		
SPREKELIA FORMOSISSIMA (Jacobean lily)			●									●	●	●						●	●			
STEPHANOTIS FLORIBUNDA (stephanotis)	●				●	●			●			●	●	●						●		●		
STRELITZIA REGINAE (bird-of-paradise flower)					●								●	●						●	●			
STREPTOSOLEN JAMESONII (marmalade bush)		●											●	●	●					●		●		
TETRANEMA MEXICANUM (Mexican foxglove)				●					●		●					●				●	●	●	●	●
THUNBERGIA ALATA (black-eyed-Susan vine)				●					●	●		●	●	●						●			●	●
TILLANDSIA CYANEA (pink quill)				●	●				●			●			●					●	●	●		
TRACHELOSPERMUM JASMINOIDES (star jasmine)	●			●		●			●	●		●	●	●						●		●		
TRICHOCENTRUM TIGRINUM (trichocentrum orchid)				●	●	●			●			●			●					●	●	●		
TROPAEOLUM MAJUS (common nasturtium)	●	●	●		●				●	●		●	●	●				●	●			●	●	
TULBAGHIA FRAGRANS (sweet garlic)			●			●						●			●					●		●	●	●
TULIPA 'FANTASY' (parrot tulip)				●							●			●				●	●		●			
VALLOTA SPECIOSA (Scarborough lily)			●									●	●	●						●		●	●	
VELTHEIMIA CAPENSIS (forest lily)			●									●			●			●	●					●
VRIESEA X 'MARIAE' (painted feather)				●								●			●					●	●	●	●	
ZANTEDESCHIA ELLIOTTIANA (golden calla lily)		●					●					●	●					●	●	●	●	●	●	
ZEPHYRANTHES ROSEA (zephyr lily)			●							●	●	●		●					●			●	●	●
ZYGOCACTUS TRUNCATUS (Christmas cactus)	●		●					●		●		●		●					●	●				●

Picture Credits

The sources for the illustrations that appear in this book are listed below. Credits for pictures from left to right are separated by semicolons, from top to bottom by dashes. Cover—Leonard Wolfe. 4—Keith Martin courtesy James Underwood Crockett; Clem Harris courtesy Francis Perry. 6—Evelyn Hofer courtesy Mark Twain Memorial. 10, 11—(top) Giuseppe Mazza; pictures 2, 3, 4, Harry Smith Collection; A-Z Collection—(second row) A-Z Collection; Harry Smith Collection; A-Z Collection; Harry Smith Collection; Giuseppe Mazza—(third row) Harry Smith Collection; Harry Smith Collection; Giuseppe Mazza; Giuseppe Mazza; Harry Smith Collection—(bottom row) all Harry Smith Collection except picture 2 Giuseppe Mazza. 13, 15, 16, 17—Drawings by Vincent Lewis. 19 to 27—Derek Bayes except page 25 Elizabeth Whiting. 28—Ted Streshinsky. 29, 31, 33, 36, 37—Drawings by Vincent Lewis. Credits for pages 38, 39, 40 are for photographs only. 38—Top, New York Public Library Picture Collection—Bibliothèque Nationale, Paris; Hunt Botanical Library Collection, Carnegie-Mellon University, Pittsburgh, Pa. 39—Hunt Botanical Library Collection, Carnegie-Mellon University, Pittsburgh, Pa.; Bettmann Archive—Hunt Botanical Library Collection, Carnegie-Mellon University, Pittsburgh, Pa.; New York Public Library Picture Collection. 40—New York Public Library Picture Collection except bottom centre left Staatsbibliothek, Berlin Bildarchiv (Handke). 42, 45—Drawings by Vincent Lewis. 46—Peter Gautel courtesy Badisches Landesmuseum, Karlsruhe. 48, 50, 52, 53, 54, 55—Drawings by Vincent Lewis. 57—Property of American Orchid Society Inc. except right second from top Phil Brodatz. 58—Rutherford Platt except bottom left property of American Orchid Society Inc. 59—Phil Brodatz; property of American Orchid Society Inc. except third from top Don Richardson. 60—Property of American Orchid Society Inc. except top left Orchid Jungle. 62, 63—Drawings by Vincent Lewis. 64, 65, 66—Illustrations by Rebecca Merrilees. 68—By Gracious Permission of Her Majesty, Queen Elizabeth II. 71—Drawings by Vincent Lewis. 73 to 75—Patrick Ward. 76, 78, 80, 82—Drawings by Vincent Lewis. 84—Richard Jeffrey. 87, 89, 90, 91, 93—Drawings by Vincent Lewis. 96 to 151—illustrations by Allianora Rosse except where otherwise indicated next to illustration.

Acknowledgements

The editors would like to extend special thanks to the sub-editor, Mrs. Lizzie Boyd, Kingston-on-Thames, England. They also wish to thank the following: Airguide Instrument Company, Chicago, Ill.; Mrs. Iris August, Bayshore, N.Y.; Podesta Baldocchi, San Francisco, Calif.; Mrs. Ernesta Drinker Ballard, Executive Director, Pennsylvania Horticultural Society, Philadelphia, Pa.; Mrs. Robert I. Ballinger Jr., Villanova, Pa.; Mrs. Pearl Benell, President, American Begonia Society, Whittier, Calif.; Theodore W. Bossert, Curator of Portraits, Carnegie-Mellon University, Pittsburgh, Pa.; Gunn Brinson, London, England; Mike Brown, London, England; Mr. and Mrs. William Crane, New York City; Mr. and Mrs. Warren F. Cressy, Falls Village, Conn.; Mrs. Edith Crockett, Librarian, Horticultural Society of New York, New York City; Mrs. Muriel C. Crossman, Librarian, Massachusetts Horticultural Society, Boston, Mass.; Gene Daniels, Camarillo, Calif.; Marie Eaton, Seattle African Violet Club, Seattle, Wash.; Mr. and Mrs. David Eisendrath, Brooklyn, N.Y.; Mrs. Wanda Elin, Fullerton, Calif.; Audre Fiber, Fiber Jehu, Inc., New York City; The Gazebo, New York City; Miss Marie Giasi, Librarian, Brooklyn Botanic Garden, Brooklyn, N.Y.; The Green Thumb, New York City; Dr. Arthur Grove, Houston, Texas; Miss Elizabeth Hall, Senior Librarian, Horticultural Society of New York, New York City; Ben Heller, New York City; Mrs. Hugh Hencken, Newton, Mass.; Merle Hernandez, London, England; Mr. and Mrs. Harold Howard, Los Angeles, Calif.; Colin Hunt, London, England; Donald Leaver, Bromley, England; Mr. and Mrs. Paul Lee, San Diego, Calif.; Miss Lornie Leete-Hodge, Devizes, England; Emory Leland, Seattle, Wash.; Mrs. Sheila Macqueen, Hemel Hempstead, England; Mark Marko, Monrovia Nurseries, Azusa, Calif.; The Neal Street Shop, London, England; Ronnie Nevins, Fullerton, Calif.; New York Botanical Garden Library, Bronx, N.Y.; Mrs. Thelma O'Reilly, La Mesa, Calif.; Desmond Paul, The House of Rochford, Broxbourne, England; Mrs. Henry Parish II, Hadley-Parish, Inc., New York City; Mrs. Ruth Pease, Judging Course Director, American Begonia Society, Los Angeles, Calif.; Walter Pease, Past President, American Begonia Society, Los Angeles, Calif.; Mrs. William Piel Jr., New York City; Plantamation, Inc., New York City; Mr. and Mrs. Herbert H. Plever, Jamaica, N.Y.; Mrs. Diane Powers, San Diego, Calif.; C. Rassell Ltd., London, England; Sylvania Lighting Centre, Danvers, Mass.; Charles Tagg, Past President, American Begonia Society, Fullerton, Calif.; Wills and Segar Ltd., London, England; Mrs. Alma Wright, Editor, *Gesneriad Saintpaulia News*, Knoxville, Tenn.; Rudolf Ziesenhenne, Nomenclature Director, American Begonia Society, Santa Barbara, Calif.

Bibliography

*Ballard, Ernesta D., *Garden in Your House*. Harper & Row, 1958.

*Brooklyn Botanic Garden, *Gardening in Containers*. Brooklyn Botanic Garden, 1958.

*Brooklyn Botanic Garden, *Handbook on Propagation*. Brooklyn Botanic Garden, 1965.

*Brooklyn Botanic Garden, *House Plants*. Brooklyn Botanic Garden, 1965.

*Brooklyn Botanic Garden, *Plants & Gardens: Gardening Under Artificial Light*. Brooklyn Botanic Garden, 1970.

Cherry, Elaine, *Fluorescent Light Gardening*. Van Nostrand Reinhold Company, 1965.

*Cruso, Thalassa, *Making Things Grow*. Alfred A. Knopf, Inc., 1969.

*Elbert, George and Edward Hyams, *House Plants*. Funk & Wagnalls, 1968.

*Everett, Thomas, *How to Grow Beautiful House Plants*. Arco Publications, 1953.

*Fennell, T. A. Jr., *Orchids for Home and Garden*. Holt, Rinehart and Winston, 1959.

*Free, Montague, *All About African Violets*. The American Garden Guild and Doubleday & Company, Inc., 1951.

*Free, Montague, *All About House Plants*. The American Garden Guild and Doubleday & Company, Inc., 1946.

*Free, Montague, *Plant Propagation in Pictures*. The American Garden Guild and Doubleday & Company, Inc., 1957.

*Graf, Alfred Byrd, *Exotic Plant Manual*. Roehrs Company, 1970.

*Kains, M. G., *Plant Propagation*. Orange Judd Publishing Company, 1931.

*McDonald, Elvin, *World Book of House Plants*. The World Publishing Company, 1963.

*McDonald, Elvin, *Complete Book of Gardening Under Lights*. Doubleday & Company, Inc., 1965.

*Moore, Harold E., *African Violets, Gloxinias and Their Relatives*. The Macmillan Company, 1957.

*Nehrling, Arno and Irene, *Propagating House Plants*. Hearthside Press, 1962.

Northern, Rebecca Tyson, *Home Orchid Growing*. Van Nostrand Reinhold Company, 1962.

Rector, Carolyn, *How to Grow African Violets: A Sunset Book*. Lane Books, 1962.

*Schuler, Stanley, *1001 House Plant Questions Answered*. Van Nostrand Reinhold Company, 1963.

Selsam, Millicent E., *How to Grow House Plants*. William Morrow and Company, 1960.

*Sunset Books, *How to Grow House Plants*, Lane Books, 1968.

*Sutcliffe, Alys, *House Plants for City Dwellers*. E. P. Dutton & Co., Inc., 1964.

*Wilson, Helen Van Pelt, *African Violet Book*. Hawthorn Books, Inc., 1970.

denotes U.S. publication only.

Index

*Numerals in italics indicate an illustration of
the subject mentioned*

Printed and bound in Hong Kong **XXX**